QUEER WHISPERS

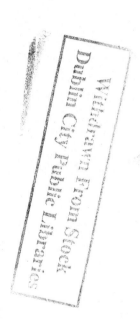

Queer Whispers

Gay and Lesbian Voices of Irish Fiction

by

JOSÉ CARREGAL

UNIVERSITY COLLEGE DUBLIN PRESS
PREAS CHOLÁISTE OLLSCOILE
BHAILE ÁTHA CLIATH
2021

First published 2021
by University College Dublin Press
UCD Humanities Institute
Belfield
Dublin 4
Ireland

www.ucdpress.ie

ISBN 978-1-910820-88-9 pb

Cataloguing in Publication data available from the British Library

*The right of José Carregal to be identified as the
author of this work has been asserted by him*

Typeset in Scotland in Plantin and Fournier by Ryan Shiels
Text design by Lyn Davies
Printed on acid-free paper by Bell & Bain Ltd,
Glasgow G46 7UQ, UK

Contents

To my academic mentor and friend
Professor Teresa Caneda Cabrera

Acknowledgements

I wish to thank Professors Anne Fogarty and Eibhear Walshe for their guidance and generosity during my research stays at University College Dublin and University College Cork. My research for this book was possible thanks to a postdoctoral grant given by the Xunta de Galicia, Spain (ED481 2017/042). This study is also part of a research project funded by the Spanish Ministerio de Economía y Competitividad and AEI/FEDER UE (FFI2017-84619-P).

In Chapter 7, I draw on two of my previously published articles on Colm Tóibín and Keith Ridgway: in *Atlantis: The Journal of the Spanish Association of Anglo-American Studies* (issue 37.1, 2015) and *New Hibernia Review* (issue 23.1, 2019).

My gratitude extends to the editors of UCD Press, Noelle Moran and Conor Graham, for their patience and enthusiasm, to designer Daniel Morehead and indexer Jane Rogers, and to the reviewers of my manuscript for their constructive criticism. A special thank you to Mary Dorcey for writing the introduction to this collection. All remaining errors are my own.

JOSÉ CARREGAL
August 2021

Foreword
by Mary Dorcey

'As for me I have cared too much about people and places. Cared too hard. It made me as a writer. It will break me in the end.'

Willa Cather, American Novelist

Could it be the case that we writers in general care too much? It may well be that in order to observe and describe our fellow human beings accurately, we have to care about them more than is common. And if we also happen to be gay, then in most periods and in most places, we will have to fight hard for the freedom to express this love. We all know how many in the past have been broken by just this struggle.

I grew up in the fifties and sixties in Ireland, a period of profound social conservatism; silence, repression, guilt and fear. A Catholic State for a Catholic people. Poor food, drab clothes, hospitals and schools run by priest and nuns, censorship of books and films. The contraceptive pill was unspeakable, condoms had to be procured in Belfast, abortion was unknown.

But I lived in a place of wild, natural beauty and spent a large part of my time out on the sea. I also had the good fortune to live in a household where books were prized. I began to read voraciously. I do not know what age I was when I first noticed that 95 per cent of fiction available in shops and libraries at that period were written by men.

My mother who loved literature, urged me to read, Austen and the Brontes but she also recommended Willa Cather and Somerville and Ross. The first mention I heard of homosexuality was that two of Ireland's heroes, Wilde and Casement, were gay. And both of these came to bad ends. But for whatever reason, very early I sensed some echo in myself, something mysterious in my nature that would demand of me particular courage. Was this a vague understanding that I was destined to be a writer or was it a glimpse of where my dormant sexual nature would lead? By adolescence I knew I was attracted to my own sex. But I was also drawn to the alternative sex, so I had a sense of choice and at that stage no fear. I turned to literature to better understand myself, to the invaluable world of recorded thought where generations of women and men have told the truth about their lives. I read Wilde and Colette, Baldwin, Genet, Virginia Woolf, later on to Rich, Oliver and Lorde, the great names of 20th-century literature who dared to write about same sex love. And in immersing myself in their lives I discovered I was in good company.

In Paris where I was studying and living with my boyfriend of the time, I mixed with an exciting tribe of civil rights and black power activists. Returning to Dublin I was determined somehow to uncover radicals and bohemians. Three months later with seven new friends, in 1973 we set up the first Gay Rights Group in Ireland, 'Sexual Liberation Movement' and a few weeks later a new feminist grouping: Irish Women United.

I was invited to address 'UCD Women's Week' on sexuality. It took place in the largest lecture hall in the new Belfield, a virtual arena. As we were setting up the panel, young students, mostly male, were already crowding in. When the seating filled up, they spilled out into the corridors. I rose to speak alongside another activist and a psychiatrist . I began by declaring: 'I am a lesbian and proud of it.' This outrageous, forbidden word, never before spoken at a public gathering in Ireland was incendiary. The huge crowd instantly erupted in anger. They stood on their seats and screamed abuse at me. Some had been far sighted enough to bring bags of fruit, oranges and apples to be used as missiles. They hurled them at the stage, most fortunately, falling short, roaring like bulls to drown me out. Their outrage fired my defiance and drove me on to dizzy heights of rhetoric. As their ugly names broke against my ears like hard stones, 'pervert, lezzer, fucking freak...' I looked down at my new lover (who I had met on my second day home in Dublin) smiling up at me from the front row, a foreigner detached from this Irish savagery. I focused my attention on her beautiful eyes and continued to speak the truth we had both come to tell.

The next morning the *Irish Times* ran a front page headline 'Self-confessed Lesbian denounces heterosexuality as sado-masochism'. This explosive L.word had never before publicly attached to anyone's family name. My life was changed overnight.

I had a lot of soul searching to do. A central question formed itself, if minds and hearts could slammed shut by lying, vicious words, could they be opened by powerful, truthful ones? I knew the reality of same-sex love, the ordinary human beauty, the trials and tribulations, tenderness, the passion . Was it possible that I – who had always planned to be a writer – had found the subject that could spur me into action? A conviction that would give urgency to each day spent alone in a quiet room, choosing words, composing sentences. The belief that writing – if it offered unflinching and truthful witness – could be a form of revolution?

Unflinching witness, could be the watchwords for Carregal's exploration of Irish Gay literature in *Queer Whispers*. In this remarkably wide ranging study of Irish queer writing from the twentieth and twenty first centuries, Carregal combines a breath of vision and detailed analysis that has not I think been matched before. Some of the stories gathered here are shocking, others are deeply romantic, all are passionate and honest.

Carregal has read extensively and with extremely close attention. Through eight chapters under a variety of aptly chosen headings he discusses fiction by 21 Irish writers. His desire for inclusivity is seen, first of all, in the near equal representation of writing by women and men. Although only three of the female writers discussed are gay, this is a commentary on Ireland's gender politics, I suspect, rather than the author's preferences. He also departs from narrow classification in his detailed consideration of work featuring gay characters written by straight authors. This allows him to include four heterosexual women: Maura Richards, Edna O'Brien, Anne Enright and Belinda McKeon.

Each chapter surveys a different aspect of gay life. Ranging from the familiar rites of passage: coming out, first love, and first loss, to the dangerous world of gay male cruising, and a tragic story set in the bitter years of the Aids epidemic. It is notable perhaps that it is women writers who turn our attention to romantic attraction, falling in love and the common human struggle to maintain love and loyalty in long term relationships.

Many writers included are familiar to all: Jamie O'Neill, Joseph O'Connor, Enda O'Brien,Colm Toibin, Emma Donoghue, John Boyne. Others such as Keith Ridgeway, Pádraig Standún and Desmond Hogan will be new to some.

In Chapter One 'I don't even know how to be a lesbian' Carregal discusses four novels that describe the isolation of same-sex lovers before the campaign for Gay Rights in the seventies. Two of these authors are straight and two gay. Edna O'Brien takes an unusual route in concentrating on a purely romantic attraction between two women. But in this telling we are reminded that the word lesbian is often rejected in studies of gay authors if it is unclear whether or not their characters have sex. This debate still continues with any woman who writes about same sex love. Including the celebrated American writer Willa Cather whom I quote above, who had two deeply committed, beloved women partners in her lifetime, would the same demand for evidence be upheld if all heterosexual couples had to demonstrate an active sex life before being acknowledged?

Men Without Refuge': looks at the writing of three gay men and one straight who describe the scene of 'Cottaging'. the dangerous ground of cruising for casual sex between strangers. An interesting addition to this world is Joseph O'Connor's story which describes the danger of gay lives lived in northern Ireland during the 'Troubles.' when those involved were routinely spied upon by the RUC.

The chapter 'Love is War' deals with the work of three writers on that most traditional topic of gay life: 'Coming Out' Might the equivalent for straight fiction be 'First Love' The difference between these two phrases aptly describes the stark difference in attitudes to alternative romance and 'orthodox'.

In the section entitled: 'The room looks warmer when you're in it...' Emma Donoghue provides a welcome contrast to the grief of the Aids epoch (discussed in 'Cultural Narratives of AIDS'; which describes life in the fear ridden years of the epidemic which dominated the gay male world in the nineties, largely hidden from straight brothers and sisters.) Though situated in the same time frame, this chapter offers a love story. Donoghue came to international attention with her first two books which concerned the problematic lives of young women in love with one another, in the 1990s and, yes extraordinary as it may seem – six years on from the achievement of Marriage Equality – in the 90s the majority of all Irish gay girls and boys lived in the closet.

In a chapter entitled 'The Feminist Politics of Mary Dorcey's Lesbian Fiction,' my own work is explored through three short stories and an extract from my novel *Biography of Desire*. I am pleased to say that the writing chosen concentrates on relationships between women lovers which even when framed by an outside climate that is hostile, are illuminated by emotional and sexual rapport.

In Chapter Four, under the heading: 'Narratives of Gay Life and Identity in Celtic Tiger Ireland.' the writing of Jarlath Gregory is discussed and lifts the mood onto a more light hearted plane. His novel' G.A.A.Y.: One Hundred Ways to Love a Beautiful Loser. takes readers to a radically different scenario, set in the gay scene of 2000s Dublin. The novel teems with references to gay culture and, as an early reviewer points out, Gregory offers here fresh insights into Dublin life, as G.A.A.Y. depicts a side of the city - 'the straight world never sees' (Leonard, 2005: 95).

In conclusion, may I say that I am more than proud to realise that Irish writers have produced since the 1980s, a body of work describing gay life as we know it, that is confident, distinctive and illuminating. The 21 writers here tell us stories of lives often concealed, not always celebratory, but powerful, determinedly clear eyed, often passionate, sometimes joyous and frequently humorous. José Carregal by gathering together so many disparate voices has done us all a service. We are fortunate indeed that our literature has attracted such a generous and meticulous witness as Jose Carregal.

MARY DORCEY
August 2021

Introduction

In Micheál Ó Conghaile's 'Athair' (1998), 'Father',[1] a young man struggles to confess his homosexuality to his father. Upon the realisation that his son is gay, the grief-stricken and embarrassed father breaks into tears and refuses to look at him, except for 'a stray watery glance' (20). After a long moment of silence, the father attempts to ask his son a question, finding it impossible to finish:

> 'And you. . .' he said, as if the word stuck or swelled up in his throat until he didn't know if it was safe to release it or rather he hoped, perhaps, that I would say it – the word that popped in his ears just now, a word he was never likely to form in his rural throat unless it was spat out in some smutty joke for the lads down the pub. A word there wasn't even a word for in Irish, not easy to find anyway. (1998: 21)

A similar but somehow inexact and offensive term for 'gay', reserved for insults and 'smutty jokes', seems to exist in the father's Irish language. Its derogatory implications, though, render this term too painful and humiliating to utter, leaving the father and son in shameful silence. This lack of an adequate language exemplifies the entrenched homophobia of twentieth-century Ireland, both in the Irish and English-speaking areas. Whereas modern Irish language was injurious towards homosexuals (as Ó Conghaile shows), old Irish was 'fairly rich in words that describe homosexual or effeminate men and lesbian or mannish women, as well as homosexual activity' (Lacey, 2008: 3). This richness of vocabulary seemingly evinces a non-suppression of same-sex desire in Gaelic Ireland before the language of Christian sexual morality became dominant.[2]

Far removed from old Ireland, the present volume concentrates on the contemporary moment, from the late 1970s until the late 2010s, tracing the ways in which a number of Irish authors challenged a public language of homophobia[3] and heterosexism.[4] *Queer Whispers: Gay and Lesbian Voices in Irish Fiction* thus concentrates on a (non-exhaustive but wide) selection of

I

twenty-four novels and eleven short stories which have given voice to gay and lesbian issues, experiences, and identities in Irish society, against a background of non-recognition and silence. Because it does not provide the vocabulary to understand them, silence distorts (or impedes) our perception of certain subjects, feelings, personal relationships, and social structures, and usually reinforces society's cultural codes (present in stereotypes and wide-spread prejudice, injurious language, taboos, a generalised lack of empathy towards the suffering of some social groups, etc). Taken together, the works analysed in *Queer Whispers* consistently expose the limitations imposed by silence, and, while doing so, articulate a new language of resilience and recognition of the particular struggles faced by homosexuals.

Embedded in everyday language and public discourse, silence – as Michel Foucault reminds us in his *History of Sexuality Vol. 1* ([1976] 1998) – is not just an absence of communication, but 'an element that functions alongside the things said', manifesting itself in 'the thing one declines to say, or is forbidden to name, the discretion that is required between different speakers' (27). Robin Patric Clair provides a further helpful conceptualisation of the social uses of silence: 'Silence and language create and re-create our social realities. From interpersonal relationships to the structuring of organizations, silent practices are pervasive and interwoven with linguistic practices [. . .] The issues of power, politics, aesthetics, and economics are all part of the organizing of silence' (1998: 21). This binary between language and silence participates in the ways in which dominant discourses establish the limits between knowing and unknowing, promote some values and principles over others, and channel public responses and emotions towards specific social realities.

If language and naming are often associated with power and authority, silence can easily flourish in situations of hiddenness, marginalisation, and public shaming (silence, though, can function as a strategy of resistance in some circumstances). Considerations on 'cultures of silence' continue to impact Irish society as it comes to terms with a history of cruelty against its most vulnerable citizens. In January 2021, in response to the Mother and Baby Homes Report,[5] Minister for Children Roderic O'Gorman declared that 'for decades, Irish society was defined by its silence' (Leahy), while the *Irish Times* attributed the prolonged concealment of abuse to 'a conspiracy, not just of silence, but of silencing'. Until recently, many of those who did not conform to the prevailing norms of sexuality were exiled in public opinion, driven to migration (expatriation, as we shall see, emerges as an important topic in Irish gay and lesbian-themed fiction), or confined to state-run insti-tutions, like Mother and Baby homes and Magdalene laundries[6] (it is worth noting that the current Direct Provision scheme, which houses asylum seekers, has been described as a continuation of previous coercive systems of exclusion).[7] Complicit in the nation's architecture of silence, these institutions have served to conceal members of society whose plight and need for an equal, humane treatment destabilised the moral regime and class system of the nation. An effect of this silencing is what Emilie Pine calls 'agnosia' (a term she borrows from medical language), which is a 'cognitive inability to recognise or understand the significance of what is being seen' (2013: 6). Pine quotes from the 2009 Ryan Report to argue that a form of 'social agnosia' helped maintain the historical silencing of child abuse in Ireland, because 'the general public was often uninformed and usually uninterested', so 'these pools of unknowing reinforced each other' (6).

This widespread social agnosia, as may be presumed, did not operate on its own. As several sociologists have remarked, among them Tom Inglis (1998, 2005), Catholic Ireland's culture of prudery and chastity, as well as its idealisation of the nuclear family, enforced Victorian values on domesticity, social respectability, the body, and sexuality (especially oppressive for women),[8] so those realities which transgressed the aforementioned principles were either relegated to secrecy or harshly condemned when publicly exposed. For most of the twentieth century, many of the 'uncomfortable' truths of Irish society – among others, unmarried women's pregnancies, abortion,[9] prostitution, the physical and sexual abuse of women and children within families, communities, and religious institutions – remained shrouded by shameful silence, because they contradicted the 'language of national identity formation', with its emphasis on Catholic moral values (Smith, 2004: 214). Within this cultural scenario, gay sexuality was not only criminalised until 1993, but was also considered inimical to the heterosexist institution of the family,[10] anti-Irish and a 'foreign pollution' until the 1980s (Conrad, 2004: 25).[11] Like gays, lesbians had no legitimate place in society, due to a heteropatriarchal culture which disempowered women (economically and psychologically speaking), consigning them to the romanticised roles of mothers and wives[12] (in many cases, the alternative was emigration due to poverty and lack of marriage prospects),[13] making lesbianism socially (and oftentimes personally) unrecognisable.[14]

GAY AND LESBIAN LIFE IN IRELAND FROM THE 1970S TO THE 2010S

To understand the value and subversiveness of the works analysed in *Queer Whispers*, we need first to delve into the social contexts where these texts are grounded. As indicated above, the languages of Irish Catholicism and national identity by no means facilitated the recognition and dignification of gay sexuality and lesbianism in twentieth century Ireland. Of course, the silence and stigma attached to homosexuality has a history which precedes the creation of the Irish State, exemplified by the late nineteenth century's emergence of homosexuality as gender inversion and the 'antithesis of respectability' (Mosse, 1985: 37),[15] the unspeakable nature of gay sex in Victorian times and Oscar Wilde's requirement to define at court 'the love that dare not speak its name' before being condemned of 'gross indecency',[16] and the absence of lesbianism in public discourse due to women's lack of social power until the last decades of the twentieth century.[17] Because same-sex desire was shameful and unmentionable, relevant figures like Wilde, Roger Casement[18] and Eva Gore-Booth[19] were only recently reclaimed as queer icons, as their sexual dissidence had been for long 'subsumed into broader debates and discourses concerning Irish nationalism' (Walshe, 2005: 57). In mid-twentieth century Ireland, while women's same-sex passions were largely unknown, gay sex was judged as sinful and an abject vice, and was talked about in hushed voices, as a dirty secret. Whereas many same-sex attracted men shared a subterranean knowledge of cruising sites where they could meet, women enjoyed less freedoms and often had their lives controlled by family and society, even though, as Katherine O'Donnell points out, some lesbians did benefit from the widespread silence of lesbian love: 'Oral histories report that many lesbian relationships went undetected, as it was popularly assumed that spinsters were asexual' (2003: 11).

Thanks to the advancement of a language of feminism and sexual rights, this underground situation slightly changed in the course of the 1970s, when gay and lesbian groups appeared in places like Cork, Dublin, Galway, Clonmel, Limerick, Kilkenny and Sligo.[20] The emergence of these groups, O'Donnell notes, was also paralleled by the beginning of Irish gay and lesbian activism, in associations like LIL (Liberation for Irish Lesbians), which was 'strongly inspired by feminism and, to a lesser extent, gay liberation and socialism' (2008: 2), political languages that had been developing in Ireland and elsewhere. Tina O'Toole (2013) highlights the contributions of the Irish queer diaspora, and how, through transnational networks, terms associated with the gay liberation movement in America, like Radicalesbians's 'woman-identified-woman' (1970) and Adrienne Rich's 'compulsory heterosexuality' (1980), made their way into the Irish lesbian and feminist communities, who now found new value in the example of precursors like writer Kate O'Brien.[21] Gay activists, on their part, benefitted from Irish feminists' fight for reproductive rights and the separation of sex from married reproduction, as this would lessen the moral and legal policing of all sex, 'including gay sex' (Ryan, 2006: 88). While IGRM (Irish Gay Rights Movement) campaigned against criminalisation and offered legal assistance and support to men accused of gross indecency,[22] LIL considered feminism fundamental for women's emancipation in all facets of life, including sexuality awareness.[23] Though there was cooperation between Irish gay and lesbian activists, hostilities arose in the contexts of the 1980s referenda on abortion (1983) and divorce (1986), due to the sexism of a significant proportion of gay activists.[24]

Despite occasional conflict, gay and lesbian associations worked together against the vilification and pathologisation of homosexuality, developing a language of resistance. If, as suggested above, there was a need to import a vocabulary of gay and lesbian liberation, it was because there were no neutral, respectful terms to name the reality of homosexuality. Recalling her early days as a feminist and lesbian activist, author Mary Dorcey claims that, before the 1970s, words like 'gay', 'lesbian' or 'bisexual' did not exist in Ireland (1995: 28). As a non-offensive word to designate homosexuals, 'gay' came to be used with a higher frequency in the course of the 1980s, and proved influential in the shaping of public opinion, since 'slowly, the word and the idea began to make its presence felt in the Irish public consciousness' (Lacey, 2008: 246). As a reaction to social change, the lay Catholic group Family Solidarity published in 1990 *The Homosexual Challenge* in their attempt to prevent the decriminalisation of male homosexuality:

> Our original vocabulary for describing homosexual conduct –we are speaking of polite and academic discourse, not abusive language– expressed and reinforced the perception of homosexual acts as immoral, contrary to the law, and often needing medical treatment, when it described them as 'unnatural', 'indecent', 'abnormal', etc. The new vocabulary, which suggests that homosexual behaviour is natural, legitimate, and normal, is in many cases terminology that developed within the homosexual movement, which has now become the accepted norm or dominant terminology. (1990: 19)

Family Solidarity thus attempted to keep the public language of homosexuality inside a discourse of moral condemnation. Their claim that the 'new terminology' became dominant at the time is debatable; the fact that Family Solidarity viewed terms like 'unnatural' as polite language suggests that people's everyday speech included even more derogatory names to refer to homosexuals (like 'perverts' or other words that encapsulated the stereotypes of the time). As gay and lesbian activists demanded the end of discrimination, they had to reclaim a new language of dignity, tolerance, and inclusion.

The decade of the 1980s had been characterised by a marked polarisation of opinion in an Ireland which saw the reassertion of conservative values, followed by Pope John Paul II's 1979 visit,[25] and epitomised by the anti-feminist outcomes of the referenda on abortion and divorce (in both campaigns, the Church was heavily involved), and David Norris's 1983 failed legal battle to have gay sex decriminalised after suing the Irish State[26] (his appeal to the European Court achieved victory in 1988).[27] In those years, homophobia became vociferous in public discourse (e.g. in Irish priests' warnings against sexual 'immorality'),[28] but lesbian and gay activists also raised their voices louder than ever before, especially after the 1982 murders of Charles Self[29] and Declan Flynn,[30] because of the indignation caused by the ways in which these cases were mishandled by the judiciary and the police.

The situation for gay and lesbian activism in 1980s Ireland may remind us of Judith Butler's idea that, in social movements, vulnerability does not equal passive suffering, as it brings an awareness of injustice which articulates a 'language contrary to accepted norms of authority' (2016: 16). It therefore transpires that resistance requires the politicisation of vulnerability, since 'without being able to think about vulnerability, we cannot think about resistance' (Butler, 27). Whereas in previous decades homosexuality and anti-gay violence were silenced and hardly acknowledged (Ferriter, 2009: 391), in the 1980s homosexuality became more visible and publicly exposed, due to a discourse of homophobia whose effects now increased a shared sentiment of grievance and vulnerability among Irish gays and lesbians. The deaths of Flynn and Self, as suggested, became 'catalysts for gay mobilisation' (Casey, 2018: 223), and a call for action. In 1988, dozens of gays and lesbians staged a 'kiss-in' outside the *Dáil* (one symbol of state-sponsored homophobia), defying the heteronormative construction of the public sphere.[31] Protests of this nature, Butler explains, become particularly relevant to cement group solidarity, as forms of nonviolent resistance which, through bodily exposure to police coercion and social recrimination, 'mobilize vulnerability for the purposes of asserting existence, claiming the right to public space' (2016: 26).

Within this situation of reenergised activism, the Gay and Lesbian Equality Network (GLEN) appeared in 1988 to campaign for gay decriminalisation.[32] Led by Kieran Rose, GLEN adopted a strategy of non-confrontation, as it emphasised the inherently tolerant nature of the Irish, while presenting the 1861 Victorian law only as a residue of British imperialism. GLEN in this way avoided linking gay discrimination to the highly moralistic and Church-dominated ideology of twentieth-century Ireland. Moreover, GLEN referred to gay men as heterosexual people's sons and brothers, who deserved to be loved and respected equally (a similar discursive tactic was employed in the same-sex marriage referendum campaign). Gays were thus presented as rightful members of their biological families (rather than as part of their queer ones), which reaffirmed the nuclear family's cultural prominence (it must be said, though, that numerous Irish homosexuals still suffered violence and exclusion within their families of birth, so GLEN's strategy may have helped ease familial homophobia).[33] Ultimately, GLEN's message was that '"Ireland as family" would and should show [. . .] compassion towards its children in general who were gay' (Dunphy, 1997: 256). Because of this emphasis on inclusion within mainstream society, notions of sexual dissidence and difference were, to a significant extent, neutralised. GLEN's campaign thus silenced some aspects of gay and lesbian life, but proved effective to achieve decriminalisation in 1993.[34]

The incidence of external factors on Irish life further contributed to decriminalisation. Aside from the 1988 European ruling against the Irish State, one important influence was the World Health Organisation's declassification of homosexuality as a mental disease, as well as their recommendations for the adoption of liberal approaches to sex health education to prevent the spread of HIV/AIDS (O'Connor, 1995). As Diarmaid Ferriter further argues (2009: 10), the 'sexual liberalism' already experienced in other Western countries arrived in Ireland in the early 1990s, propelling major debates and social transformations on issues such as women's role in society and access to work, support for unmarried mothers, the wider availability of contraceptives, and the progressive separation between the State and the Church (this coincided with revelations of cases of abuse against women and children in religious institutions, which seriously undermined the Church's moral and political authority).[35]

One consequence of the Church's gradual loss of power was the 1995 legalisation of divorce by referendum (by a very narrow margin),[36] a legal reform for which feminists and lesbians had been campaigning for so long. The 1990s was also a time of increased political assertion for Irish lesbians,[37] who began to organise separately: in 1991, Lesbians Organising Together (LOT) was founded, and in 1993 the first Lesbian Lives Conference was held at University College Dublin, organised by Ger Moane, Ailbhe Smyth, and Rosemary Gibney. Despite the liberalism of these years, lesbian activism was still needed to confront the traditional silences and constraints of hetero-patriarchal Ireland,[38] as demonstrated by the numerous calls LOT received by women confused by their sexual identity, afraid of losing child custody, or even trapped in dysfunctional marriages and unable to remake their lives as lesbians (in the mid-1990s, a majority of married women did not work outside the home). As was the case for gay men, there were sharp generational divides at the time, as many younger lesbians participated in a culture of sexual liberalism where feminism was perceived as outdated (Moane, 1995: 94). Lesbianism, nonetheless, remained relatively invisible when compared to gay sexuality.[39]

Unlike lesbians, gay men were positioned within a discourse of Irish modernity that promulgated values of individualism, sexual freedom, and consumerism, capitalised by the liberal economy and ideology of Celtic Tiger Ireland[40] (from the early 1990s to the 2008 economic crisis), which equated itself with notions of social progress and justice, but disregarded issues of class oppression and racism. As Michael G. Cronin argues (2004), popular representations of gay men became intimately linked with the life-style principles of liberal capitalism, which explains why they were customarily portrayed as urban, young, white, economically empowered, invested in middle-class values, and supportive of the established social order (in line with notions about the socially acceptable type of homosexual). Building on Cronin's work, Susannah Bowyer (2010) identifies this imported stereotype as a 'global gay brand', which relies on 'a covetable sense of sexual ease and enjoyment' (805), as if homosexual lives had suddenly become problem free. Allegedly, Celtic Tiger Ireland promoted this exaggeratedly optimistic icon of gay liberation in order to highlight its differences from conservative, sexually repressive Catholic Ireland. This dichotomy between tradition and modernity – as shall be explored in chapters ahead – was fraught with contra-dictions, silences, and occlusions of aspects of gay and lesbian existence that went beyond issues of personal sexual freedom, like the persistence of homo-phobia[41] (at times unacknowledged), class oppression and exploitation, HIV/AIDS stigma, or homonegativity[42] towards queer kinship.

In the late 1900s and 2000s, though there was in Ireland a discourse of modernity and sexual freedom, the dominant language of heterosexism still impeded the recognition and valorisation of same-sex parenthood, a silence that was reflected in the law, since, as the Equality Authority remarked in 2003, 'lesbian and gay couples have no guarantee of fair treatment under the law because legally their relationships do not exist' (20). LOT activist Patricia Prendiville noted that there were 'no legal provisions to cover the rights of the non-birth lesbian mother', who received no next-of-kin status, which caused serious problems in case of separation or the death/severe disease of the biological mother (1998: 89). Other benefits enjoyed by married people, like tax deductions or pension and bereavement rights, were simply not available to same-sex couples. This legal discrimination was brought to public attention in 2006, in a High Court case where Ann Louise Gilligan and Katherine Zappone sought to reclaim the validity of their Canadian marriage under Irish law. Gilligan's and Zappone's legal battle was unsuccessful, but, vitally, their challenge sparked 'public discussions about what a family is' (Kavanagh, 2009: 173). The institution of the family – for long a bastion of Irish identity, heterosexuality, and Catholicism – was now open to inquiry and redefinition. Generally considered the preamble to the same-sex marriage referendum, the Civil Partnership Bill was passed in 2010, granting State recognition to same-sex couples, even though adoption rights remained as limited as before.[43]

To circumvent society's heterosexist anxieties, issues of same-sex parent-hood and adoption rights were also marginal in the context of the 2015 same-sex referendum. As Emer O'Toole explains, activists[44] favoured testimonies of heterosexual parents advocating on behalf of their homosexual children, rather than focusing on same-sex parents themselves: 'Queer subjectivities and kinship had to be camouflaged' (2017: 118). Judging by the success of the Yes vote,[45] activists developed an effective campaign to expand the concept of marriage but failed to protest against the discrimination surrounding other alternative forms of queer kinship, which are not so easily 'digestible' by the majority. Occlusions like this one were, probably, seen as the only possible way to gain the necessary support for legislative change.

The official campaign for same-sex marriage was, in fact, seen by some observers, among them Anne Mulhall, as a clear manifestation of 'homonormativity', as it developed along the lines of a 'familiar white middle-class neoliberal register' (2015). Mulhall herself, drawing on the work of queer theorists Sarah Ahmed and Jasbir K. Puar, explains how queer activism in twenty-first century Ireland began to use an assimilationist language of homonationalism, or homonormativity, which constructed a 'model of the disciplinary homo-subject', which eventually converged with dominant liberal values and 'enforc[ed] love for the imaginary family, community and nation' (2011: 110). This scenario reflects general trends in other Western nations. Writing in an early 2000s American context, Lisa Duggan (2002) had already warned against a homonormative culture (focusing on 'respectable' issues like same-sex marriage or inclusion within the army), which domesticated queer activism by 'privatizing gay politics and culture for the new liberal order' (188). Contrary to what happened in the early years of activism, today there are no radical attempts to reform the established social system, nor is there a vision of 'a collective, democratic public culture' among the LGBTI+ population (Duggan, 189).

A similar opinion with regard to liberalism and gay life is put forward by Cormac O'Brien (2020) in his analysis of Ireland's homonormative 'post-AIDS culture' (emerging after 1996, after the development of the antiretroviral therapy ART, which highly reduced the mortality rate of the disease), which stigmatises HIV-positives outside and within the gay community, a situation of exclusion aggravated by a predominant gay aesthetic that emphasises 'white, young, muscled perfection', and where 'less-than-perfect health is disavowed and shamed in this culture of the ideal lifestyle and body' (125). This ideal of gay life, as Cormac O'Brien (2020) suggests, often silences realities of body-shaming, stigma, or derision of those who do not fit into the ideals of the homonormative body. Arguably, the liberal stereotype of homosexual life has exacerbated a kind of social behaviour where the body is perceived as central to symbolic capital, due the proliferation of stereotypes that reduce LGBTI+ identities to a number of sexual behaviours and body types which affect the identity formation of homosexuals, and reinforce the same gender binaries against which early gay and lesbian movements had protested.[46] Shaped by market-oriented forces and propagated in the media, LGBTI+ identities have allegedly been commodified and deprived of their potential to challenge dominant values of race, gender, and social class.

Though problematic in some respects, the liberal culture of contemporary Ireland has helped many homosexuals achieve a higher degree of wellbeing and self-respect, and there is not the same sense of vulnerability and isolation as in previous periods. According to Gráinne Healy, Brian Sheehan and Noel Whelan in their *Ireland Says Yes* (2016: 41), there are notable generational gaps today, as younger people grew up at a time when sexuality was more openly discussed, and thus generally became supportive and enthusiastic about marriage equality. Yet, even though younger generations are perceived to be more tolerant, recent studies reiterate that homophobic bullying continues to be endemic in primary and secondary school environments. The 2016 *LGBTI Ireland Report* revealed unexpected findings, since 'a very significant number of those aged under 25 did not experience the same levels of positive mental health and wellness as those older than them', as among the younger generations there were 'very elevated levels of suicidal behaviour and self-harm' (Higgins et al., 3). It therefore transpires that the gender anxieties of heterosexism remain deeply entrenched in Irish society, despite recent legal changes like marriage equality, which created a public image of Ireland as a nation that embraces sexual diversity. There is therefore a need to continue exploring, denouncing, and combating the stubborn, and at times silenced, homophobic discrimination and prejudice damaging the self-image and mental health of the LGBTI+ population.

MAPPING THE BOOK

By calling attention to the ways in which public discourse shapes subjectivity and social perceptions on homosexuality, the previous overview on Irish homosexual life and activism will, I hope, enrich my analyses of the gay and lesbian-themed fiction produced in Ireland in the last four decades. The overriding focus of analysis shall be language and silence (including: how language and culture mediate our (self)perceptions of gender and sexual identity, the need to resist the languages of homophobia and heterosexism, and the effects of social agnosia and non-recognition provoked by silence), in relation to a diversity of socio-cultural contexts (for example, the Catholic sexual morality of 'traditional' Ireland and homonormativity in the years the Celtic Tiger period and today).

Queer Whispers: Gay and Lesbian Voices in Irish Fiction explores these works of fiction in union with their contexts of production and their interaction with current debates and social realities. The lesbian and gay experiences explored in the pages of *Queer Whispers* certainly illuminate key aspects of the Ireland's evolving recent story of gender and sexual politics; however, the author is mindful that the stories of other parts of the rich LGBTI+ community are not explored in this current study (including bisexual and transgender), leaving space for much needed further work in these equally important areas of our queer story. The present volume is the first book-length study of Irish gay and lesbian-themed fiction; the door is thus pushed open to more research to add to this ongoing dialogue.

Considerations on gender identities, and their connection with issues of language and silence, will become recurrent in the chapters that follow, since, as Judith Butler puts it, there are 'sexual and gender norms that in some ways condition what and who will be "legible" and what and who will not' (2009: iii). In an interview with Sarah Ahmed (2016), Butler remarks that we become subjectivated by a language which, through gender assignment, acts upon us prior to our development of any notions of gender or sexual dissidence. Deviance, Butler argues, may bring with it anxiety, fear, and a sense of vulnerability, which, when mobilised, may lead to resistance, and become 'the beginning of new forms of solidarity' (Ahmed, 484). Of particular interest to this book is how Butler understands vulnerability and resistance in reference to their 'linguistic register' (486), given the possibilities that we may have to 'speak out and against those who address us in ways that are radically unacceptable, or against those who really fail to address us and, in that way, potentially imperil our existence' (485). In Butler's configuration, vulnerability – which relates to precarity and forms of power that determine what lives are more 'liveable' than others – triggers a reaction of 'responsiveness' towards silence and injurious language (486), where we accept, refuse, or resist the modes of address, or the silencing, to which we are subjected. The novels and short stories analysed here explore situations of vulnerability – among them, religious and familial homophobia; the pressures of masculinity for gays; lack of material conditions to live as a lesbian; enforced migration; HIV/AIDS stigma; heterosexist discrimination against queer kinship – which do not always lead to resistance, but nonetheless dramatise important issues of gay and lesbian life in contemporary Ireland.

Gay and lesbian voices and concerns have indeed been silenced in Ireland for too long, even in the academic field, since, as Eibhear Walshe points out in the 2013 *Queering the Issue* volume of the *Irish University Review*, until the last years of the twentieth century 'LGBT perspectives simply did not exist as possible areas of teaching or research' (O'Rourke et al., 36). To counteract this tradition of silence, relevant work in the field of Irish Queer Studies has been published by scholars, including Joseph Valente, Margot Backus, Anne Mulhall, Michael G. Cronin, Kathryn Conrad, Ed Madden,

Eibhear Walshe, and Cormac O'Brien; and, thankfully, the list keeps growing. In the area of literary studies, there is one book-length study of queer performance and theatre in Ireland by Fintan Walsh: *Queer Performance and Contemporary Ireland: Dissent and Disorientation* (2016). This study of Irish drama shares crucial concerns with my own work, as Walsh explores the ways in which queer performance 'articulates experiences of oppression, exclusion, and displacement, while imagining and cultivating more accommo-dating, inclusive, and sustaining modes of interpersonal intimacy, social support, public participation and cultural belonging' (1). But, while Walsh's book concentrates on the Celtic Tiger period and its aftermath, *Queer Whispers* delves into the contexts of both Catholic and liberal Ireland. Walsh's main critical concepts are dissent and disorientation; as he explains, when indi-viduals openly and publicly dissent, as in queer performance, they 'unsettle the very opposition between the dominant and the subordinate' (14), a process that is followed by disorientation, which is of particular relevance for LGBTI+ people, 'who often have to wilfully find each other, and actively construct their own social worlds, having no ready-made map to follow or reproduce' (15). While similar to Walsh's approach, *Queer Whispers* wants to emphasise how, in much of the fiction analysed here, for characters be able to dissent and reduce their vulnerability, they first need to overcome silence and find a language of resistance.

In my readings of fiction, I draw on variety of sources in the wide arena of Irish cultural studies, literary criticism, queer and feminist studies, sociology and history, journalism, as well as looking at the rich archival material from the National Library of Ireland's Irish Queer Archive (curated by Tonie Walsh), which contains valuable insights given by Irish LGBTI+ activists. This volume examines not only the work of widely acclaimed authors (such as Emma Donoghue and Colm Tóibín), but also the fiction of lesser-known writers who deserve the critical attention given here (such as Keith Ridgway and Belinda McKeon), and other (almost) forgotten titles, which broke new ground in Irish literature (such as Maura Richards's *Interlude* and Desmond Hogan's *The Ikon Maker*). Although *Queer Whispers* concerns itself with gay and lesbian themes and identities in Irish fiction, this does not mean that the works included here are either written by queer writers specifically (there are texts by non-queer identifying writers such as Edna O'Brien, Pádraig Standún, Sebastian Barry and others) or addressed to a gay and lesbian readership in particular . Classifications vary and change over time: a book like Edna O'Brien's *The High Road* is classified as Irish (not lesbian) fiction, but a title like Tom Lennon's *Crazy Love* would be deemed gay fiction, and, while the collection *Quare Fellas* (edited by Brian Finnegan in 1993) focuses on queer subcultures,[47] some of the 'educative' novels of the 1990s, like Donoghue's *Stir-fry* and Tóibín's *The*

Blackwater Lightship, take a more 'polite' approach to lesbian and gay issues, and were published for a wider audience. By bringing together a wide range of literary texts, the present volume intends to valorise the richness and diversity of the writings and writers of gay and lesbian lives in Ireland.

Chapter One describes the cultural climate of isolation and vulnerability for lesbians in the 1980s and early 1990s, in a staunchly hetero-patriarchal Ireland that seriously restricted women's autonomy, censoring their desires for self-fulfilment. This chapter analyses Maura Richards's *Interlude* (1982); Edna O'Brien's *The High Road* (1988); Linda Cullen's *The Kiss* (1990); and Padráig Standún's *A Woman's Love* (1994), focusing on topics such as lesbian awakening, the effects of cultural invisibility, social class, romantic friendships, and expatriation as a chance for sexual liberation. Reflecting the constraints of heteronormativity, these novels dwell on the unfulfillable: lesbian lovers either fall victim to patriarchal violence (*The High Road*), have to separate (*Interlude* and *The Kiss*) or must remain hidden from the community (*A Woman's Love*). Even though these novels do not articulate a language of lesbian feminism nor provide models of lesbian empowerment, they do produce important cultural representations of lesbian love and sensuality against a background of silence and non-recognition.

Chapter Two is devoted to Mary Dorcey, a relevant figure of the early Irish gay and lesbian movements, and the first Irish woman to be an openly lesbian public figure. Dorcey is also a widely acclaimed poet, but this chapter shall concentrate on two of her works of fiction, the stories of her collection *A Noise from the Woodshed* (1989) and her novel *Biography of Desire* (1997). As shall be argued, Dorcey develops a language of lesbian feminism which foregrounds notions of lesbian community and solidarity, creating a woman-centred world that defies both male-dominated images of femininity and heterosexual conventions on romantic love. Her lesbian characters – unlike those of the novels in Chapter One – become politically empowered by other women. In her fiction, Dorcey undermines cultural silences and emphasises the joys and freedoms of lesbianism, while portraying feminism as the gateway to self-discovery and self-expression.

Chapter Three engages with the sexual subculture of 'cruising' (a type of anonymous, depersonalised sex in public spaces, like parks or lavatories). This chapter concentrates on times of secrecy and sexual shame, when, in Ireland and Northern Ireland, cruising areas were the main (and, sometimes, the only) social and sexual outlet for gays and other same sex attracted men. As the exact opposite of ideal heterosexuality, of sex confined to the home and the straight couple, cruising came to be defined as the prime example of gay 'depravity'. Read together, the four short stories analysed in this chapter – Keith Ridgway's 'Graffiti' (1994); Eamon Sommer's 'Nataí Bocht' (1994); Micheál O' Conghaile's 'At the Station' (2012); and Joseph O'Connor's

'The Hills are Alive' (1992) – describe a variety of contexts that contradict popular notions on this sexual subculture. These stories thus provide a new language to understand the reality of cruising, as they remove moral considerations and highlight possibilities for empathy and connection within cruising sites.

Drawing on Michael G. Cronin's work on the Bildungsroman and the coming-out story, Chapter Four concentrates on four novels – Desmond Hogan's *The Ikon Maker* (1976); Damien McNicholl's *A Son Called Gabriel* (2004); Tom Lennon's *When Love Comes to Town* (1993); Jarlath Gregory's *Snapshots* (2001); and *G.A.A.Y.:* (2005) – that highlight the particular challenges of growing up gay in the recent Irish and Northern Irish past, in the years between the 1970s and early 2000s. Published at a time when there was scarce recognition of the loneliness and harassment suffered by many young homosexuals, these texts prefigure public debates on homophobic bullying and the LGBTI+ youth's mental health. In these novels, the family and the school emerge as sites of struggle, disaffection, and conflict. The protagonists contend with two sources of homophobia: religion – with its view of homosexuality as pathological, filthy, and sinful – and hegemonic masculinity – with its feminisation of the gay body, a gendering which becomes the justification for derision and abuse. In all cases, the young protagonists need to remake a received language of gay identity in order to resist internalised homophobia and lead healthier, more fulfilling lives as homosexuals.

Chapter Five addresses the impact of the AIDS crisis on the Irish gay community, from a local and transnational perspective, as reflected in Mícheál O'Conghaile's 'Lost in Connemara' (2012); Keith Ridgway's 'Andy Warhol' (2018); Anne Enright's *The Green Road* (2015); Desmond Hogan's *A Farewell to Prague* (1995); and Colm Tóibín's *The Blackwater Lightship* (1999). As discussed in the chapter, at the outbreak of AIDS in the 1980s, sex, sexuality and sexual health were taboo subjects in Ireland. In later decades, despite the growing sexual liberalism of Ireland, the situation did not change much for HIV-positive people, as the general public has remained largely prejudiced and misinformed. This chapter draws on Cormac O'Brien theorisation of the 'post-AIDS' culture of contemporary Ireland, and also consider to what extent the texts analysed here conform to the 'punishment paradox' (a way of representing HIV-positive people which, while promoting empathy towards their predicament, ultimately endorses moral condemnation), which O'Brien himself identified in his study of Irish theatre.

Chapter Six offers an analysis of Emma Donoghue's contemporary-set lesbian novels: *Stir-fry* (1994); *Hood* (1995); and *Landing* (2007). Whereas Dorcey's fiction is inspired by lesbian feminist principles which discard gender roles and stress sameness and mutuality, Donoghue's *Stir-fry* and *Hood* depict a time, the 1990s, when liberal ideas of individualism began to replace feminist notions of equality and woman-bonding. Paradoxically, Donoghue's young lesbian characters, who live at a time of greater sexual freedom, display much more conservative attitudes than Dorcey's middle-aged protagonists. Contrary to what happens in *Stir-fry* and *Hood*, the protagonist of *Landing* is a postfeminist, highly consumerist, and hyper-feminine lesbian, whose behaviour reflects the limitations of the 'gender repolarisation' of Celtic Tiger Ireland (Ging, 2009). Aside from analysing some of the shortcomings of Ireland's liberal culture as shown in Donoghue's fiction, this chapter examines other relevant topics, such as lesbian awakening against a background of invisibility (*Stir-fry*), the silence and non-recognition suffered by a recently widowed closeted lesbian (*Hood*), and the contrasts, in terms of gender and sexual issues, between the Canadian and Irish liberal societies (*Landing*).

Chapter Seven focuses on Celtic Tiger Ireland and how, in those years, new cultural representations of gay men – as urban, carefree, sexually liberated, middle-class consumers – promoted notions of personal fulfilment and social progress that were clearly connected with the lifestyle principles of liberal capitalism. An exaggeratedly optimistic icon of gay life served the political agenda of the Celtic Tiger economy, which obviated issues of class oppression and poverty, while establishing rigid distinctions between a dark, repressive Catholic Ireland, and a tolerant, open-minded Irish modernity. In multiple and illuminating ways, the texts analysed in this chapter – Tom Lennon's *Crazy Love* (1999); Belinda McKeon's *Tender* (2015); Colm Tóibín's 'The Pearl Fishers' (2010); Ridgway's *The Long Falling* (1998), 'Angelo' (2001), and *The Parts* (2003); and Frank McGuiness's 'Chocolate and Oranges' (2018) – challenge the celebratory icon of gay life promoted by Celtic Tiger Ireland. These texts consistently undermine the correlation between gay identity and the sexual freedom and middle-class values of the Celtic Tiger ideology, and emphasise how, below a veneer of modernity and progress, silenced prejudices and homophobic assumptions remained entrenched.

Finally, this volume closes with a chapter devoted to four historical novels – Jamie O'Neill's *At Swim, Two Boys* (2001); Emma Donoghue's *Life Mask* (2004); Sebastian Barry's *Days Without End* (2016); and John Boyne's *The Heart's Invisible Furies* (2017) – which effect a cultural revisioning of the past, destabilising the heterosexual consensus that has traditionally dominated historiographical accounts. In Ireland, this queering of the historical novel has opened up a space for the exploration of early examples of sexual dissidence and resilience against heteronormativity, including the construction of a lesbian identity in eighteenth-century England (*Life Mask*), the retelling of the 1916 Rising from a gay viewpoint (*At Swim, Two*

Boys), gender fluidity and transgenderism as a philosophy of life (*Days Without End*), and gay emigration as a means of evading the rampant homophobia of Catholic Ireland (*The Heart's Invisible Furies*). The analyses of the novels draw on Norman W. Jonas's study on the three characteristic topoi of gay and lesbian historical novels: identification, transformation, and chosen community. As shall be explained, the four novels foreground contexts of silence, self-suppression, and non-recognition of homosexual love, just to depict how their protagonists progressively acquire a language adequate to express and understand their same-sex passions and senses of self. Taken together, these novels help build and reinforce a sense of a queer history and tradition, which aptly exemplifies the growing cultural recognition of lesbian and gay identities in contemporary Ireland.

Through its focus on fiction, this book offers a much needed exploration of gender and sexual dissidence, queer empowerment and social change in Ireland from the 1970s until the present moment. Aside from revitalising contemporary Irish fiction, the queer stories analysed here have effectively challenged the historical silencing and oppression not just of homophobia, but of our heteronormative systems. Being the first comprehensive survey of gay and lesbian-themed Irish fiction, *Queer Whispers* will hopefully lay the foundations for future expanded work on the ever-evolving story of queer Ireland.

I Don't Even Know How to be a Lesbian

Isolation and Vulnerability in the 1980s and early 1990s Irish Lesbian Fiction

In a 1985 article, Irish scholar and activist Carol Lannigan, writing under the pseudonym Carol Laing, argued that lesbians were everywhere, but most of them chose to wear 'the cloak of invisibility' due to a patriarchal culture that either denied their existence or portrayed them as 'sad unfulfilled women, ugly half men who relate to women because of an inability to involve themselves in real adult relationships' (17). In 1980s Ireland, lesbian lives did occasionally come to public attention, but these discussions where short-lived and did not undermine the social silencing of lesbianism. In 1980, activist Joni Crone came out on the *The Late Late Show*, the same TV programme where, five years later, American scholars Nancy Manahan and Rosemay Keefer Curb publicised their book on lesbian nuns, *Breaking Silence* (1985), while 'a protest was waged outside the Montrose studios' (RTÉ Written Archives). This animosity reflects hetero-patriarchal Ireland's need to keep lesbianism silenced, repressed, and condemned. Derided as a kind of infantilism and a non-viable lifestyle, lesbianism, when acknowledged, was stigmatised, as it challenged notions of women as emotionally and sexually dependent on men.

A primary reason for lesbian invisibility was that women's sexuality was largely censored and controlled by a punitive, conservative Catholic morality,[1] which enforced ignorance and shameful silences on women's own bodies and sexual desires. Given this socio-cultural context, many same-sex women chose to conform to hetero-patriarchal norms, but often confronted the frustrations of sexual unfulfillment, or an inability to understand their desires.

Aside from sexual oppression, most Irish lesbians experienced economic and legal disadvantages. In non-mainstream Irish publications like the 1980s magazine *OUT*, activists addressed the needs of married women who wanted to start a new life as lesbians, offering them advice as how to deal with their separations[2] (divorce was not legal until 1995). In cases involving children and custody rights, lesbian mothers became highly vulnerable to moral judgment and unfair treatment, since, as Patricia Prendiville notes in her 1990s study, '[Irish] women are rightly fearful of declaring their involvement with another woman in court, as they may lose custody [of their children]' (1997: 136). Firmly sustained by law and moral doctrine, patriarchy has been one of the main impediments to women's personal freedom. In the early years of activism, Irish lesbians associated mainly with the feminist movement, and their contributions to it were crucial, as Anne Mulhall observes: 'Many lesbian women were centrally involved in the Irish feminist movement that achieved massive gains during the 1970s, and [. . .] groups such as Irish Women United included a vocal radical lesbian feminist membership' (2011: 102).

In the 1980s, while joining forces with gay liberationists to have male homosexuality decriminalised, lesbians continued to campaign for other legal issues, such as birth control, abortion, and divorce, so, at the time, lesbian and feminist concerns seemed hardly discernible. A lesbian life requires women to be independent from men, and this was not always possible in a society where women faced much higher rates of unemployment: 'Women's employment stagnated or declined from the 1920s to the 1980s' (Meaney et al., 2013: 106). If in 1973 only seven per cent of married women were employed (see Kennedy, 2011: 114), 20 years later, a majority of Irish married women, 60 per cent, still depended on a male breadwinner (see Coulter, 1997: 286). This general situation of economic disadvantage may partly explain why, even in the 1990s, it was widely believed that lesbian relationships were only a type of middle-class privilege.[3] Apart from suggesting a necessary link between lesbianism and female emancipation, this class-based assumption undermined the notion of lesbianism as a fully formed, autonomous, sexual identity.

Activists encountered numerous obstacles in their attempt to construct a more visible public identity for lesbians. Created in 1991, the Irish organisation LOT (Lesbians Organising Together) aimed to 'promote a positive identity and/or positive image for lesbians' in order to 'encourage and support the "coming out" of all lesbians' (LOT Annual Report, 1993), but they quickly found that a large number of same-sex attracted women, far from regarding themselves as lesbian or bisexual, were struggling with self-definition. In their 1993 report, LOT remarked that their helplines received the calls of numerous married women and young women in heterosexual relationships. Writing about her experiences working for LOT, Ger Moane relates that most of these women were 'dealing with their lesbian feelings for the first time', their words revealing 'shame, ignorance, fear and self-hatred'

(1995: 87). Many Irish lesbians therefore suffered a sense of entrapment, finding it difficult to escape from their old selves and heterosexual relationships.[4] Still in the late 1990s, in a more liberal society where gay men became icons of Irish modernity, 'lesbians were largely concerned with issues of coming out and making visible a lesbian identity' (O'Donnell, 2008: 18). Thus, as has been discussed so far, silence, self-suppression and fear of disclosure have been commonplace in the lives of too many Irish lesbians in the 1980s and 1990s.

Drawing on cultural contexts similar to those described above, the four novels in this chapter – Maura Richards's *Interlude* (1982), Edna O'Brien's *The High Road* (1988), Linda Cullen's *The Kiss* (1990), and Pádraig Standún's *A Woman's Love* (1994) – evoke situations of isolation and non-politicised vulnerability for Irish lesbians. Referring to gender norms, Judith Butler theorises this type of vulnerability as a condition of silence and unintelligibility, as there are forms of sexuality for which 'there is no good vocabulary precisely because the powerful logics that determine how we think about desire, orientation, sexual acts and pleasures do not admit certain modes of sexuality' (2009: iii). The four novels recreate a time when Irish lesbians faced a lack of role models and visibility, and this absence of (using Butler's words) 'good vocabulary' on lesbian life and identity disorients these characters as they come to terms with their same-sex desires. Silence, secrecy and the characters' inability or refusal to identify as lesbians hence become important topics in these texts. Except in Cullen's *The Kiss*, where one of the protagonists reveals her lesbian relationship to some friends and family members, lesbian relationships develop within the confines of the strictly private, due to the fear of social recrimination and/or the renunciations an open lesbian life would entail. At least one of the lovers in each of these stories is in a heterosexual relationship, and some of the characters do not or cannot even name the nature of their same-sex desires, long repressed or newly discovered.

MAURA RICHARDS'S INTERLUDE

The important topic of sexual discovery is already foregrounded in the opening scene of Maura Richards's *Interlude*, where the protagonists engage in a passionate sexual relationship in the dressing-room of a Dublin store: 'Lust for the bodies of all the women she had never known exploded in Martha' (14). When she published *Interlude* in 1982, Richards, a writer of popular fiction, was already known for her book *Two to Tango* (1981), which denounces the hypocrisy of patriarchal Ireland by presenting the predicament of a single mother in a daring way, 'provoking annoyance and high sales' (O'Cuilleanáin, 1984: 119). Her second novel, *Interlude*, describes a short but intense affair between two women in their forties, Sheila Segal, a nun, and Martha Stephens, a married Irish woman on holidays from England. Critic Rebecca Pelan includes Richards within a generation of female authors – like Ita Daly, Catherine Brophy and Evelyn Conlon – who, in the 1970s and 1980s, broke the 'codes of literary niceness' and produced non-sanitised accounts of Irish women's lives (1999: 127). Pelan regards *Interlude* as 'one of the earliest examples of Irish erotic/lesbian fiction' (137), indicating that, had it been a straight novel, Richards's text would have similarly challenged social mores because of its explicit sexual content.

Interlude is a first-person, linear narrative which revolves around Martha's experiences with Sheila and her evolving perceptions of them. Because of the novel's numerous and graphic sexual scenes, an early reviewer remarked that *Interlude* 'degenerate[s] into soft porn', adding the complaint that 'the teller of the tale doesn't even understand [herself]' (Sweetman, 1983: 14). Given the vulnerable situation for lesbians at the time, Martha's confusion is not only relatable, but also adds some complexity to the story. While *Interlude* may not be remembered alongside the finest of Irish literature, the novel is certainly worthy of exploration because of its sexual politics in the context of early 1980s Ireland.

Richards's protagonists desire each other fervently, and their lesbian attraction breaks two of the norms of their conservative Catholic milieu: the notions that sex had to be inseparable from procreation within marriage, and that, for women, 'even within marriage lust was a sin' (Beale, 1986: 91).[5] Arguably, in a culture that censored female sexual desires, 'sexual acts between two women were unimaginable' (Irish Council for Civil Liberties, 1990: 7). Showing an in-your-face aesthetics, Richards's *Interlude* creates a language of lesbian eroticism:

> Martha was gasping, breathless, begging. Wanting the orgasm to start and never wanting to reach it. Sheila stroked the edge of the vagina with her right hand, still pressing the clitoris with the left one, then when Martha thought she could bear no more, her mouth came down and her tongue pressed on the swelling clitoris. Martha burst into orgasmic screaming which went on in wave after wave. (47)

Throughout the book, Richards provides detailed descriptions of their lovemaking, including images of how Martha and Sheila stimulate each other's genitalia. Hence, in the figures of Richards's protagonists, *Interlude* radically undermines the social silences on lesbianism, the female sexual body, and women's sexual pleasures.

The pleasures of lesbian sex, though, do not alleviate Martha's fears now that she perceives herself changed by her relationship with Sheila. In this way, Richards addresses the consequences of what American lesbian feminist Adrienne Rich called 'compulsory heterosexuality' (1980), whereby, because of the influence of patriarchal cultural institutions, people assume that men and women are innately attracted to each other, as if heterosexuality were intrinsic to functional human behaviour. Though a feminist, Martha had internalised this sexual dichotomy between normality and abnormality, so her self-image as a 'normal' woman starts to crumble (22). She reassesses her heterosexist biases and realises how in the past she 'got twinges' when she heard gays and lesbians claim that their sexuality was normal, when, in actuality, 'they should be pleased to be tolerated' (23). But, for Martha, the most devastating effect of compulsory heterosexuality is her vulnerability and lack of role models as she faces a new life as woman-loving: 'I can't go to Richard after this, and I don't even know how to be a lesbian' (130).

The consequences of compulsory heterosexuality are also explored through Martha's initial unawareness of society's homophobia and the impact it has on homosexuals' daily existence. Her ignorance reflects broader attitudes of 1980s Ireland, as one recent study demonstrates: 'Most of Irish society at the time did not consider the treatment of Irish homosexuals to be in fact oppressive [. . .] If homosexuals felt insecure or like second-class citizens, then that was a result of their own actions, rather than society's' (McDonagh, 2017: 80). Having lived all her life as a heterosexual, Martha is accustomed to expressing affection in public, but feels vulnerable and frightened by a straight couple's raw hostility when she kisses Sheila on the street: 'Everything was there, horror, revulsion, accusation, condemnation, soundless screaming loathing' (58). In *Interlude*, Richards dramatises how, for long, homophobia has constructed public space into heterosexual territory, making heterosexuality the only visible and valid option.[6]

Interestingly, aside from raising awareness of homophobia in 1980s Ireland, Richards presents her readers with different varieties of feminism. If Sheila features as a Christian feminist who wants to reform the Irish Catholic Church from within, Martha is a more liberal feminist whose hostility against the Church 'bordered on the obsessional' (89). Their worldviews clash when Sheila reveals that she is a nun, and that she wishes to return to her religious community. Enraged, Martha condemns her as a complete hypocrite:

> Going back to what? You, a raving lesbian, going back to a convent full of women like you, is that it? What do you do? Come out every now and again and prey on some helpless woman like me, destroy her life and then return to the safety of your stronghold? (124)

Martha, who had begun to identify as a lesbian, now voices the stereotype of homosexuals as sexually predatory, seeing herself as a victim of a 'raving lesbian'. Nonetheless, due to her bafflement and sense of entrapment, her predicament excites the reader's sympathy. At a time when there was a lack of social outlets for lesbians, Martha sees no option other than returning to her previous life: 'Did she want to go back to him? She couldn't answer the question; she couldn't think of any place else' (136). Paradoxically, Sheila – a nun who, according to Martha, belongs to 'the most patriarchal, woman-destroying institution' (125) – appears as a more independent woman than the heterosexually married Martha.

In the figure of Sheila, the nun, Richards gives voice to a non-main-stream type of feminism. This is important since, as Jenny Beale argued in *Women in Ireland: Voices of Change* (1986), Catholic feminism was largely ignored, and most Irish feminists 'found it hard to see nuns as thinking, feeling people like themselves' (174). Richards's text was published in an early 1980s context where Irish Christian feminists, nuns, and lay women, became more vocal; in 1983, a mother-superior publicly denounced the 'totally patronising, condescending manner' in which Irish bishops treated women (Beale, 178). These criticisms were not only directed against male authority, but also against the perceived anti-religious ethos of the lesbian feminist movement. Eileen Brady, a Sister of Mercy nun, declared: 'I may define my identity as a lesbian differently than others do [. . .] I'm not going to let either the Catholic Church or the lesbian caucus define who I am' (Douglas, 1984: 19). In *Interlude*, as a Christian feminist, Richards's Sheila is highly eloquent on her opinions against women's oppression and artic-ulates liberal views on sexuality when she argues that compulsory celibacy is psychologically unhealthy, because 'sex becomes an obsession' (130). Sheila tells her lover how, in her early career, she experienced the rigid discipline prior to Second Vatican Council (1962–5), when nuns lived in enclosed orders,[7] which made her suffer 'frightful crises' (129). But now, after Vatican II, Sheila informs an incredulous Martha that there are 'groups of strong-minded independent women' within the Church (128).

Richards abruptly concludes her story when Sheila decides to abandon Martha, invoking the moral authority of her Christian feminism. As an experienced lesbian, Sheila surprises Martha by telling her that, because she had relationships with one woman, she should not consider herself a lesbian, just to add later that her willingness to identify as a homosexual originates from the dictates of lesbian feminism (Martha is familiar with the movement that developed in Britain): 'You are *not* a lesbian [. . .] Militant lesbian feminists do not speak for the majority of women in the movement, even though their voice is sometimes louder than all the rest put together' (emphasis in the original; 131). Richards characterises Sheila as morally ambiguous; it is not clear whether she actually believes her own words, or if she is making an excuse to abandon Martha, encouraging her to go back to her husband. Sheila's idea that Martha is still heterosexual cannot be ascertained, as *Interlude* finishes the moment she drives home to her husband, aware that she has nowhere else to go.

Perhaps because this novel is a product of its time and culture, *Interlude* offers its readers a politically disempowering ending, which hinges on acts of betrayal (Sheila initially deceives and then abandons Martha) and conformism (Martha returns to her heterosexual life). At the same time, Richards emphasises Martha's vulnerability and inability to start a lesbian life. For the reasons here described, Richards's *Interlude* should be regarded as more than 'a holiday romance' (Quinn, 2000: 146) or 'soft porn' (Sweetman, 14). The encounter between the two women – who belong to opposite worlds but become united by their lesbian desires – gives way to provocative reflections on sexual and feminist identities within the conservative milieu of 1980s Ireland.

LINDA CULLEN'S THE KISS

Another work of popular fiction that provides meaningful commentaries on public perceptions on lesbianism is Linda Cullen's *The Kiss*, which, while being less subversive than Richards's *Interlude*, also represents same-sex love and desire as prominent in the story. The novel describes the failed love relationship of Joanna Maloney and Helen Ryan, two friends who fall in love with one another, discovering the thrills of lesbian sex: 'Their lovemaking was passionate in a way neither of them knew woman and woman could be' (86). *The Kiss* is a third-person narrative focalised on Joanna and follows a linear storyline except for the first chapter, which portrays the couple's breakup while on a trip in the West of Ireland. Cullen withholds the gender of Joanna's lover until the end of the chapter, so the reader may get the impression that the protagonist is grieving her separation from a man, not from another woman. In this way, Cullen presents lesbian love as equal by nature, but unequal due to social constraints: '[Joanna] couldn't help thinking it was like a ludicrously friendly divorce. Without the marriage. There could have never been a marriage' (16). In spite of this initial criticism of heterosexism, *The Kiss* reads as a rather conservative narrative in some other aspects.

As shall be explained, though published by Attic Press (an Irish feminist publishing house), *The Kiss* endorses a postfeminist, rather than a feminist, sensibility. Cullen's only novel appeared in 1990 and excited much media attention, and, while the story is 'based on [Cullen's] experiences of a lost love with a woman', in interviews the writer 'skitted the issue of any identity politics' (O'Donnell, 2008: 20). This lack of lesbian (and feminist) identity politics permeates the novel in its entirety. Arguably, Cullen's protagonists do not become politicised in the course of the story because their family and friends feature as broad-minded and enlightened, free from prejudice. In her review of *The Kiss*, Emma Donoghue judged Cullen's portrayal of Irish society as unrealistic and politically disempowering:

> Bland, semi-closeted heroines who always shave their legs, never pose a social problem, living in a mythical new Ireland where homophobia is never heard louder than a murmur [. . .] Yuppie employees are understanding, mothers are open-armed, and Catholicism never rears its homophobic head. This is an Ireland where I have never been. (quoted in Quinn, 2000: 148)

As Donoghue remarks, homophobia is not an issue in *The Kiss*, even though Joanna herself knows that '"homosexual" or "lesbian" were dirty words in Ireland' (111), which explains why she refuses to hold hands with Helen on the streets of Dublin: 'I refuse to be called names. I refuse to create problems for myself' (152). Joanna never encounters those problems, though. For example, when she timidly confesses her love for Helen to Kathy, this friend perceives lesbian love as positive and equal: 'Don't *ever* put me into a box that says this woman is so damned straight she couldn't see love if it bit her on the nose' (emphasis in the original, 115). The protagonist's social circle displays similar attitudes to those of Kathy, so Joanna's fears prove delusional. At a time, 1990, when homophobic prejudice remained strong and by no means hidden, Cullen's depiction of lesbian acceptance in a new, modern Ireland seems excessively optimistic.

Though the story does not engage with society's sexism and lesbophobia, *The Kiss* does challenge stereotypes about lesbians' appearance and behaviour. A mid-2000s study found that the popular image of the lesbian as 'unattractive and butch' persisted in Ireland, especially among heterosexual women, who were much more accepting of gay men than of lesbians (O'Higgins-Norman, 2009: 10). Far from looking unattractive and butch, Helen and Joanna are svelte and sophisticated, and take good care of their physical appearance and personal style.

Paradoxically, whilst rejecting the stereotypes of lesbianism, Cullen seems to draw on some clichés of modern femininity, or the so-called postfeminist culture. According to Yvonne Tasker and Diane Negra, a postfeminist culture commodifies feminism 'via the figure of the woman as an empowered consumer' (2007: 2). Postfeminism, Tasker and Negra add, emphasises women's 'sexual empowerment' and 'freedom with respect to work', but this liberal culture is 'white and middle-class by default', since it 'set[s] aside economic disparities' and regards 'consumption as a strategy for the production of the self' (2). Characterised as positive role models, Cullen's postfeminist protagonists are independent women who radiate self-confidence, especially Helen, who proclaims: 'We are the women of today. Young, successful, bright, gorgeous and happy' (55). Being 'the women of today', Joanna and Helen prioritise their professional career over their relationships with men, and regard Catholic sexual morality as totally irrelevant to them. Because theirs is the first lesbian relationship both had, Helen asks Joanna:

> So if someone asked you were you homosexual or heterosexual what would you say?
> I'd say it was none of their business. (86)

Joanna invokes here one mantra of individualism: the right for privacy and self-fulfilment away from other people's moral judgments. This culture of individualism helps the two women 'savour their time together and marvel at themselves' (77), but they develop no political convictions on account of their transgressive affair. Cullen presents Helen and Joanna as the beneficiaries of a more liberal Ireland, as it is their middle-class status that allows their lesbian relationship to blossom and remain private: Joanna owns a house, and they spend holidays together in places like San Francisco. This model of sexual liberation is hardly available to a large number of lesbians who cannot enjoy the same freedoms, especially those trapped by patriarchal and social-class constraints.

At the same time, Cullen's *The Kiss* aptly illustrates a common situation for many same-sex attracted women in 1980s and 1990s Ireland, a time when 'the formulation of a [lesbian] sexual identity [was] often fragmentary, incomplete and involve[d], to a large extent, self-censure' (Gibney et al., 1995: 166). This 'fragmentary', precarious formulation of lesbian identity manifests itself in the text's lack of feminist politics, and how the protagonists' same-sex love hardly transforms the concept they have about their relationship (they still call each other 'friends', in spite of their passionate attachment). Joanna, unlike her lover, is ready to call herself a lesbian, but only because of what she *does* with Helen – 'What we are doing is called lesbianism. So if that makes me a lesbian then I'm a lesbian' (86) –, a partial identification which further evinces her non-politicisation as woman-loving. Helen, the other friend, consciously rejects a lesbian identity when she tells Joanna that their relationship has 'nothing to do with lesbianism' (93), insisting that she also loves Laurent, the man she eventually marries. The possibility exists that Helen is a bisexual, but this idea never crosses her mind (or Joanna's). *The Kiss* in this way dramatises how, where a rigid dichotomy between heterosexuality and homosexuality is established, people generally lack the language and awareness of bisexuality.[8]

As the novel closes, the lesbian bond dissolves and the protagonists return to their previous heterosexual lives. Even if Cullen's novel portrays this relationship as extremely significant to both women,[9] Helen and Joanna do not develop a new understanding of themselves as same-sex attracted women who challenge hetero-patriarchal values. Their freedom to enjoy the relationship emerges from their social status and belief in individualism, so, as explained, Cullen's story contains elements of a postfeminist narrative. One positive aspect of *The Kiss* is its promotion of a language of lesbian passion and romantic love, but the story ultimately offers no models of lesbian empowerment.

EDNA O'BRIEN'S THE HIGH ROAD

Whereas in Richards's *Interlude* and Cullen's *The Kiss* lesbian passion features as too explicit as to be dismissed, in *The High Road* Edna O'Brien adopts a much more subtle approach to same-sex desire, and her novel's lesbian content has often been overlooked. A well-establish author by the time *The High Road* came out, Edna O'Brien – one of the most celebrated contemporary Irish writers – had her first novel, *The Country Girls* (1960), banned in Ireland, accused of being 'a smear on Irish womanhood' (Adachi, 2014: 51). An Irish literary exile after the banning of *The Country Girls*, Edna O'Brien has often written about expatriation in her fiction (*The High Road* is an example), essays and memoirs, as in *Mother Ireland* (1976) and *Country Girl, a Memoir* (2012). Often by depicting the new possibilities brought by migration, O'Brien has produced vibrant portrayals of Irish women's emotional and sexual lives, as well as their desires of personal freedom. As critics have observed, O'Brien's feminism denounces the patriarchal obsession to possess and control women, and thus her 'canon testifies to the failure of heterosexual relationships and nuclear families, and instead suggests that women's salvation lies in their relationships with each other' (Thompson, 2003a: 23).

This female union is a sexual one in *The High Road*, but the author herself circumvented the issue of lesbianism when discussing her novel, noting that 'every woman, like Anna, wants the love of a woman as much as the love of a man' (Adachi, 2014: 51). O'Brien evades here her novel's lesbian content, just to highlight the 'meeting of minds' which she mentioned in another interview; an interpersonal connection where there is not only 'sexual excitement', but also 'creative stimulation' between two individuals (Thompson, 2003b: 203). Like O'Brien herself, reviewers of *The High Road* 'relegated the lesbian themes' and, subsequently, refrained from using the word 'lesbian' to describe the sexual attraction between Anna and Catalina (Thompson, 2003a: 24). In this respect, one may wonder whether, had the protagonists of *The High Road* been men, the topic of gay sexuality would have remained as diffused as lesbianism was in many of the reviews and analyses of the novel.

Set in an unnamed Spanish town on the Mediterranean coast, *The High Road* describes the affair between a foreigner, Anna (the first-person narrator of the story), and a younger local woman, Catalina, the hotel's chambermaid. Their bond saves a depressed Anna from despair, making her reassess her past failures and disappointments about her married life with her husband. Tellingly, O'Brien portrays these personal recognitions in the context of Anna's infatuation with Catalina, whom she constantly eroticises as 'a picture of radiance, herself a flower, a lotus, unfolding' (107). In another passage, Anna describes one of her sexual fantasies with Catalina:

> In the evenings when I had a drink or two I would allow myself to think of her, as I might a painting or a beautiful garden. I would dwell on her body the way I never allowed myself to dwell on my own, exploring it with invisible hands, invisible eyes, touching her tentatively without shame. (77)

While acknowledging her sexual passions, Anna uses here a language that denotes vulnerability, self-censure, and restraint ('I would allow myself. . .', 'touching her tentatively without shame'). Much as she tries, Anna cannot conceal her desires, as her sexual attraction to Catalina becomes visible to others. She experiences much shame when another woman warns her that they live in a small village where nothing goes unseen: 'I felt the colour rise in my cheeks, imagining that she saw into me, saw my own desire mirroring hers, wild, inchoate, covert' (120). Though easily perceived by others, same-sex desire remains 'covert', dangerous and unspoken, only transmitted through gestures and indirection. Even though many commentators have not interpreted *The High Road* as a lesbian-themed novel, the text teems with references to same-sex desire and the homoerotic.

In her analysis, Kathryn Conrad neglects the presence of the homoerotic, and remarks that O'Brien subordinates here lesbian concerns to feminist ones, since 'the connection between the two women works against the pain and lack of fulfillment that women get from their [heterosexual] relationships' (2004: 60). For Conrad, another significant issue is O'Brien's depiction of lesbian sex not as explicitly sexual, as in the following excerpt:

> Boundaries burst, bursting, the mind as much as the body borne along, to this other landscape, that was familiar yet unfamiliar, like entering a picture, or a fresco, slipping through a wall of flesh, eclipsed, inside the womb of the world, and throughout it all her words, faint, sweet as vapour. (157)

Lesbian sex, rather than passionate, is described as a fusion of bodies and souls, a return to safety and female communion. Conrad further argues that, because O'Brien does not have Anna naming her desire as lesbian, 'the ambivalence of the "sex" sequence gives us the opportunity to deny the scrawl, to plead a kind of innocence on the narrator's behalf' (61). Though it is true that the story avoids lesbian awakening, O'Brien does foreground Anna's conscious same-sex desires, as in the scene when she recalls the moment she was to have sex with another woman, but then felt unable and began to weep, terrified that 'something would alter in her' (156). Lesbianism thus emerges as a personal transformation the protagonist has been repressing. From this, we may conclude, following Helen Thompson, that Anna 'fears the permanence of her sexual re-orientation, the inability to return to the safety of desiring men' (2003a: 27). Because *The High Road* gives us insights into the protagonist's past struggles, Anna's vulnerability and all her fears seemingly relate to the difficulties of autonomy and self-definition derived from the pressures and limitations of her hetero-patriarchal culture.

If these personal limitations can be momentarily transcended, the novel implies, this is because Anna finds herself far away from home. *The High Road* belongs to a tradition of Irish novels, such as John McGahern's *The Leavetaking* (1984) and Colm Tóibín's *The South* (1990), which 'pay tribute to the traditional sexually liberating power attached to exile and expatriation' (Wondrich, 2000: 10). When it comes to Irish gay and lesbian fiction (though *The High Road* may be considered a lesbian-themed novel, O'Brien is no lesbian fiction author), expatriation, too, has counted as one central topic, since, as Ed Madden points out, previous to the 1990s same-sex desire was 'insistently displaced abroad in Irish literature and culture' (2012: 75), a notable example being Kate O'Brien's work, in novels like *Mary Lavelle* (1936) and *As Music and Splendour* (1958).

In *The High Road*, Anna's experience abroad becomes a process of self-discovery, and a quest for a new life. In Spain, O'Brien's protagonist projects on Catalina her own desires for freedom, and her attraction to her clearly revives her hitherto suppressed lesbian self. As a foreigner, Anna exoticises the Spanish landscape and its people, including Catalina: 'There was something untamed about her, a sort of recklessness' (48). Anna describes her Spanish friend as a 'free spirit' (48), but Catalina features as a much more oppressed woman than her. Anna, not Catalina, is the one who adopts a 'reckless' behaviour and breaks the rules of social intercourse when, uninvited, she repeatedly visits Catalina's family home in search of her.

Issues of power and social class colour the locals' perceptions of their friendship as sexually charged, but Anna, as an outsider, remains blinded to the consequences of her actions, to the extent that Catalina has to remind her that, to avoid people's suspicions, she cannot accept expensive presents from her. If their time together gives raise to people's 'looks', 'nudges' and 'innuendoes' (118), tragedy becomes inevitable when a graffiti appears: '"Lesbos" had been painted on [Catalina's] wall for all to see' (160). This accusation of lesbianism unleashes the violence that kills Catalina in the hands of her brutal husband, but O'Brien is careful to link lesbophobia with the oppression exerted by the patriarchal and social class systems, which establish a set of moral principles that make this female friendship deviant and suspect in the eyes of the community. For example, Catalina's sister, Rosario, sees the protagonists' lesbian transgression in terms of the violation of social class boundaries: 'Why the presents to Catalina? Why the lunches and dinners? Why go to the mountain, why insist on staying all night? Why? Why?' (161). With this tragic ending, the exotic Spanish land loses its aura of adventure and romanticism, and Anna is brutally reminded of the rigid codes of behaviour governing the lives of women.

As explained above, readings of *The High Road* have generally deviated from Anna's recognition of her same-sex desires, obviating the numerous instances of homoeroticism, and opting to see the two women's union only as a strategy of resistance against patriarchy.[10] To avoid confusions: O'Brien's protagonist, Anna, is not affected by men's domination during her time in Spain; she rather experiments an unprecedented freedom as a result of her expatriation and social class. Though O'Brien's text refuses to fix the protagonist's sexual identity as lesbian, lesbian desire features here as the suppressed 'other' of Anna's inner self, which flourishes in her tragic relationship with Catalina.

PÁDRAIG STANDÚN'S A WOMAN'S LOVE

Like O'Brien's Anna and Catalina, the lesbian couple in Pádraig Standún's *Cion Mná*, or *A Woman's Love*, is characterised by social class differences, and by the challenges lesbian love poses to the patriarchal authority of a jealous, violent husband. *A Woman's Love* is a third-person story focalised on Bridie, a battered wife in her early twenties, who has returned from London, where her husband, John, remains imprisoned for nearly killing her. Bridie is also the housekeeper of the 35-year-old Therese, who works as a member of the Gaeltacht Board in Galway, and whose authority and assertiveness in a man's world cause the resentment of her male colleagues. Published in 1993, Standún's *Cion Mná* came out a year later as *A Woman's Love*, translated by the author himself, an English translation where the Irish text's lesbian content, according to Emma Donoghue, was 'disappointingly watered down' (1995b: 167).

Standún's lesbian novel, Brian Ó Conchubhair notes, has been regarded in the Gaeltacht as a 'counter-narrative' to the old nationalist mould that presented Ireland and the Irish language as 'a symbiosis of strict Catholic morality [and] traditional culture' (2005: 216).[11] As a Catholic priest, Standún may be considered a Christian feminist who has, for instance, advocated for the priestly ordination of women, the possibility of marriage for priests and, consequently, the abolition of compulsory celibacy (Standún, 2004: 506–08). His views on Christianity, which filter into his fiction,[12] clearly deviate from established norms and orthodoxies, as in his first novel, *Súil le Breith* (1983), translated as *Lovers* (1991): a story of an illicit affair between a priest and his housekeeper, which ends up in scandal when she becomes pregnant, and he admits being the father. *A Woman's Love* may be read as a lesbian version of *Lovers*, as Standún explores the same topics in both texts; namely, the clash between the private and the public, as well as the validity of non-normative love and alternative family configurations.

Together with Mary Dorcey's *Biography of Desire* (1996), analysed in Chapter Two, Standún's novel is one of the few texts – both in the Irish and English languages – exploring lesbian motherhood in an Irish literary tradition where 'there has not been an extended examination of [this issue]' (Palko, 2016: 208). Standún's protagonists raise Caomhán, Bridie's little son, whom Therese treats as her own child. Weary of town gossip, of people telling her that '[Therese] looks more like a man than a woman' (161), Bridie initially rejects Therese's notion that they are a 'family' (15), but she eventually embraces this new life and the comforts it brings. After their trip to Ballinahinch Castle, Bridie confesses that she felt 'as if the three of [them] were [their] own little family' (71).

Even though Bridie becomes ready to accept Therese as a co-parent, ideological factors inevitably impact on the private realm of their family. A study carried out in 2000s Ireland found that there was a strong element of heterosexist prejudice concerning same-sex parenting: 'The assumption is that children may be prone to gender confusion, to confusion over sexual orientation or any number of social problems such as stigmatisation' (Kavanagh, 2009: 167). Social acceptance of same-sex parenting is therefore made difficult because of the gender and sexual anxieties of heterosexism, expressed through the generally accepted moral superiority of the heterosexual nuclear family. This widespread prejudice of course affects Standún's character, Bridie, who voices the moral reserves of heterosexism:

> [Bridie] worried aloud that being reared by two women might be bad for [Caomhán] in the long term.
> 'What harm could that do?'
> 'He might turn out gay, or something.' (98)

In spite of her unacknowledged homophobia, Bridie becomes a much less prejudiced character as the story progresses. In the final chapters, Standún moves from dramatising Bridie's reservations about same-sex parenting to highlighting the two women's fears that Caomhán will suffer discrimination. Having anticipated the ways the child may suffer, they consider abandoning their town to settle in London, where they would be anonymous: 'It'd be better than being here with the other children teasing him about us' (223). In the context of his story, Standún calls attention to how, whereas a homosexual relationship may remain private and out of social control, same-sex parenthood becomes a much more public issue, subject to numerous pressures affecting the private life of the family unit.

Bridie's acceptance of Therese's role as co-parent goes parallel with her development of romantic and sexual feelings towards her. In order to dramatise this, Standún traces the growing physical intimacy between the two, which culminates one evening when they dance together at home, doing it 'cheek to cheek, as if holding each other up' (144), and then sleeping in the same bed together, holding one another. Their sexual relationships are not described but only suggested, something which, according to Seán Mac Risteaird, damages the novel's 'realism' and 'silences lesbian sexuality' (2020: 71). The writer, though, inserts numerous intimations that their friendship has turned into a love relationship,[13] even if Bridie insists that she is not a lesbian. Unlike Bridie, the more experienced Therese does identify as a lesbian, and speaks freely about a past relationship in England (the text thus underlines the importance of expatriation and the availability of a new language of same-sex love for this character's lesbian awakening). Bridie's initial qualms about Therese's lesbianism progressively disappear, and she starts calling their relationship a 'marriage' (213), which marks a turning point in her self-perception as woman-loving, though not as a lesbian yet.

In the final part of the story, the protagonists' relationship becomes threatened when Bridie's brutal husband, John, returns to town. Like O'Brien's *The High Road*, Standún's *A Woman's Love* illustrates how women's romantic friendships (not necessarily lesbian) have caused a stronger social disapproval in cases where they were considered a 'dangerous affront to

male sexual prerogatives' (Vicinus, 1996: 3). Standún, thus depicts lesbophobia in connection with the patriarchal control of women's lives and
sexuality. Social hostilities against Therese dramatically increase the moment
Bridie refuses to quit her job and move in with John as his wife. Emasculated,[14]
a furious John blames Therese for getting 'her filthy claws in [Bridie], turning
her against him' (235), an accusation that brings negative consequences on
Therese's personal life and professional career.[15] In a final turn of events, a
drunken John attempts to burn down Therese's office, but fails. Therese
decides not to press charges under the condition that John leaves the town.
She tells Bridie:

> 'It's not John's skin I'm saving.' Therese looked Bridie in the eyes. 'But mine,
> yours, ours. Can you imagine what a defence lawyer would make of the rumours
> that were going around a few weeks ago if it was to come up in court? Or the
> headlines, "Father takes revenge on gay mums?"' (238)

A trial would give John a chance to explain himself and justify his actions
before a court that may be biased in his favour. Due to the support John
received from others, Therese's fears are not unfounded, so she understandably regards John's enforced exile as a self-defence strategy.

Bridie and Therese's is a condition of vulnerability, given that public
opinion is heavily influenced by a homophobic language that can hardly
value or understand the positive nature of their attachment. In the novel,
there is no lesbian identification on the part of Bridie, and the text implies
that, for this character, same-sex love may simply become a refuge from
male violence. Bridie accepts her love for Therese, but remains 'unable to
identify with lesbianism, let alone understand it' (Mac Risteaird, 71), a
situation that exemplifies the unintelligibility of lesbianism in a highly
hetero-patriarchal community like the one portrayed by Standún. The other
protagonist, Therese, does identify as a lesbian, but her lesbian awakening
happened away from Ireland, in London, which highlights the importance
of queer expatriation in those years. All in all, Standún's *A Woman's Love*
can be deemed a story of lesbian love that, unlike the other novels analysed
in this chapter, offers a positive resolution for the protagonists (including the
child, who prefers Therese over his father), who remain together as a family.
Interestingly, as a Catholic priest, Standún rejects traditional notions of the
so-called Catholic family – with its exclusion of homosexuals and patriarchal
ideology – and offers instead an alternative model, advancing public debates
about family equality and the social acceptance of same-sex love.

CONCLUSION

This chapter has explored four novels that depict the isolation and vulnerability of lesbian life in the 1980s and early 1990s, a time when lesbianism remained largely invisible in Irish society. The novels stage the predicament of various characters who, having led heterosexual lives, engage in their same-sex passions for the first time, but can hardly find social outlets to develop a lesbian identity. This vulnerability, as explained in the introductory paragraphs, connects with an Irish context where there was no public language of lesbian life and experience, and where there were 'no structures to protect or accommodate [lesbians]' (Laing, 17). There is no sense in these texts of an Irish lesbian community or subculture either. This lack of a solid lesbian identity in Ireland connects with the sexual ambiguity displayed by some of these characters, who do not or cannot identify as lesbian or bisexual even though they love and desire their female partner.

Because the dominant hetero-patriarchal system defined notions of social and sexual respectability, same-sex attraction was generally judged as deviant and unnatural. A character that explicitly articulates this idea is Richards's Martha, who asks herself: 'Had she become abnormal?' (23). In more subtle ways, O'Brien depicts the silence and unacceptability of lesbian desire through the shame that Anna experiences as she comes to terms with her attraction to Catalina. Like O'Brien's Catalina with Anna, Standún's Bridie finds love and protection in her close friendship with Therese, but, as a vulnerable married woman, lacks the language, awareness, and personal freedom to regard herself a lesbian. Given the situation of patriarchal oppression in Ireland at the time, feminist concerns become relevant in these novels, except in Cullen's *The Kiss*, which articulates a liberal culture of postfeminism and individualism as the (failed) promise for lesbian empowerment. As discussed, though not really providing models of lesbian politicisation or resistance, these four novels do promote a language of lesbian love, which counteracts the general climate of homophobia and non-recognition of lesbianism. Taken together, the novels of this chapter accurately reflect the submerged nature of lesbian desire in 1980s and early 1990s, as well as the social constraints impeding the protagonists from leading open lives as lesbians.

TWO

Coming Clear of Years of Camouflage

The Feminist Politics of Mary Dorcey's Lesbian Fiction

The first high profile Irish woman to be publicly and proudly a lesbian, Mary Dorcey grew up in an Ireland where words like 'sex', 'condoms', 'divorce' and 'abortion' were dirty and sinful, and where there was fear and suspicion surrounding anything that deviated from the sexual norms of conservative Catholicism. In this context, as Dorcey indicates, specific, non-offensive terms to refer to sexual diversity were virtually non-existent:

> The word 'lesbian' was never spoken. The word 'homosexual' was not spoken or written in Ireland before the 1970s. The word 'gay' didn't exist. I had never heard of a bisexual. I had never seen one or spoken to one. (1995: 28)

There was therefore no public language from which to reclaim the equality of same-sex love, a silence which Dorcey and others undermined after their foundation of the Sexual Liberation Movement (SLM) in 1973, the first group to address lesbian and gay issues in Ireland (a year later, David Norris and others set up the Irish Gay Rights Movement, IGRM, to campaign for gay decriminalisation). As an activist, Dorcey volunteered, together with Fergus Martina, to speak at 'UCD Women's Week', but her openness as a lesbian feminist had a personal cost, as she was 'vilified in the media' (Weekes, 2000: 141), and her mother, a widow living alone, received hate mail and abusive phone calls and was shunned by her Parish priest. This response fueled her activism and her determination to educate and enlarge the public discourse on Gay and Women's Rights. Joining forces with Anne Speed and other feminists, Dorcey participated in the creation of Irish Women United, which held meetings where lesbian activists could discuss their sexuality more openly.

Dorcey, whose politics and sexual identity had been first formed by her time in Paris as a college student, moved to London in the 1980s and later to the US. Referring to Dorcey and poet Cherry Smyth among other Irish lesbians, critic Tina O'Toole emphasises the positive effects of diasporic experience on the 'language and politics' of late twentieth-century Irish lesbian activists and writers (2013: 133). As also discussed in Chapter One, too many Irish women suffered the vulnerability of not being able to define themselves outside the parameters of patriarchal, conservative Catholic discourse. That is why, O'Toole insists, international feminism proved crucial: 'As Irish lesbians and bisexual women looked for role models, cognate communities elsewhere, and ways to read themselves into representation, the distinctive logos of UK publishers such as Virago and Women's Press became prevalent on Irish feminist bookshops' (134). These transnational networks strengthened feminist activism in Ireland, creating a cultural scenario which grew in parallel with the establishment of the homegrown feminist presses, most particularly Attic Press and Arlen House, the latter contributing to the 'resurgence' of author Kate O'Brien as a 'role model' for Irish feminists coming of age in the 1980s (O'Toole, 134).

Arguably, Dorcey's diasporic experience in London and the US became a primary influence on her writing, as illustrated by the radical and confident perspective she maintains in both her poetry and fiction in an Irish context where such writing was still viewed with suspicion. Dorcey's first two books were published by the British press Onlywomen, and, whereas her poetry collection, *Kindling* (1982), was judged as 'scandalous' in Ireland due to its lesbian content (Coppola, 230), some years later her short story collection, *A Noise from the Woodshed* (1989), enjoyed a much more positive reception, and received the prestigious Rooney Prize for Irish Literature. Though this chapter focuses on her fiction, more specifically on her novel *Biography of Desire* (1997) and three of her short stories in *A Noise from the Woodshed*, Dorcey is also the author of acclaimed poetry collections, including *Moving into the Space Cleared by Our Mothers* (1991) and *Perhaps the Heart is Constant After All* (2012).

The present chapter approaches Dorcey's work from the perspective of its feminist politics, and how her characters manage to discover and embrace their lesbian selves once they unlearn patriarchal stereotypes about women. According to the writer, there is an essential link between lesbianism and feminism, because '[lesbians] want to live as equals and in a patriarchal world this is condemned as neurotic' (1995: 33). Due to the cultural influence of hetero-patriarchy, Dorcey adds, many women have willingly suppressed their 'instincts and personalities' (1995: 33). This is what had happened to a young Dorcey before her discovery of feminism and lesbianism in the company of a female lover, an event that 'changed a private sexual encounter into a cultural happening, a psychic image, a way of seeing, a way of being in the world' (Dorcey, 1995: 30). In her fiction, some of her protagonists experience the same sense of personal transformation thanks to their acquisition of a language of feminism and lesbian love. Dorcey's texts do not centre so much on the dangers and consequences of homophobia, but dwell on the joys and rebelliousness of lesbianism, thus providing positive and politically empowering representations of Irish lesbians, which reverse damaging stereotypes of lesbians as angry, sad, and unfulfilled women.[2]

As shall be argued, lesbian relationships in Dorcey's texts are characterised by emotional nurturance, sameness, and mutuality, in contrast to a hetero-patriarchal culture that creates rigid gender boundaries between men and women. At the same time, while also addressing specific lesbian experiences and concerns, her characters' emotional conflicts and desires for personal freedom feature as profoundly human and relatable. Another central aspect of Dorcey's fiction is that 'her lesbian lovers are not isolated but integrated into a wide spectrum of Irish life' (Weekes, 2000: 147). Whereas, as seen in Chapter One, some of Richards's, O'Brien's, Cullen's and Standún's characters confront isolation, vulnerability, and incomprehension of their own sexuality, Dorcey's protagonists find their place within a lesbian and feminist community, accept their same-sex desires, and become transformed by the experience.

'A COUNTRY DANCE'

As indicated above, this chapter offers a feminist reading of Dorcey's novel and selected short stories from *A Noise from the Woodshed*, one of them being 'A Country Dance', where the author locates lesbian love in a rural setting, avoiding the 'geographical clichés' of lesbianism as a product of urban subcultures (Donoghue, 1995b: 166). Set in a dancehall, 'A Country Dance' is the first-person narration of an unnamed woman who addresses herself to her younger lover as they look at one another, silently communicating their mutual desire and affection. Their seduction is interrupted by several men whose behaviour illustrates the objectifying power of the male gaze.[3] 'A Country Dance', Anne Fogarty observes, depicts with 'painful realism' the oppressive nature of patriarchy and lesbophobia, foregrounding the lesbian characters' 'rebellion against those conditions with constrain [them]' (1997: 195). In this story, as in many others by Dorcey, the two women's bravery, defiance and resilience eventually prevail, allowing them not to become hapless victims of male aggression.

Unaccompanied by men, the two women become a curiosity in the dancehall, and receive the unwanted attentions of their male onlookers, who hardly understand the real bond between them. The protagonists consciously evade their watchful eyes – 'you ignore them, your gaze holding mine' (44) – , but one of the men, having grown impatient, interrupts their conversation:

'"Is it a drink you want?" [. . .] He has been listening to us for some time, his gaze flickering between us like a snake's tongue' (51). The barman, on his part, simply ignores the narrator's presence and talks to her companion, but, when he suddenly becomes aware of the narrator's wary eyes on him, he gives 'a deferential nod' and 'place[s] [her] then as protector, older sister' (47). Because of their agnosia, or inability to understand what they are seeing, these men register the two women's lesbianism and disinterest towards them as signs of prudishness, innocence or even vanity, perceptions which, so far, fit into their schema of acceptable female behaviour.

In Dorcey's text, the sexual passivity that the male gaze assigns to women clashes with the reality of lesbianism as an active, passionate manifestation of female sexuality. Moreover, as Todd W. Reeser theorises, if the male gaze is often thought to be 'a metaphor for – or extension of – the penis', men may react with aggression when deprived of such power, as this emasculation can be experienced as a form of 'castration', a threat to their masculinity (2010: 110). In the course of Dorcey's story, the male gaze evolves from unwanted seduction into a potent mixture of disgust and fascination. When the two women dance together, their physical intimacy clearly transmits their lesbian desires:

> Our cheeks touch. I smell the scent of your shirt – the darkness of your hair. Your limbs are easy, assured against mine. Your hands familiar, hold me just below the waist [. . .] I open my eyes. The music has stopped. Behind you I see a man standing; his eyes riveted to our bodies, his jaw dropped wide as though it had been punched. (54)

The sexual attraction between both women is finally rendered obvious, and this provokes the shocked reaction of these men who, far from restraining themselves, now see the two women as oversexualised and unworthy of their respect. A man accosts them and gives a 'lascivious' look, asking querulously: 'Would one of you lesbians give me a dance' (56). When the narrator energetically refuses his request, she becomes the victim of his misogynist fury: '"You fucking cunt!" he screams' (56). Allegedly, since the male gaze fetishises women as sexually available, this man understands the narrator's assertiveness and sexual independence as an attack against his male ego, a metaphorical castration.

From then on, the male gaze changes meaning and now transmits male power through aggressiveness and intimidation. In meaningful ways, Dorcey constructs patriarchal and lesbophobic violence as two sides of the same coin. 'A Country Dance' becomes a stark reminder of how, at this time in Ireland, lesbians had to face 'a form of double prejudice: as women challenging the dominant male order and as lesbians taking on the heterosexual establishment, [which] makes them particularly vulnerable to physical assault' (Irish Council of Civil Liberties, 1990: 9). Dorcey's protagonists experience an increased sense of fear when they spot a group of men standing in a circle: 'Their gaze has not left us, I know, since we walked off the dance floor, yet they have made no move. This very calm is what frightens me [. . .] Hunters letting the hounds play before closing in?' (57). Aware that the group of men continue to watch them in a 'patient, predatory' way (59), both women decide to leave, moving 'stealthy and cautious as prisoners', and, when they reach the door, they hear a man shout: 'Fucking whoores – you needn't trouble yourselves to come back' (59). Identified as lesbians and exiled from the rural dancehall, Dorcey's protagonists are named 'whores', an insult which is also used against many other women who, regardless of their sexual identity, are judged as sexually transgressive and, consequently, unreliable to male power.

'THE HUSBAND'

This interconnectedness between patriarchal and lesbophobic oppressions is further explored in 'The Husband', a third-person narrative focusing on the emotions, impressions, and thoughts of a married man coming to terms with abandonment. The story develops the same day his wife, Martina, leaves him for another woman, Helen, a lesbian feminist whom she met in a women's group. In 'The Husband', Dorcey 'interrogate[s] heterocentric Irish culture' by challenging the conventional 'intolerance and ignorance' of patriarchal Ireland (Hanafin, 1998: 424). Dorcey focalises the story through a male perspective which enables the reader to see through the husband's prejudices and condescension while he claims to be a victim of his wife's schemes and deceptions.

This analysis draws on Raewyn Connell's concept of 'patriarchal dividend' (1995), a type of male privilege that remains almost invisible and unchallenged due to its being part of the status quo. Rather than involving blatant oppression, the patriarchal dividend is present in men and women's socialisation, constructing their everyday expectations. For that reason, most men believe that the patriarchal dividend is 'given to them by an external force, by nature or convention, or even by women themselves, rather than by an active social subordination of women' (Connell, 1995: 215). Connell's notion is relevant to Dorcey's feminist critique in the story since the husband's emotional turmoil relates to his damaged patriarchal dividend. As the wife exits the house, he experiences a clear sense of emasculation:

> A flood of blind terror had swept through him, unmanning him [. . .] He knew what all this was about – a drama, a show of defiance and autonomy [. . .] She

could not throw away ten years of his life for this – to score a political point – for a woman! But he had not said it, all morning. It was too ridiculous – it dignified the thing even to mention it. (79)

Even though his pain is real and heartfelt, his words reveal that he does not consider his wife his equal in terms of intelligence and temperament. Neither does he show any signs of self-criticism; according to him, the reason for Martina's recriminations is only a whim to 'score a political point'. Given that the patriarchal dividend renders male privilege natural and largely unexamined, the husband feels deprived of some kind of male prerogative: 'He could not accept that, could not resign himself to being a mere cog in someone else's political theory' (65). His observations are biased and, as the story progresses, readers become increasingly aware of the husband's misconceptions.[4] Moreover, Dorcey's story suggests that, as the bearer of privilege, the husband barely knows his wife as an individual because their relationship was not based on equality and mutuality. Invisible to him, the patriarchal dividend acted here as a barrier to a genuine emotional connection between wife and husband.

In her feminist analysis of Irish society, Pat O'Connor also draws on the notion of the patriarchal dividend, explaining that: 'In Ireland, the social subordination of women was, until very recently, seen as "natural", "inevitable", "what women want". It was reflected in women's allocation to the family arena, where their position and status was given rhetorical recognition and validation' (2000: 83). This cultural validation of female subordination is precisely what Dorcey explores in her story, as it blinds the husband to any recognition of his male arrogance and shortcomings. In a more sinister way, the husband machinates that, once he threatens Martina with a child custody case, she will give up her lesbian affair and return home as his wife. He is also sure that, if he tells Martina's parents about the situation, they will do the 'dirty work' for him: 'The instant they discovered the truth, who and what she had left him for, they would snatch Lisa [their daughter] from her as ruthlessly as they would from quicksand' (67). Dorcey hence accounts for the ugly mechanisms of the patriarchal dividend. Unlike Martina, the husband has institutionalised power behind him – in this case, the family, and the law –, which, in turn, builds up his confidence, self-righteousness and sense of entitlement to control his wife's life.

The effects of the patriarchal dividend are also felt in the realm of sexuality. The husband regards Martina's 'rebellion' – that is, her lesbian affair – first with disbelief, and then with amusement and curiosity, 'allow[ing] himself delicious images of [the two women's] tentative, childish sensuality' (72). The writer draws here on the sexual culture of 1980s Ireland, and how lesbianism was perceived not only as infantile, but also as vague, ambiguous – 'tentative', in the words of Dorcey's character – and 'incomplete' because of the absence of a man. Views like that one fed the patriarchal fantasy of 'lesbians titillating each other for the pleasure of an onlooking male', eventually becoming available to him (Boyd et al., 1986: 33). Fetishised by the male gaze, lesbianism is understood here as subservient to the patriarchal dividend.

Martina's lesbian awakening, however, is no 'schoolgirl's pap' (78) since it helps her deconstruct and denaturalise the male privilege that she and her husband have always taken for granted. As his patriarchal dividend progressively weakens, the husband's derision of lesbianism turns into fear and hostility. When he watches his wife leave, the emasculated husband is filled with spite for her: 'He hated her then. He hated her body, her woman's flesh' (80). Significantly, Dorcey chooses to close the story with Martina's most relevant act of defiance so far; the moment she finally leaves the house. Yet the conflict is far from being resolved, as the story dramatises the numerous social constraints that lesbian women must confront in their attempt to reclaim their own sexual and personal independence. In this process, 'The Husband' critically exposes the gender politics of the patriarchal dividend, which trivialises women's experiences and favours male self-centredness.

'INTRODUCING NESSA'

Like 'The Husband', Dorcey's 'Introducing Nessa' describes the lesbian awakening of a separated married woman but doing so from the viewpoint of the female protagonist, Anna. Typical of Dorcey's fiction, the character's discovery of lesbianism is linked here to her feminist politicisation, when, in the context of the 1986 divorce referendum campaign,[5] Anna attended feminist debates and met Nessa, with whom she fell in love. In Nessa's company, Anna found the bliss that is stereotypically attached to the romanticised rites of passage of heterosexuality – 'All that my mother, in her innocence, had thought I would discover in marriage and motherhood, I discovered in those weeks with you' (140) –, yet she is still reluctant to come out publicly as a lesbian, so she hides Nessa from her family, friends, colleagues, and neighbours. Dorcey's protagonist is affected by society's heterosexist values, and therefore feels 'compelled to deny her love for the sake of appearing respectable and normal' (Quinn, 1992: 227). 'Introducing Nessa' is a second-person narrative addressed to the protagonist's lover, a technique which intensifies the confessional tone of the story, where Anna assesses how damaging her behaviour was towards Nessa.

In various ways, Dorcey's story deals with the complex realities of the closet, exploring the tensions between Anna's private self and her public persona. As Eve Kosofsky Sedgwick reminds us in her seminal *Epistemology of the Closet* ([1991] 2008), the social knowledge about same-sex desire has been customarily enmeshed within 'wider mappings of secrecy and disclosure' (71), with homosexuals being forced to negotiate the spaces where they can freely express their sexual identity. Central to Sedgwick's formulation, the closet – a symbolic space of confinement and self-suppression which contains the secret of same-sex desire – is a defining element in the lives of many homosexuals. In many of its manifestations, Sedgwick remarks, the closet becomes essential for the maintenance of 'the gender, sexual, and economic structures of the heterosexist culture at large' (71).

In 'Introducing Nessa', nowhere is this clearer than in Anna's fear of losing her teaching position. Due to Section 37.1 (operative until 2015), Catholic schools could dismiss employees if they were perceived to transgress the religious ethos of the institution.[6] One of the effects of Section 37.1 was to reify schools as heterosexist spaces where non-heterosexual teachers would remain closeted, and where no open discussions of homosexuality or sexual diversity was encouraged. Recent sociological studies, for example, stress the fact that a large number of Irish teachers have avoided addressing LGBTI+ issues in class because this could lead to 'accusations of "undermining" the denominational ethos of the schools' (Fahie, 2016: 404). In 'Introducing Nessa', as a teacher, Dorcey's protagonist is 'haunted by the fear of exposure' (144). When a male colleague spots Anna and Nessa holding one another on the street, she becomes terrified that he may have perceived the lesbian bond between them, even if Nessa reminds her that, unless made obvious, lesbianism usually remains unintelligible to the wider society: 'You said he would just think we were nice affectionate girls' (144). No matter how real or exaggerated the danger may be, the truth is that Anna feels under a pressure she is not ready to handle, so she chooses to remain closeted in her social life.

The closet does not always appear as a figure of oppression in Dorcey's story, as the secrecy of this secluded space provided Anna with a degree of personal freedom to explore her lesbianism in the first place, and thus initiate her personal rebirth:

> You said I was coming clear from years of camouflage. Out of the closet, as you all called it. But to me [. . .] it felt more like emerging from a chrysalis – a slow, laboured process of self-discovery. Every day casting off layer by layer the outworn pretences: weakness, passivity, dependence on men – centuries of artifice sloughed away – the quick, vital core released. (137)

Unlike most of the characters in the stories analysed in Chapter One, Dorcey's character has already acquired a new language which makes her psychological transformation possible, even if she remains trapped by old versions of herself – the old layers of 'outworn pretences' – and the constraints of heterosexism (social appearances of respectability, the threat of losing custody of her child, Section 37.1, and so on). These pressures of the closet are particularly strong in her case and threaten to destroy the women's relationship when Anna tells her heterosexual friends that Nessa is only her housemate, not lover, provoking her anger.

The story, being a second-person narration, reads much like an intimate conversation where Anna explains herself, declares her love, and asks for Nessa's understanding. Despite their conflict, the story ends in a positive note and hints at reconciliation when both women engage in a friendly conversation over the phone. Much in the style of her other stories, lesbian love in 'Introducing Nessa' features as a solid bond that cannot be easily broken by either patriarchal, lesbophobic or heterosexist oppressions. All in all, Dorcey's stories in *A Noise from the Woodshed* clearly differ from the texts analysed in Chapter One, because they insist on the protagonists' politicisation as lesbians, portray their positive transformation and renewed sense of freedom, and provide a feminist language of solidarity. These portrayals of lesbian life transcend vulnerability and victimisation. In Dorcey's stories, lesbians empower one another and build a sense of community.

BIOGRAPHY OF DESIRE

This sense of mutual empowerment, which permeates the stories of *A Noise from the Woodshed*, also becomes prominent in Dorcey's 1997 novel, *Biography of Desire*, which concentrates on the troubled but intensely passionate love affair between Katherine Newman and Nina Kavanaugh, whose relationship makes them reassess their personal histories and conflictive senses of loyalty to each other and to their respective families. Whereas Katherine is a mother and a married woman who has recently discovered her lesbianism, Nina lives with her partner, Elinor, and her child, Lizzy, whom she loves as her own. The protagonists' relationship is described through acts of memory and self-reflection, as Nina and Katherine remain separated throughout the present time of the story (Katherine waits alone, in a Galway town, for Nina's decision to leave home and join her).

Much of the text concerns Katherine's 'biography of desire', a diary she writes for Nina, where she intimates that 'all my life now, in retrospect, seems to have been a journey towards *you*' (emphasis supplied, 363). Also present in 'Introducing Nessa' and 'A Country Dance', the second-person narration is a stylistic device which, in its closeness and specificity, 'makes a particular aesthetic, emotional or political point' (Conan, 2014: 8). Dorcey's use of this device helps her strengthen her feminist discourse and create, in Antoinette Quinn's words, a 'female imaginary', where 'women's presence to each other is a primary feature of narrative' (1992: 228). In *Biography of Desire*, as in much of her other writings, this stylistic choice connects with the author's desire to create a woman-centred world that reconfigures male-dominated images of femininity.[7]

As also occurs in 'The Husband' and 'Introducing Nessa', in the novel Dorcey opts to give central stage not to the experienced lesbian, but to the woman who has re-discovered herself through the embrace of feminism and lesbianism. Though some chapters are devoted to Nina, the main voice of the story is Katherine's, and it is through this character's transformation that Dorcey most clearly articulates her feminist politics. Fascinated by Nina's spontaneity and disregard for conventional behaviour (for instance, her non-gendered attire), Katherine instantly admires this new friend's personal independence, an admiration that precedes her lesbian awakening and feminist policitisation. Inspired by Nina, Katherine begins to recognise the restrictive nature of her heterosexual culture: 'All my ill-defined criticisms and frustrations with the social order made sense to me at last' (39). The emotional connection between the two women grows sexually charged, and lesbian love offers Katherine a new understanding of sexuality and intimate relationships.

In *Biography of Desire*, this type of woman-to-woman intimacy – on a formal level reinforced by the consistent use of the second-person narration – provides a contrast with a heterosexual culture that keeps gender boundaries safe and turns lovers into 'creatures gazing at each other across a fence' (45). In the novel and also in *A Noise from the Woodshed*, Dorcey accomplishes one of her purposes in fiction, which is to express 'the multifaceted reality of women's lives – the fusion of emotional, sensual and intellectual experience that women take for granted but that is foreign to men' (1995: 39). Such fusion is also present in the ways Dorcey describes the sexual scenes between her two protagonists, as she develops an alternative, woman-centred, form of eroticism that undermines more conventional, patriarchal representations of the female body. In this way, the writer transcends the objectifying power of the male gaze, which often entails a 'corporeal fragmentation' of women (as sexual objects) under the eyes of a male observer (Reeser, 2010: 110). Instead, Dorcey describes lesbian passions as a fusion of minds and bodies:[8]

> Your body was the sum of these parts and the sum of mine. And my body was the sum of all I had lived before touching you. It was not any one thing about you, not one quality or physical feature that made me love you as I do [. . .] The suck and heat and grasp of you. It wasn't the bud between the swollen lips; the clitoris rising like what to the caress of my tongue? Like the beating pulse of my heart. (342)

In all aspects, from the emotional to the sexual, lesbianism comes to be characterised by mutuality and reciprocity, making Katherine the 'object' and 'subject' of desire at the same time (46). As is made clear, lesbian love provides Katherine with a sense of self-realisation unavailable to her in her heterosexual marriage.

Contrary to the popular beliefs about women turning to lesbianism because they suffered male violence (lesbian love in O'Brien's *The High Road* is often read through this lens, while in *A Woman's Love* Standún does appear to characterise one of the character's lesbianism as an escape from her husband's brutality), Dorcey's Katherine simply starts to perceive a heterosexual life as less satisfactory than a lesbian one. Just like Anna in 'Introducing Nessa', Katherine becomes aware of the constraints of heterosexual culture, and how it enforced her self-suppression, converting her into 'an institution, a function [. . .] Mrs Malachy Newman' (321). Even if she eventually returned to her husband, Katherine knows that she would no longer conform to Malachy's expectations of her. Because heterosexuality romanticises women's subservient roles as wives and mothers, Malachy remains blinded to his patriarchal dividend, and thus cannot truly understand neither Katherine's marital dissatisfaction, nor her sexual transformation as woman-loving.[9] Far from being cruel, Malachy is characterised as a 'benevolent despot' (88), and for years, Katherine lived 'cocooned in his devotion', adapting herself to 'his great plans, his enthusiasms,' at the cost of self-expression (62). As Dorcey depicts it, Katherine herself participated in her husband's sense of patriarchal dividend but has now identified the sources of her frustrations. Her repudiation of heterosexuality is not only portrayed on sexual and affective terms, but also on socio-cultural ones.

Paradoxically, even if she separates herself from this heterosexual culture, Dorcey's character experiences a process of sexual redefinition which is irremediably influenced by society's heterosexism. As a result, Katherine's sexual redefinition becomes entangled in a whole world of moral considerations and a re-evaluation of past experiences. The author's dramatisation of this reality does not differ much from what several studies indicate, which insist that there is a certain degree of fluidity in people's sexual development and identity, an aspect which contradicts the concept of sexual orientation as fixed and innate.[10] Christine Gaffney (2014) found that mid-life Irish women transitioning to lesbianism usually experiment a 'radical, deeply emotional and profoundly significant change in their sense of identity' (219), as they 'are faced with trying to explain – both to themselves and to others – a personal experience that is absolutely contrary to the prevailing social norms of sexuality' (238).

In *Biography of Desire*, Dorcey has Katherine re-assessing these well-known social norms of sexuality, realising that, instead of being a natural manifestation of human behaviour, heterosexuality is a type social conditioning. Because of this culture of (using Rich's term) 'compulsory heterosexuality', Katherine had no language to understand previous experiences of the homoerotic; lesbianism belonged to the realm of the unspeakable. Now that she is in love with Nina, Katherine revisits her past and revives a long forgotten adolescent infatuation with a schoolmate, Barbara, when she learnt that 'there was desire beyond the fringe of the speakable', present 'in everything that went unsaid' (173). Having same-sex desires during adolescence does not necessarily lead to the development of a bisexual or homosexual orientation, as 'uncertainty over sexuality is common for adolescents' (Goggin, 1993: 103). However, the customary silence, shame, and denial surrounding same-sex attraction remains a consequence of society's heterosexism. Having understood the mechanisms of compulsory heterosexuality, Katherine expresses the idea that bisexuality should be people's first sexual identification, 'to find out when we are young how we really feel' (149). Of all the works of fiction included in this volume, *Biography of Desire* is the one that articulates the most positive, politically transgressive view of bisexuality.

Considerations about heterosexism (or compulsory heterosexuality) move from issues of sexual subjectivity to the arena of the family when Katherine reflects on her situation as a married mother of two children. In several scenes, Katherine imagines herself being denounced by Malachy and becoming involved in a custody case,[11] an imagined legal battle presided by a judge who sides with the husband:

> 'And may we ask if you consider that this was a healthy atmosphere for young boys?'
> 'Yes I do. They were very happy.'
> 'You cannot, surely, expect to have them live with you while you openly flaunt this abnormal liaison?'
> 'It's not abnormal.' (20)

Katherine is now aware of the vulnerability provoked by heterosexism in the realm of the family, as a social institution where 'proper' gender and sexuality should be taught, and where same-sex parents may become suspect of 'indoctrinating' their children into homosexuality (these prejudices still today inform widespread objections against same-sex parenthood). As noted in Chapter One, the same issue is also addressed in *A Woman's Love*, but while Standún depicts Bridie's reservations and insecurities, Dorcey's Katherine only fears social recrimination and loss of custody now that she plans to have a future domestic life with her children and Nina.[12]

Much as Katherine, as a mother, sees herself as a possible victim of heterosexism, she is not free from heterosexist prejudices herself, since she initially assumes that her biological motherhood is a more significant and fundamental bond than Nina's adoptive parenthood: 'The fact that there was a child involved I discounted because I didn't see you as an equal parent' (127). Paradoxically, Katherine dismisses Nina's status as a mother while admiring her mothering role with Lizzie, Elinor's daughter. Observing Nina playing games with the child, Katherine exclaims:

> 'You're so good with children – have you ever thought of having one of your own?'
> I wanted to bite my tongue the second the words left my lips.
> Lizzie stared at me in amazement for a moment and then in a small, patient voice said simply: 'She has me as her own.' (113)

From her innocent perspective, Lizzie understandably reacts with surprise at not being considered Nina's child. Dorcey dramatises here a common example of a 'microaggression'. Unlike insults or other instances of overt discrimination, microaggressions are often unintentional and non-aggressive, but they nonetheless express 'a lack of recognition of LGBTQ family relationships' (Haines et al., 2018: 1143). As her microaggressions demonstrate, Katherine, without fully realising it, diminishes the importance of Nina's non-biological motherhood.

Instead of having her character decide between one lover or the other, Dorcey constructs Nina's dilemma as that between her passion for Katherine and her maternal devotion to Lizzie: 'This child who was not her own aroused the closest thing she knew to devotion. Could she feel more strongly if it belonged to her?' (231). Non-biological lesbian motherhood thus emerges as an important topic in *Biography of Desire*, since, as Abigail Palko remarks, Dorcey privileges the relationship between Lizzie and Nina, 'with scenes of Nina and Lizzie together that illustrate ways that theirs is in actuality the strongest mother-child bond of the novel' (210). While Katherine and Elinor are the biological mothers in the story, Nina is the one portrayed in a motherly role. Dorcey therefore brings to the forefront a common LGBTI+ reclamation: the equal moral significance of non-heterosexual kin relationships.

Biography of Desire hence draws on a social context of silence and discrimination against non-biological homosexual parenthood. In 1998, LOT (Lesbians Organising Together) activist Patricia Prendiville denounced the inexistent legal recognition of homosexual families in Ireland. The non-biological lesbian mother, for instance, could lose access to her child if she became a widow, as the deceased mother's blood relatives would always gain custody. Similarly, in case of a breakup, 'the non-birth mother would have little or no legal rights regarding custody or access' (Prendiville, 1998: 89). As a non-biological lesbian mother, Dorcey's Nina would undoubtedly find herself in a vulnerable position after her breakup with Elinor. Even though she never voices her concerns,[13] Nina appears to be acutely aware of her precarious status as a mother, so, for her, the vital issue would be how to remake her relationship with Lizzie if she definitely abandoned Elinor. Throughout the story, Dorcey not only points at her character's genuine maternal feelings for her non-biological child, but also her need to stake her claim as a legitimate mother.

Finally, even though Nina quits her relationship with Katherine, Dorcey opts for a poetics of reconciliation, depicting lesbian love as generous and non-possessive (both women come to a new understanding of their future relationship as friends), in marked contrast to patriarchal obsessions to control women's lives (seen in Malachy's insistence for Katherine to return home immediately, without considering her opinion). As usual in her fiction, in *Biography of Desire* Dorcey resolves the protagonists' sentimental conflict by foregrounding the empathy, mutuality, and solidarity between lesbian lovers.

CONCLUSION

To recapitulate, it is worth considering that, in Mary Dorcey's early years as an activist and literary figure, the feminist and gay liberation movements were still judged as a foreign influence and, therefore, a threat to Ireland's cultural identity. For this reason, following Heather Ingman, we may conclude that Dorcey's work as an activist back in the 1970s, as well as her poetry and fiction from the 1980s onwards, can certainly be deemed as 'a deliberate intervention in her nation's life in order to prevent the term Irish being defined solely by conservative ideologies' (2007: 61). These 'conservatives ideologies', like ultramontane Catholicism, patriarchy and heterosexism, not only silenced and deprecated lesbian love and relation-ships, but also repressed women's self-expression and autonomy, increasing their vulnerability. A much-admired collection, *A Noise from the Woodshed* became a literary landmark within Irish fiction, a book which the younger lesbian author, Emma Donoghue, commended for its social realism, avoidance of clichés, and frank portrayal of lesbian experiences: 'Dorcey's women are rooted in real places and moments that are sharp with delight and danger' (1995b: 166). Whereas the novels in Chapter One presented lesbian couples as isolated women, Dorcey's fiction develops a feminist language of lesbian identity, community, and solidarity.

As discussed, in *A Noise from the Woodshed* Dorcey insists on women's right to assert a lesbian identity within their familial, professional, and social lives, but, in *Biography of Desire*, the author focuses on the personal histories and private world of two female lovers. The novel belongs to a more liberal time, a moment when women began to enjoy a greater degree of freedom, as demonstrated by Katherine's economic independence as a married woman, and her possibility to remake her life as a lesbian. In *Biography of Desire*, Dorcey addresses many issues of lesbian life which, by the mid-1990s, had not received public attention, like the validity of homosexual families, the precarious legal status of non-biological lesbian mothers, or the difficult psychological process that mid-life women undergo when they transition to lesbianism. Most significantly, in the ways her stories allow her characters to reflect on their past and unlearn their heterosexist prejudices, Dorcey – already an established author by the time *Biography of Desire* was published – promotes a deeper understanding of lesbian lives and relationships.

THREE

Men Without Refuge

The Subculture of Cruising in Irish Gay Short Stories

For most of the twentieth century, the practice of cruising – sex in public spaces – was the main social and sexual outlet for gays and other same-sex attracted men.[1] At a time of secrecy and gay criminality, many same-sex attracted men shared a subterranean knowledge about cruising areas where they could meet, social venues which, until 1990s Ireland, 'remained an important feature of gay men's lives' (Ryan, 2003: 80). The (often) depersonalised, anonymous sex of cruising was closely identified with a lifestyle of promiscuity and degeneracy. From the early years of the Irish State, public authorities targeted cruising areas – in 1929, there were 86 prosecutions, and the general impression was that homosexuality was 'spreading with malign vigour' (Gallagher, 2016). Similar judgments persisted until the 1980s, a time when the (scarce) media coverage of gay life 'confined [itself] to what might be conceived as the negative aspects of the gay community, such as cruising' (Byrne and Larkin, 1994: 120). Cruising thus became synonymous with a gay life, and was considered extremely degrading.[2] Whereas many participants internalised strong feelings of shame and self-loathing, other men simply enjoyed the thrills of cruising, despite the dangers they confronted.

From the 1990s onwards, as Western societies were growing more tolerant, a liberal explanation for the persistence of cruising was that most participants were still in the closet, 'sad' and 'confused', 'groping their way towards a gay identity' (McKenna, 1998: 8). Paradoxically, such liberal viewpoint, while advocating for the coming out of cruisers, draws on conservative, heterosexist assumptions about cruising as morally wrong and lacking in social respectability. In today's allegedly homonormative gay culture, cruising has fallen out of favour,[3] a 'sacrifice' which has been made 'in the drive towards the assimilation and commodification of homosexuality by the wider society' (Mowlabocus, 2008: 434). Yet the same rationale of cruising remains prevalent in today's gay scene (saunas and darkrooms are clear examples), and has gained acceptance (both in the heterosexual and homosexual worlds) through the use of dating websites and phone applications. Additionally, whilst a need for secrecy may still today explain the reasons why some men engage in cruising (or similar sexual behaviours), notions of homosexual repression fail to account for the whole truth of this subculture.[4]

Though deemed a gay subculture, cruising appears to strike a deep chord in many men regardless of their sexual identity, since these public sexual encounters are 'defined in "masculine" terms of orgasm, its complete separation from procreation, its partial separation from some forms of affection and emotional bonding' (Edwards, 1994: 114). In the 1990s, the sexual category SMSM (Straight Men who Have Sex with Men) was created by AIDS organisations and sex researchers who discovered that there are numerous self-identified heterosexual men practicing cruising. SMSM are primarily attracted to women in sexual and romantic ways, but they occasionally engage in homosexual experiences (see Kort, 2008). Commenting on this phenomenon, Neil McKenna, an AIDS researcher, writes about cruising in the following terms:

> [Cruising] is a form of instinctive, unspoken, sexual communion between men, older than the veneer of our late 20th century sexual civilisation [. . .] This kind of sex between men challenges both our comprehension and our tolerance. How can a man go out, meet another man, have sex, and then go back to his heterosexual life as if nothing had happened? If we cannot comprehend it, our instinct is to condemn it. (1998: 8)

Cruising, McKenna underlines, cannot be appropiately understood by applying the sexual categories and values of 'our late 20th century sexual civilisation'.[5] As a clear challenge to the norms of social and sexual respectability, cruising not only destabilises heteronormativity, but also subverts the cultural confinement of sex to the space of the home and the romantic couple. It is therefore no surprise that cruising came to be regarded as a moral danger and a criminal sexual behaviour. In Ireland and elsewhere, this behaviour was identified with the 'depravity' of gay life, as the exact opposite of ideal heterosexuality.

Set in various Irish towns and cities, the short stories in this chapter provide a new language to understand the reality of cruising, one which opposes the vulnerability of internalised shame, removing moral considerations on sexual identities or illicit sex, while engaging in a careful exploration of the different contexts where this type of relationships occur. The short stories analysed in this chapter – Keith Ridgway's 'Graffiti' (1994), Eamon Somer's 'Nataí Bocht' (1994), Mícheál Ó Conghaile's 'At the Station' (2012) and Joseph O'Connor's 'The Hills Are Alive' (1992) – recreate conservative contexts, accounting for the disruption caused by homophobic violence. Because short stories usually concern themselves with a 'single effect' conveyed through 'economy of setting' and the characters' actions and 'dramatic encounter[s]' (Hansen, 2020), this genre becomes one apt vehicle for the representation of the intermittent but intense relationships in cruising sites, offering a glimpse into what this sex means to the men who enter this subterranean sexual world.

MICHEÁL Ó CONGHAILE'S 'AT THE STATION'

While the short stories in this chapter describe cruising as being shaped by the constraints of heteronormativity, the same narratives also subvert such ideology. These stories, with the exception of Keith Ridgway's 'Graffiti', show how cruising can become a space of empathy and connection, creating chances of human communion which would have been impossible in other social interactions. This proves especially relevant in Micheál Ó Conghaile's 'At the Station'[6] – included in *Colours of Man* (2012), his collection of English-translated stories –, which describes the existence and destruction of an old train station, which served as a cruising site. A well-known writer to Irish-language readers, Ó Conghaile published his first short story collection in 1986, *Mac an tSagairt*, and became a representative of a generation of intellectuals who not only modernised Irish-language written culture, but also broke deep-seated taboos and silences of the time, like abortion, child abuse, suicide, and homosexuality. This subversiveness pertains to the openness with which this generation of writers represented sexual matters; one of Ó Conghaile's early short stories was about homosexuality and male rape, and it provoked 'outrage in certain sections of society which referred to it as *brocamas* or dirt' (Ó Siadhail and Ó Conghaile, 2005: 56). Despite this negative reaction, in the Gaeltacht Ó Conghaile's gay fiction has generally been well-received and regarded as culturally innovative, since the author 'g[a]ve expression to the experiences of a section of his Conamara Gaeltacht community whose voice had not been heard out loud previously' (Ó Siadhail, 2010: 156).[7]

In Ó Conghaile's work, gay sex is depicted in connection to the characters' search of freedom and self-expression, 'as a facet of the intellect, the imagination, and the physical, in a portrayal that gives prominence to the integration of the whole self' (de Brún, 2017: 24). Ó Conghaile's gay Bildungsroman, *Sna Fir* (1999), still unpublished in English, illustrates such point. The novel follows one year in the life of a young man from the Connemara Gaeltacht, whose maturation and self-acceptance largely relate to his sexual experiences at home and away from it, in Dublin and London.[8] In one of the scenes, John Paul – ironically, a namesake of Pope John Paul II – goes cruising to a London cemetery and has sex on a tomb:[9]

> And for five pulsating minutes, that tomb was ours, myself and the Cockney's. We were close to death, and miles away from it. Sex is life affirming, reminding us we're here, alive, able. It's a little victory. Let the dead bury the dead. Carpe diem. It was hard to feel sorry for the dead –we'd be long enough with them ourselves. (quoted in Madden, 2013: 201)

Surrounded by crosses and headstones, the protagonist transcends the moral constrictions of his Catholic upbringing, and takes delight in cruising. Far from being disrespectful, this lust for life, Ó Conghaile's protagonist suggests, honours the memory of the people buried in the graveyard: 'The earth sucks in the dripping semen of gay men, giving relief to one another under the discreet shade of headstones and high tombs' (quoted in Madden, 2013: 203).

Similarly, in 'At the Station' Ó Conghaile describes gay sex as cathartic and life affirming, and there is a 'strong sense of spirituality and wonder' attached to the cruising site which numerous men visit deep at night (Ó Conchubhair, 2012: 13). The story is a third-person narration focalised on a station – which is personifed as a kind of maternal, nurturing figure – that cherishes these men's presence, their 'loving company' (137), which contrasts with the 'poverty of spirit' (134) and 'mechanical leave-taking' (135) of its other visitors in the past, passengers who just passed by. If in the past the station stood 'cold, empty' (134), now it glows with warmth: '[The station] welcomed the deep desires of their hearts and bodies. Their hidden loneliness. The gentle respect they showed the station until they left at first light, before dawn. They were its lifeblood' (137). Cruising provides these men a way out of 'their hidden loneliness', so their sex, far from being furtive or a 'vice', is described as a key aspect of their humanity and affective needs. The station keeps the men safe inside its walls, and celebrates 'their eager arrival, their lack of haste, their appointments and intentions' (137). Social networks develop within this cruising area, which becomes a homely place which fosters homosociality.

Yet once rumours spread about the old station and the men who visit it at night, the voices of institutional authority (the clergy, politicians, and the police) eventually interfere to destroy their refuge. 'Arrogant and masterful', an 'army' of bulldozers smashes the building (138), while, up on a slope, a group of men silently mourns the loss of the old station: 'They stood their ground there in a brave semicircle right to the end. Staring and staring. Men without refuge' (139). While much of the story reads as a celebration of sexual freedom, in the end, public space is redefined as heteronormative. As a needless and vengeful attack, the destruction of the station illustrates the inflexible, authoritarian nature of a dominant ideology which suppresses alternative forms of love, community and sexual relationships.

EAMON SOMERS'S 'NATAÍ BOCHT'

Like Ó Conghaile's 'At the Station', Eamon Somers's 'Nataí Bocht' recreates homosociality within a cruising area, with its regular visitors, together with the occasional tourists and 'curious' men. In Somers's story, these regular visitors not only come from Galway city and nearby towns, but also 'from Connemara and Mayo and as far north as Ballina' (22). Published in a 1994 short story collection edited by Brian Finnegan, *Quare Fellas: New Irish Gay Writing*, Somers's 'Nataí Bocht' is set in Galway city, at a public lavatory in Eyre Square. The author, Eamon Somers, had been actively involved in the 1980s gay and lesbian movement, and was President of the National Gay Federation before moving to London due to Ireland's late 1980s economic crisis.

Finnegan indicates how 'cottaging' (the type of cruising activity taking place in public lavatories) has had a 'strong tradition in Ireland', 'for years, and even now, cottages were often the only guaranteed sexual outlet for gay men in rural areas and small towns to meet other men' (9). In many ways, Somers characterises this cottage as a place of social contact and interaction, as the protagonist readily confides that '[he] shar[es] the toilet with several men who come in regularly', and that he usually has 'someone to talk to' (18). Somers's story is a first-person narration of a middle-aged man, and the main event is the appearance of a new visitor, a teenager – whom the narrator affectively calls Nataí Bocht (Poor Little Nat) – that constantly locks himself up in a cubicle, alone. Much of the story concentrates on the narrator's growing concern and protection of the teenager, even if, initially, he only considers the youngster a potential sexual partner.

Somers's story requires to be read in light of common assumptions not only about cruising, but also about the presumably negative influence of adult gays on underage males. In different cultural contexts, cruising has customarily been condemned because of the 'potential moral harm that may be caused to an unwilling observer of such acts', a preoccupation often expressed 'in relation to children' (Ashford, 2007: 509). As was also discussed in previous chapters with regard to lesbian motherhood, these concerns about children and teenagers frequently relate to heteronormative anxieties, as the dominant culture has attempted to preserve 'ideal representations of pure, normal, untainted and, crucially, heterosexual citizenship in need of protection from the imagined horrific impact of homosexuality' (Johnson,

2007: 530). A recent example of this in Ireland was a 2015 leaflet against same-sex marriage, whose headline – 'Should children be exposed to the sounds of sodomy?' – revived 'the widespread belief in the hyper-sexualisation of gay men' (Finnegan, 2015), while exploiting the old stereotype of homosexuals as corruptors (or even possible abusers) of the youth.

In Somers's story, far from requiring protection from homosexuals, the teenage Nataí Bocht seems to be struggling with his own sexuality, searching for companionship and understanding from adult gays.[10] Because Nataí looks 'broken' and 'miserable' (16), the narrator sees the teenager as a younger version of himself: 'Out of what awful, decent home was Nataí Bocht trying to find love? In spite of what anger was he willing to wait for the unknown?' (20). Somers foregrounds here the emotional pain of familial homophobia, an experience of suffering shared by many young people, especially in the 1980s and 1990s.[11]

As indicated above, in Somers's configuration, the cottage is not just a meeting place for casual sex, but also provides an opportunity for socialisation and human communion. This is demonstrated by the narrator's relief and satisfaction as he watches Nataí Bocht's emotional healing in the company of Peadar,[12] 'ideally suited' to the teenager because he is 'generous' (23). A sense of a queer kinship is built now in the story; while Nataí Bocht and Peadar spend time alone inside the cubicle, the narrator takes up a paternal role as a protector, 'stand[ing] guard' for them (22), and even compares Nataí's sexual experience to a type of rebirth: 'I walked up and down along by the urinals like an expectant father at an old-fashioned birth waiting on news' (22). In his story, Somers reverses a language of gay depravity and corruption of the youth: Nataí's relationship with Peadar is portrayed as nothing but positive.

Yet the cottage is not free from the threat of homophobic violence. Somers addresses here the threat of gay-bashing, and how, as several studies found out, this type of violence is usually 'motivated by its social function; by engaging in anti-LGB behavior men reaffirm heterosexual masculinity and strengthen their bond with other men' (Bell and Perry, 2015: 102). Like the gang who in 1982 gay-bashed and killed Declan Flynn (whom they regarded as a cruiser) in Dublin's Fairview Park, the attackers in Somers's story, instead of being unwilling observers of gay sex, purposely go to a cruising area to find gay men, their victims being viewed as 'representatives of the greater population of LGB people to which [they] wish to send a message' (Bell and Perry, 117). In the story, a gang of gay-bashers, who had been watching Peadar and Nataí Bocht walking outside on the street, follows them to the toilet to attack them: 'There were three of them –"Come out you fucken queers"– and kicking the door and then throwing one of the concrete blocks [. . .] on over the door' (25). Gang violence is confronted by

Nataí, Peadar and the narrator, a fight which reinforces a sense of queer kinship between them, saving them from severe physical damage.[13]

Significantly, Somers's story stresses notions of intergenerational solidarity as a form of resistance. Aside from being protected from physical violence, Nataí Bocht finds in Peadar and the narrator a support that had been unavailable to him within his family and immediate community. Concurrently, within the setting of the cottage, Somers addresses the (controversial) issue of the sex and desire that may arise between adult and teenage gays, a reality which, being largely associated to notions of abuse and sexual corruption, is presented here from the perspective of an adolescent's affective needs.

KEITH RIDGWAY'S 'GRAFFITI'

Contrary to the two stories previously analysed here, where cruisers establish emotional connections, Keith Ridgway's 'Graffiti' adopts an impersonal, neutral tone to describe, graphically, the quick and anonymous sexual trans-actions taking place in a Dublin public toilet. Critic Katherine O'Donnell describes Ridgway's style in a way that fits 'Graffiti' and his other works to be analysed in Chapters Five and Seven: 'The narrative is led not so much by plot but by the complexities of the characters, their mixed motivations and the claustrophobic drama of their dialogue. Ridgway manages to make the reader feel a foreboding sense of dreadful violence' (2020: 264–5). Although a critically acclaimed author, Ridgway, whose work earned him important awards and several translations, has not received the popular recognition he deserves in Ireland. 'Graffiti' is one of Ridgway's earliest publications.

Like Somers's story, Keith Ridgway's 'Graffiti' (1994) is included in Brian Finnegan's *Quare Fellas*, but differs from 'Nataí Bocht' in style and approach to the reality of cruising. Ridgway's story is narrated from the perspectives of three men – named as 1st Person, 2nd Person and 3rd Person – who experience a mixture of excitement, pleasure, fear, and shame as they engage in cruising. 'Graffiti' opens the moment 1st Person perceives 2nd Person's sexual interest in him as they use the urinals, a desire transmitted through a silent language of signs: 'A pulse of something caught his eye, just a bright stab of something in the corner, like a face turned differently or a reflected button or the small sharp movement of a hand' (31). Because the cottage is a sexualised space, this silent language initiates a series of unspoken invitations which lead to their moving together into an empty cubicle.

Though pleasurable, gay sex is described in Ridgway's text as mechanical and totally depersonalised, as also happens in his London-set novel *Hawthorn and Child* (2012),[14] in a scene where the anonimity of a darkroom allows the protagonist to feel that he is given a fellatio by a 'mouth', and not by another man: 'It is doing it too well' (97). Ridgway's Hawthorn – like many of his other gay characters – feels uneasy about his sexuality, so these quick, impersonal sexual encounters help him partake of a 'comfort that predates anything his mind might think about it' (98). Similarly, in 'Graffiti' cruising helps 2nd Person disengage personally from the sexual acts he is performing, which, for him, 'seemed a fiction' (37).[15]

If 2nd Person experiences cruising in this way, Ridgway implies, is because he is affected by moral values which judge gay sex as degrading. The graffiti he writes on a cubicle door – 'Did you ever think you'd sink this low?' (37) – might well be directed to himself as much as to other men like him. Ridgway in this way brings attention to the feelings of sexual guilt some cruisers suffer, which may lead to unexpected violent reactions against their sexual partners. This unease, as remarked in a 1990 English study, 'emerges crudely in cases where men expiate their guilt by attacking or robbing their partners' (CHE, 1990: 32). Reactions like this one were not rare – Somers's 'Nataí Bocht' also refers to this[16] –, as several studies on cruising (conducted in different countries) have demonstrated. Troubled by his same-sex desires, this type of tormented cruiser, according to Stefano Ramello, cannot escape his internalised homophobia, and typically leads a double life which impacts negatively on 'his self-worth and esteem' (2013: 90).

This archetype defined by Ramello fits Ridgway's characterisation of 2nd Person in 'Graffiti', who, right after their sexual relationship, attacks and robs 3rd Person, loudly accusing him of sexual assault. Presenting himself before the police as a victim, 2nd Person draws on the language of homophobia: 'This faggot tried to fucking rape me. You can't come into one of these places without some pervert drooling all over you' (40). Defenceless, 3rd Person tries to report the attack he suffered, but he only encounters the policeman's scorn and non-cooperation: 'I suggest you cut your losses and fuck off home before I lose my temper.' (42)

Ridway thus accounts in the story for the police regulation (or lack thereof) of violent incidents within cottages and cruising sites (being published in 1994, 'Grafitti' may recreate a pre-decriminalisation time). In those years, though some Gardaí did assume a 'humane and sympathetic approach' to these problems (Kelly, 2017: 210), too many of them showed reluctance to act on reports of gay-bashing in cruising areas, and this was one common complaint voiced by 1980s associations,[17] like the Dublin Lesbian and Gay Men Collectives: 'If a gay man reports being beaten up, he is usually told "it's your own fault" or that "it's not the guards' job to protect criminals"' (Boyd, 1986: 190). The same sense of vulnerability, humiliation, and disprotection is felt by Ridgway's 3rd Person, victim of the policemen's derision and 2nd Person's assault.

'Graffiti' thus concentrates on the reality of cruising from the viewpoint of 'the dangers that come with the territory' (Finnegan, 1994: 9). Because homophobic attacks were not rare, the three stories so far analysed here deal with the irruption of violence and the disruption it causes. In the case of Ridgway's story, this violence seems more difficult to predict or understand, as it comes from a cruiser himself. As he also does in some other gay narratives, like 'Andy Warhol' (2018), Ridgway foregounds, in the figure of the main character, the effects of sexual guilt and internalisation of negative judgments on gay sex.

JOSEPH O'CONNOR'S 'THE HILLS ARE ALIVE'

As in Ridgway's 'Graffiti', in Joseph O'Connor's 'The Hills are Alive' the cruising site features as a space outside language, governed by silent codes of behaviour, a no-man's land where the sense of community depicted in Ó Conghaile's 'At the Station' and Somers's 'Nataí Bocht' is nowhere to be seen. 'The Hills are Alive' is included in O'Connor's 1992 collection *True Believers*, where unpalatable, often silenced realities of 1990s Ireland remain as open secrets in the stories ('Mothers were All the Same', for instance, dramatises the silence of Irish women's abortions in England). A well-established author, O'Connor had made his debut with *Cowboys and Indians* (1990), which was followed by many other successful publications, among them the novels *Star of the Sea* (2004), *Ghost Light* (2010) and *Shadowplay* (2019). O'Connor is no gay fiction writer, though 'The Hills are Alive' may be considered a gay short story worth studying for its complex, politically challenging portrayal of cruising in the late 1980s Belfast during the Northern Irish Troubles (1968–98).

O'Connor's 'The Hills are Alive' revolves around the secret relationship between IRA member Danny Sullivan and English soldier Henry Woods, two eighteen-year olds who meet each other while cruising in Belfast's Victoria Park. Like many other novels and short stories about the Troubles from the 1970s onwards, 'The Hills are Alive' uses a 'style of stark realism', which portrays 'violence in a context larger than the ideological one', focusing on human issues, such as 'the dehumanizing aspects of sectarian violence; the disruption and loss of lives caused by the violence; and the profound physical, social, and psychological effects inflicted on its victims' (Storey, 2004: 151). O'Connor's story emphasises the human tragedy of terrorism in the figures of two male lovers, portraying 1980s Belfast as 'a city full of secrets' (159), whose citizens scurry 'into shadows' (159), and look 'over their shoulders' (164), imagining 'enemies, both real and imaginary' (166). O'Connor's text has a third-person omniscient narrator, and the story is sometimes interrupted by short scenes highlighting the close surveillance the two young protagonists are under. O'Connor deploys here a graphic but reticent style that emphasises the characters' inarticulacy on their homosexual feelings.

During the Troubles, as O'Connor depicts it here, homophobia became extremely threatening, by no means hidden. Bolstered by nationalist ideologies and religious doctrines that vilify sexual dissidents, the opposing military organisations fostered the policing of local communities.[18] 'Those who have been rumoured, or proven to be gay, or indeed involved in prostitution,' Rob Kitchin argues, 'have come under pressure to leave tightly knit, local communities, and in many cases forcibly evicted' (2002: 215). Like gays, women often fell victim to sectarianism and the community's surveillance and vicious violence. O'Connor's IRA character, Danny, confesses having inflicted brutal punishments when he 'covered teenage girls in boiling pitch for befriending soldiers' (173). This violence in O'Connor's text appears as a consequence of a glorification of hyper-masculinity and its attendant hetero-patriarchal values, exposed and magnified in the murals painted throughout the city for all to see.[19]

O'Connor's protagonists can only come together thanks to the silence and anonimity of cruising, which helps them momentarily transcend not only the constraints of their heterosexual masculinity, but also the social, historical and political divides of the Troubles. The story hence illustrates how, in contexts where sharp social divides exist, 'queer counter-public spaces of cruising and sex may create possibilities for identification, affiliation, and communication across class and racial boundaries' (Madden, 2012: 193). In the story, Danny, the IRA member, and Henry, the English soldier, encounter one another for the first time in Victoria Park, and, as they have sex, 'each shivered and goosepimpled in the icy thrill of shame', and 'the entire hungry manoeuvre was completed without a single word' (165). Their need for discretion prevents them from disclosing their identities, or even talking to one another, but they continue to meet for weeks 'in the usual place, at the usual time, for the usual purpose' (171). And, though they develop 'a lovers' language of sighs, unspoken consents, silent invitations', due to their homophobic backgrounds, gay sex still feels, to some degree, repugnant: 'They simply met and grappled and groped and slipped away later, reeling with a kind of triumphant disgust' (171).

If cruising represents a space of silence and non-definition which initiates an otherwise implausible relationship, language reinserts the protagonists into their cultural contexts of political violence. The first time they ever speak, they perceive each other's accents, and now the burden of sectarianism puts them in serious danger[20] – as O'Connor's narrator presages at this point, 'in the end, it was words that came between them' (172). Despite the threat of reprisal, they are unable to quit their secret relationship. Feeling themselves observed, Danny and Henry now move to an abandoned garage where they meet once a week, as usual, and also engage in conversations about their own personal backgrounds.[21] Convinced that 'death was watching them' (181), Danny and Henry – now portrayed as terrified boys, not tough soldiers – 'clung to each other in the last weeks' (184), and 'wept like children' (183). By highlighting their vulnerability and sense of entrapment, the writer humanises the figures of the IRA terrorist and the English soldier.

Their fears, the reader soon discovers, are not unfounded. At times, the sequentiality of the story is broken by short fragments informing readers about unknown men who 'plotted and took notes and times and photographs through telescopic lenses' (184). O'Connor's omniscient narrator holds back crucial information concerning the identity of these men and their exact plans. Similar stylistic devices have been observed in other short stories about the Troubles, which dramatise 'the intrusion of political disturbance into the private or domestic realm', by deploying 'strategies of silence', like gaps, fragmentation, and obliqueness in the narrative (McDonald, 2005: 249). Though obliquely, O'Connor's story takes a close look at a reality of constant surveillance during the Troubles, and how at the time 'fears of paramilitary reprisal and leaks from the police to members of such community regulatory organisations [were] a key factor setting homophobic victimisation' (Duggan, 2012: 36). As Kathryn Conrad further argues, to combat the IRA, the RUC (Royal Ulster Constabulary) made use of state-sponsored blackmail:

> As late as 1994, more than a decade after decriminalisation, there is evidence that the RUC swept gay male cruising spots in Northern Ireland, looking for informers. As long as homosexual acts remained illegal, the RUC would have had an even easier time of it: to a closeted gay man, the possibility of legal proceedings and consequent outing was a particular threat and was an extra boon to a RUC eager to entrap possible informers. (2004: 42)

Hence, even though in Northern Ireland male homosexuality was decriminalised in 1982, the realities of surveillance and blackmail remained prevalent until the end of the Troubles.

Both factions of the conflict, as the reader eventually discovers, were perfectly aware that Danny and Henry went cruising. Their real transgression, however, was to have developed a relationship that contravenes the interests of the IRA and the British military, so both organisations decide to wait for the most convenient moment to 'get them' (184). Tragedy becomes inevitable when the two boys make plans to escape and start a new life together, as each of them is killed by friendly fire.[22] From the viewpoint of sectarian politics, Henry and Danny can only be judged as traitors, even though they are turned into symbols of martyrdom at their respective funerals. Their sexual dissidence and rebelliousness are therefore silenced by a normative language of patriotism.

In short, in 'The Hills are Alive' O'Connor stresses the horrors of the Troubles, and imagines a tragic love story between two representatives of the armed conflict. Such a love story can only start thanks to the anonimity and silence of cruising, which emerges as a queer space free of the divisions and sectarianism of 1980s Belfast. Cruising therefore gives these young men their only chance of same-sex love and comfort, while they momentarily evade their cultures of heteronormative hyper-masculinity and the oppressive rules of the community. As the story suggests, homosexual acts may go unpunished as long as they remain confined within the limits of cruising. It is only when the two lovers defy such boundaries that their relationship becomes lethal.

CONCLUSION

As is also the case in the Northern Irish context depicted by O'Connor, in Ireland cruising was generally regarded as deviant and immoral, yet it offered gays and other same-sex attracted men a much needed anonymity, and a chance of sexual release and human comfort, however fleeting. In his memoir, Senator David Norris relates that, in the Ireland of gay criminality, most same-sex attracted men feared visibility, because 'if you were visible, you were vulnerable, and the full force of public odium [. . .] would become a horrible reality' (2012: 80). As is well known, this public odium made gay sex (and homosexual affects in general) abject, something to be hidden in obscure or far-away places, so, in Norris's words, 'a hurried encounter in a public lavatory was all that was offered to gay men' (81). However, as indicated at the beginning of this chapter, it would be misleading to define cruising as the result of gay oppression only. In today's much more tolerant and liberal society, cruising (or similar sexual behaviours in commercial venues, for instance) appeals to numerous men who are either attracted to unromantic, uncomplicated sex or who are unwilling to engage in the intimacies of same-sex love and desire.

Set at times of greater gay stigma, the four short stories in this chapter defy a public language of cruising as morally degrading and an expression of sexual degeneracy. Seen in the wider context of Irish society, these stories seem to reflect Norris's words about cruising as an escape from repression, rather than an expression of sexual freedom (although Ó Conghaile's texts combine both aspects). At the same time, these texts also picture cruising as a sexual subculture that frequently entails a 'negotiation of individual practices and risks, the perceptions of partners, and the ascription of meanings to the sex act' (Ramello, 2013: 88). If, for example, Ridgway's 'Graffiti' explores the quick, clandestine sexual encounters in a busy public toilet which is subject to police surveillance, Ó Conghaile's story shows how the station becomes a relatively safe cruising area, a situation which opens up possibilities other than those sexually-oriented. In all cases, homophobic aggression disrupts the normal functioning of the cruising site, as well as the relationships developing in it. If this sexual subculture involves violence, the stories suggests, it is precisely because of the impact of external factors, such as anti-gay hate crime, political strife, and public opinion. Although cruising is often a counter-reaction to the oppression and regulation of same-sex desire, it still remains a space of vulnerability and limited possibilities, as this sexual behaviour (usually covert and anonymous) seldom emerges as politically transgressive, even if it may lead to homosociality and rebellion in some instances. Far from being a self-regulated system, cruising, as the stories in this chapter suggest, has to be understood within the socio-cultural and political contexts constructing moral codes and sexual behaviours.

FOUR

Love is War

The Irish Gay Coming-Out Novel

The present chapter centres on five novels – Desmond Hogan's *The Ikon Maker* (2013 [1976]); Damian McNicholl's *A Son Called Gabriel* (2004); Tom Lennon's *When Love Comes to Town* (1993); Jarlath Gregory's *Snapshots* (2001); and *G.A.A.Y.: One Hundred Ways to Love a Beautiful Loser* (2005) – which portray the gay teenager's emotional maturation, social world and his coming-out to family and friends. The coming-out story has been a rather popular genre in countries like the United States,[1] but not in Ireland (or Northern Ireland), where, as has been noted, the Irish homosexual remained 'relatively muted' in literature and culture until gay decriminalisation (Quinn, 1995: 560). This literary mutism on gay life ended in the 1990s, a decade which, as Michael G. Cronin argues in his *Impure Thoughts* (2012), saw a resurgence of the Bildungsroman genre (novels of formation), precisely at a moment when Catholic morality was seriously challenged by the new values of Celtic Tiger Ireland. The Bildungsroman (and the coming-out story as its subtype) in this way 'negotiates both individual and cultural crises of sexual formation and the historical crises of modernisation' (Cronin, 2012: 11). Drawing on this, the analyses of the aforementioned novels shall address generational gaps, personal and cultural crises, and the protagonists' need to resist the toxic languages of heterosexual masculinity. At the same time, these analyses shall consider the ways in which these Irish texts adopt or readapt the literary conventions of the inherited Anglo-American model of coming-out stories.

Until the early 2000s, the social silence on gay lives and experiences had clear repercussions in the lives of young homosexuals, as there was a lack of meaningful, positive role models for them. Writing in 1990s Ireland activists Suzy Byrne and Junior Larkin underlined the isolation, confusion, and vulnerability felt by lesbian and gay teenagers, as they 'receive[d] no acknowledgement of the existence of any other people like themselves as they grow up', a situation which explains why, in 2003, the Equality Authority still insisted that there was in Ireland an 'insufficient recognition of the difficulties faced by young people struggling with their sexual identity' (42).

Much has changed today, as LGBTI+ teenagers do not generally experience the same levels of isolation as in previous generations. Sources of information and support were extremely scarce before the 2000s: the Internet, social media and online dating had not happened yet, and the popular media either invisibilised homosexuals or portrayed them as grossly inaccurate and demeaning stereotypes. In contexts where homosexual identity only attracts negative attributions, many same-sex attracted teenagers have experienced feelings of self-denial and worthlessness, finding it difficult or even traumatic to see themselves in relation to the harmful stereotypes of homosexuality.

The five novels in these chapters address the sources of such stereotypes of gay sexuality, and the impact they have on the teenage protagonists. Aside from transmitting religious homophobia, which articulates a 'language of disease, sin and filth' about gay sexuality (Reygan and Moane, 2014: 309), the Catholic school[2] features in these stories as a site of struggle and gender policing. The novels show how boys who are perceived as effeminate can easily become subject to ridicule, harassment, and physical abuse. The effects of this gender regime are portrayed in varied ways, from the suicide of one of the characters in Hogan's *The Ikon Maker*, to the strenuous self-policing of the protagonist in Lennon's *When Love Comes to Town*. As the novels also illustrate, sport has traditionally been 'a space that reifies and reproduces heteronormativity, gender norms, and a masculinity that is valued above other forms of masculinity' (Cavalier, 2011: 628). In McNicholl's story, the father trashes Gabriel soundly when he refuses to play GAA at school. As a rugby hero, Lennon's protagonist receives the admiration of his equals, whereas Gregory's Oisín in *Snapshots* is ridiculed at the playground because he does not know how to kick a ball.

Significantly, these gay novels denounced the cruelty of homophobic bullying long before larger society did. In Ireland, it was in 2004 that the first in-depth study on bullying appeared, by J. Norman, whose findings revealed that 'the use of derogatory language and slurs of a homophobic nature is endemic in Irish second-level schools' (cited in O'Higgins-Norman et al., 2010: 3). After 2004, studies on the school lives of LGBTI+ youth in Ireland have underlined that discrimination was 'rarely challenged by teachers and other pupils' (Minton et al., 2008: 179), and that 'the great majority [of LGBTI+ students] reported experiencing problems in school due to sexual orientation and gender identity' (Reygan, 2009: 87). A 2011 study, based in Northern Ireland, discovered a 'disproportionately high level of self-injury among same-sex attracted young people' (Schubotz and O'Hara, 2011: 504). More recently, the results of the 2016 *LGBTI Ireland Report* surprised many people and were widely reported in the media, which highlighted that 'compared to the wider teenage population, gay teens were two times more likely to have self-harmed, three times more likely to have attempted suicide and four times more likely to have experienced anxiety or depression' (O'Brien, 2016). In spite of the increased visibility of LGBTI+ equality issues, it seems that an oppressive heteronormative culture remains deeply embedded in many Irish schools.

With the exceptions of Gregory's *G.A.A.Y.* and Hogan's novel, the novels in this chapter also portray familial homophobia as a highly damaging influence in the emotional development of gay youth. Unfortunately, in both Irish and Northern Irish societies, familial homophobia has been an extremely common reality, as attested by a 1997 survey that found that 'only 12.5 per cent of Irish people would welcome a gay person into their family' (Mac Gréil, 372). Familial homophobia has a strong negative impact on individual well-being, and is frequently expressed through shunning, a 'refusal to engage, recognize, negotiate, communicate' (Schulman, 2009: 11). A 2013 study about the young LGBTI+ population in Ireland stresses the importance of familial acceptance (more than in the case of friends and schoolmates), and how many participants felt 'hurt and grieved' when facing the non-acceptance of family members (Mannix-McNamara et al., 274). Another study, conducted in Northern Ireland, calls attention to the ways in which many LGBTI+ teenagers withdraw from emotional invest-ment in the family to minimise the pain of rejection, though this emotional distance often diminishes their 'feelings of self-worth' (Schubotz and McNamee, 2009: 199). In 2000s post-Troubles Northern Ireland, familial homophobia continued to be rampant, at least as described in a 2014 memoir essay by Northern Irish author and journalist Lyra McKee:[3]

> You watched James get thrown out of his house after coming out to his parents. You were in Michael's house the night his mum said she would 'beat the gay out of him'. You will feel guilty for being the lucky one and getting it easy in the end. ([2014] 2019)

Rather than offering images of outright rejection and aggression, the coming-out stories in this chapter depict more subtle but still damaging practices of shunning, shaming, and exclusion within the family.

DESMOND HOGAN'S THE IKON MAKER

Set from the 1970s to the 2000s in various locations, these novels, while addressing the role of the school, family, and community, also dwell on the damaged mental health of the gay teenager, an issue which is particularly relevant in Desmond Hogan's ground-breaking *The Ikon Maker*, published in 1976. Hogan's debut novel, a pessimistic account of life in 1970s rural Galway, counts as one of the very few literary inquiries into Irish gay experience prior to the 1990s. Hogan's approach to this subject matter is an indirect one. Here, the lonely, widowed mother, Susan O'Hallrahan, gathers the information that makes her learn that her young son, Diarmaid, is actually a homosexual. Narrated from the viewpoint of Susan, who goes to England in search of her exiled son, *The Ikon Maker* engages with the stigma of homosexuality in an oblique, yet powerful way, through the mother's realisation that 'long ago Ireland had mangled [Diarmaid], twisted him, embittered him' (126). The story is told in short, vignette-like chapters, full of staccato sentences which in many cases highlight Susan's troubled mind as she confronts uncomfortable truths about herself and her son.

Early in his career, Hogan received widespread admiration and critical acclaim, and his talent came to be compared to that of authors such as Salman Rushdie and Kazuo Ishiguro in Britain.[4] Hogan's celebrated short-story collections – such as *The Diamonds at the Bottom of the Sea* (1979), and novels like *The Leaves on Grey* (1980) – offer a bleak portrayal of the practices of shaming and exclusion that had for long operated in Irish society. If in the short story 'Jimmy' (which is about a gay teacher who was forced into exile) we read that 'it had been an old custom in Ireland to drive at least one of your family out, to England, to the mental hospital, to sea or to a bad marriage' ([1987] 2006: 74), in *The Ikon Maker* we learn through Susan of the terrible fate of a young pregnant girl interned in a Magdalene laundry, where 'she'd wash dirty linen' (133). Launched by the Irish Writer's Co-operative (an imprint of which Hogan was a co-founder), *The Ikon Maker*, like much of his other work, raises awareness of unpalatable, often silenced, issues of the time in Ireland.

In significant ways, *The Ikon Maker* differs from 1970s and 1980s popular models of the coming-out story, which promoted, in the figure of the gay protagonist, the notion of a 'stable self', tracing 'an interior process of self-recognition and an exterior process of making one's sexual orientation public' (Gutenberg, 2010: 73). Hogan's Diarmaid never discloses his sexuality, and the story, rather than highlighting moments of positive change, centres on the character's psychic wounds and final separation from the mother (he even refuses to see her before moving to Yugoslavia with a lover). A narrative of gaps, silences, and tacit understandings, the novel captures the unspeakable nature of homosexuality, emphasised by Susan's confusion and her son's inability to communicate his inner turmoil: 'Diarmaid was like something that had long ago silenced itself; a cry' (14). After his departure to England, Susan starts to understand her son's repressed rage, remembering that, as a child, Diarmaid used to create ikons (figures of animals made of materials like eggshells and feathers), but was constantly humiliated for it:

> He constructed these ikons, was proud of them, brought them to national school, where the old teacher praised his efforts as he praised a little girl's bunch of premature marigolds.
>
> 'Daft,' she once heard a woman say of him. 'That child should have his head examined.' (15)

As a boy, Susan insists, her gentle son was a 'dreamer' (15), but his perceived lack of masculinity made him a 'misfit' in the eyes of others (29), provoking his self-loathing.

Contrary to what happens in coming-out stories where the protagonist eventually achieves a 'recognition of the acceptability of same-sex relationships' (Gutenberg, 73), Hogan's Diarmaid remains emotionally scarred and unable to come to terms with his sexuality. Tellingly, Hogan not only addresses the cruelty society inflicts on the protagonist, but also how these experiences transform him, making him cruel to others. In the story, Diarmaid's trauma originates from a fight he had with his best friend Derek, who afterwards hung himself on a tree: 'Before he died I guess I knew he'd kill himself. We'd fought' (50). Bullied at school, Derek and Diarmaid 'made off from teasing boys' and seemed 'enamoured' of one another (18), and, while we learn that this relationship offered them mutual support, the reason for their conflict becomes a secret. As indicated above, the story is punctuated by silences that reveal the shameful condition of homosexuality, as the moment when Diarmaid nearly confesses the nature of his relationship with Derek: 'We were –, he finished [. . .] And [Susan] thought of the truth she'd heard today. The truth stated between them' (46). This 'truth' heard by Susan – the difficult, troubled love between the boys – may explain the fight between them. After Derek's tragic death, Diarmaid's taciturn behaviour is paralleled by the silences and evasions of a community that refuses to face the terrible consequences of their cruelty: 'And all the time people's voices hushed about the image of the boy, leftover, lost. Derek dangling, regretting his misfortune' (37). This social silence – which hides any public recognition of the abuse to which Derek, like Diarmaid, was subjected – fuels the protagonist's rage, an anger that, as explained, he also directs against himself.

Through the eyes of Susan, the author details how Diarmaid's victimisation leads to secrecy, anxiety, self-blame, and the repudiation of a past which includes his own mother. After his migration to England, a traumatised Diarmaid visits the town for a last time and is found crying after his visit to the old school and the tree on which Derek hung himself. Because she feels that 'something of his relationship with Derek was returning' (54), Susan wishes her son to share his secret, but Diarmaid, instead of opening up, remains estranged from her, and 'the silences between them were growing deeper' (55). As Kinga Olszewska notes, Hogan's character carries the unbearable burden of responsibility for Derek's death, and in this way 'resemble[s] Romantic heroes who suffer for crimes (in a literal and figurative sense) they have not committed' (2007: 85). Even though later in the story Diarmaid expresses, in some fits of rage, his hatred against those who had made Derek suffer, he is still unable to unburden himself of his 'crime'. Arguably, if Diarmaid cannot do so it is because he had internalised a language of sin and damnation concerning gay sexuality. As we learn from Michael, one of his lovers in England, in their relationships Diarmaid 'found – among the bed-sheets – evil in himself. That he couldn't understand or take' (111). Since Diarmaid most probably shared Derek's desires, his guilt seems inextricable from his internalised homophobia, that is, his fear of same-sex love and inability to handle their mutual attraction, which presumably led to their fight.

As in *Farewell to Prague* (analysed in Chapter Five), in *The Ikon Maker* a prominent topic is the experience of exile, when a traumatised Diarmaid, still haunted by Derek's death, decides not to return to Ireland. By writing about gay exile, Hogan was reflecting on a reality shared by many Irish men prior to decriminalisation and the more open attitudes of 1990s Ireland. London – the destination chosen by Hogan's fictional character – was not a safe haven either, but, at least, as David Norris once observed, it became a 'refuge' before decriminalisation, a place where 'a more tolerant attitude towards homosexual men prevailed' (1995: 20).[5] Hogan's character, however, fails to find such refuge in London, and emotional healing becomes impossible. Susan travels to England to find her son,[6] but soon learns about his disordered, unhappy life. There, he remains totally uprooted: he moves from being a hippy to associating with the IRA, constantly changes addresses, and engages in failed relationships where he compensates his emasculation with terrible acts of aggression – a female lover of his, Alice, tells Susan: 'He beat me up one night because I wouldn't make love to him' (115).

In another scene, Susan visits Michael, just to discover that Diarmaid had already left the house where they lived together. When Susan asks him had they been lovers, a bewildered Michael eventually confesses:

Diarmaid slept with me many times. But one night –both of us drunk on whiskey, he became hysterical and started screaming, 'You queer, you. You queer, you' [. . .] He wept. We made love. He woke in my arms. Like a young cripple.' (100)

Their homosexual relationship revives, rather than relieves, Diarmaid's turmoil, and the memory of Derek comes alive another night both lovers have a fight:

> 'Diarmaid slit his wrists. Peculiar, isn't it? And wailed "I want to get out."'
> 'Out of where?' Susan questioned urgently.
> 'Hell.' (111)

The reader is never privy to Diarmaid's thoughts and feelings (only other people's observations of him), but, even so, Hogan vividly recreates his character's troubled mind. As a young man who bears a 'grudge against life' (111), Diarmaid is deeply affected by his past, and remains incapable of expressing love and welcoming other people's affections, a frustration that makes him violent and self-destructive.

Although Hogan's *The Ikon Maker* takes the perspective of the mother, not of her exiled gay son, it nonetheless becomes a deeply humane story about the destructive power of homophobia in the context of 1970s Ireland. If Diarmaid blames himself for Derek's suicide, Susan suspects that, because of all her attentions to him as a child, she had 'made her son homosexual' (42), and thus considers herself partly responsible for his torment. Even though the source of their suffering stems from social determinants, both Diarmaid and Susan take on the burden of guilt. In *The Ikon Maker*, an early account of gay suffering in Ireland, Hogan foregrounds the insidious ways in which structural oppression affects individual psychology, and how negative social projections become internalised.

DAMIAN MCNICHOLL'S A SON CALLED GABRIEL

Similar situations of internalised homophobia are described by Damian McNicholl in *A Son Called Gabriel* (2004), where the teenage protagonist names his gay desires as an 'abomination' (180). McNicholl's novel is not as bleak as Hogan's and conforms to some of the conventions of the coming-out story, like the protagonist's eventual disclosure of his homosexuality to his family (this fails to provide him with the comfort he craves, though). Set in 1960s and 1970s rural Northern Ireland, McNicholl's work tells the story of Gabriel Harkin, detailing his sexual awakening as a gay boy, from childhood innocence to the regulated world of adolescence.[7] As a first-person, linear narrative that reflects the psychology and maturation of the protagonist, *A Son Called Gabriel* takes the form of a Bildungsroman which has as its background the social climate of the 1970s civil rights movement against the discrimination of Northern Irish Catholics. Such background somehow parallels Gabriel's personal struggles, so McNicholl's text, as Michael G. Cronin notes about the Bildungsroman genre, 'forge[s] a dynamic relationship between the narration of epochal historical transformation and the narration of self-formation' (2012: 8).

Equally relevant in the novel is the sexual culture of the time, as McNicholl relates in an interview:

> Gabriel grew up in a very conservative Irish Catholic rural culture where sexuality is repressed and certainly wasn't a subject to be aired in civilized homes [. . .] On those rare occasions when sex is discussed, it is pretty speedily and in hushed tones. Given such a situation, it's not surprising Gabriel was ignorant of sex and thus would have been utterly confused about it. (Esposito, 2005)

Sex was in this context shrouded by an aura of taboo and shame, so, when occasions of 'sin' arose, secrecy became the norm. After being abused by a priest who masturbated him, Gabriel feels defenceless and takes part of the blame, as he believes that his queerness provoked the older man to do 'wicked things on [him]' (256). Like Hogan, McNicholl explores dysfunctional silences surrounding sex, showing how the same moralistic culture that stigmatised gay men was also at the root of social maladies like the silencing of sexual abuse (a similar approach is adopted by Colm Tóibín in 'The Pearl Fishers', see Chapter Seven). Aside from the protagonist's abuse and his homosexuality, a third shameful secret is uncovered when Gabriel learns that he is an adopted child, and that Uncle Brendan – a priest who had a love affair – is his biological father. Throughout the story, McNicholl highlights the negative effects of a repressive culture that hides unacceptable sexual realities.

An alternative to this repressive language of sexuality is described in the early chapters of the novel, through Gabriel's innocence as a child. In his study of gay experiences in 1970s Ireland, sociologist Paul Ryan found that 'where there was no language to describe their activities the boys remained free from any sexual categorisation, learning only in secondary school the penalties associated with their previously carefree childhoods' (2003: 72). *A Son Called Gabriel* draws on such a scenario through the voice and perspective of the protagonist as he grows up. As a pre-adolescent, Gabriel carelessly engages in sexual experimentation, and enjoys his 'games' with another boy, experiencing no inhibitions: 'The beautiful part was the lovely pains. I enjoyed the lovely pains. They came after Noel had been playing with my thing for a while' (89).

This situation radically changes when he starts secondary school, where Gabriel learns a religious language of sexual sin. At Catholic schools, Ryan argues, the equation between sin and desire was so strong that boys were often taught that 'masturbation was the gateway to homosexuality' (2003: 76). As a teenage schoolboy, McNicholl's Gabriel is tormented by his urges to masturbate, due to his uncontrollable gay desires.[8] Gabriel's language clearly reflects his sexual guilt, when, for example, he spies an 'attractive footballer type', later 'abus[ing] [him]self' thinking about him (279). Another classmate's 'fleshy lips' and 'dark chest hair' captivate Gabriel, but he then becomes afflicted by his own 'vileness' (300). Religious morality is thus reflected by the way in which Gabriel understands gay sexuality as an evil temptation, something external to him: 'Homosexuality confronted me from every corner' (307). McNicholl's character, unlike conventional heroes of coming-out stories, never liberates himself from demeaning images of homosexuality.

As he grows up gay, Gabriel is not only affected by religious morality, but also by damaging ideas of sexual inversion. *A Son Called Gabriel* shows how popular stereotypes of gay men – in their mannerisms, voice, general behaviour and so on – have traditionally relied on a 'cultural vilification of femininity' in men, which became the 'justification for abuse' (Barron and Bradford, 2007: 241–2). Throughout his school years, Gabriel's mannerisms provoke the cruel sneering of his classmates, who 'taunted [him] unmercifully about [his] arse and addressed [him] as "poof" and "queer boy"' (282). Bullied at school, Gabriel arrives home one day, injured by a classmate, just to hear his adoptive father exhort him to 'fight back like a man' (12). A sense of shame and personal failure pervades the father-son relationship, as Gabriel knows that he will always have to hide himself from him: 'I couldn't bring myself to utter "homosexuality". It was hard to talk about something like that to a man who'd never thought of such things. He called them "fruits"' (338). The (adoptive) father's injurious language denotes his culturally induced inability to conceive of homosexuality separate from the derogatory notions attached to it. Within the school and the family, Gabriel feels diminished by his inability to live up to the expectations of masculinity.

McNicholl constantly emphasises Gabriel's difficult path towards self-acceptance, a process that is rendered even harder when he comes out to his family. Disclosure fails to lead towards psychic health and authenticity, contrary to what happens in many other coming-out stories. The moment a teenage Gabriel breaks down and confesses his fear of being gay, the mother becomes terrified of her child's 'sinful' desires and helps him the only way she knows, by taking him to the priest and the doctor.[9] If the priest says that Gabriel can still be a good Catholic 'provided that [he] do[esn't] act on [his] impulses' (314); the doctor proves equally inefficient when he asks: 'When you imagine scenes with men, Gabriel, are you active or passive?' (317). Encouraged by the priest's and doctor's advice, the mother sincerely hopes that Gabriel is only going through a phase, and that his homosexuality can disappear by means of repressing it. As McNicholl makes it clear, the highly normative and moralistic sexual culture of 1970s Northern Ireland will never allow Gabriel to become an emotionally healthy homosexual.

Despite these grim realities, *A Son Called Gabriel* is more than a story of suffering and despair. Typical of coming-out novels and the Bildungsroman genre, Gabriel makes a vital decision which originates from his personal maturation, and not from others' pressures. McNicholl's protagonist, like Hogan's, decides to migrate to England, but, whereas Diarmaid's escape is induced by trauma, Gabriel's future migration comes from his rebellion against familial expectations that he follows a religious vocation. Like Colm Tóibín, who opines that 'for young gay men in Ireland in the 1960s and 70s, the priesthood seemed to offer the only way out' (Rustin, 2010), McNicholl suggests that the most respectable option for boys like Gabriel was to join the priesthood. A more mature Gabriel, though, abandons such prospect, and discovers that studying abroad may be a better opportunity for him: 'The idea of attending an English university both terrified and attracted me. My adventurous part longed to quit Ulster and leave all the petty bigotry behind, but the quiet part was intimidated' (290). The notion of the gay migrant, in need of freedom from the community's narrow-mindedness, resonates here in the final part of the novel, bringing some hope for the protagonist's future.

A Son Called Gabriel offers its readers a carefully constructed portrayal of a boy's discovery of homosexuality at a time when sexuality itself was a social taboo. One of this novel's merits is the way in which the author contrasts Gabriel's carefree childhood with the confusion and sexual guilt of his teenage years, which he cannot dispel after his coming-out.

TOM LENNON'S WHEN LOVE COMES TO TOWN

If McNicholl's *A Son Called Gabriel* reverses some conventions of the coming-out story, Tom Lennon's Dublin-set *When Love Comes to Town* (1993) fits into most of the characteristics of the genre, in the sense that the protagonist, the eighteen-year-old Neil Byrne, not only enters a gay subculture, but also 'achieves maturity by "coming out", which is a gesture of self-acceptance and self-realization' (Jeffers, 2002: 88). Lennon's story focuses on the young protagonist's subjective world, and how he overcomes a number of personal crises, which call for gay identity validation in the early 1990s Ireland. Published in the year of gay decriminalisation, *When Love Comes to Town* has 'definite social aims in mind' (Smyth, 1997: 162), as it attempts to enlighten the Irish public about the nature and consequences of homophobia.

Probably because of his novel's homosexual content and overt critique of Catholic morality, the author adopted the pseudonym of Tom Lennon not to risk his teaching position at a Catholic school.[10] Considered subversive in 1993, *When Love Comes to Town* first appeared under the O'Brien's Press adult fiction list but was reclassified as Young Adult fiction in its reprinted editions from 2003. The book's history publication, Pádraic Whyte observes, reveals important changes concerning public attitudes towards homosexuality in Ireland, since 'it is now easier for publishers to place what may once have seemed controversial novels into their children's list' (2011: 73). As Whyte further argues, the novel has a 'unique position' (73), being, perhaps, the first gay Bildungsroman in Irish writing (the previous *The Ikon Maker* lacks the perspective of a gay protagonist).

Like Hogan and McNicholl in their novels, Lennon advances in his coming-out story social concerns with respect to the emotional health of gay adolescents. Lennon's protagonist prides himself on his masculinity and his ability to easily pass as heterosexual, since he is a rugby player and, in this text, 'rugby culture is insistently represented as oppositional and incompatible with homosexuality' (Madden, 2013b: 259). Neil is admired by his peers, but his reputation is threatened by his homosexuality, which he must repress publicly: 'Sometimes he felt like he wanted to break down and tell them all about the real Neil' (8). This situation causes much distress, so, in one of his personal crises, Neil develops suicidal thoughts: 'Down another quick whiskey. Throat burning. Head's going to explode. Imagine it. Bits of brains and flesh splattered all over the tacky bar' (186). For much of the story, Neil struggles with depression, but, while Hogan's and McNicholl's protagonists are unable to accept their gay sexuality, Lennon's character already identifies as gay, but suffers from isolation and inauthenticity.

Lennon's configuration of a stable gay identity, hidden beneath outward appearances and in need of social recognition, fits into the conventions of the coming-out story, itself affiliated with the gay and lesbian identity politics of the time. In Lennon's novel, religious morality features as one of the social pressures preventing the emergence of the 'real', gay Neil. *When Love Comes to Town* depicts an Irish context where, despite increasing opposition,[11] the moral principles of the Catholic Church remained strong. Nowhere is this clearer than in the case of Neil's religious parents, whose reaction at their son's coming-out is one of shock, fear, and grief: 'It was as though he had told them that he was going to die' (162). What disgusts his parents the most is their suspicion that their son had been having sex with Shane, an older boy, so, for the sake of reconciliation, Neil has to convince them that this relationship (or any other gay relationships) never happened: 'Now Neil understands the conditions. We'll love you, providing you hide your love away' (190). The the early 1900s reader of *When Love Comes to*

Town may have heard echoes here of well-known messages promoted by Catholic associations like Family Solidarity,[12] who claimed to accept homosexuals who, being aware of their 'abnormality', refuse to engage in gay sex, while condemning those who assert that their sexuality is 'normal' and, therefore, 'should be given free and positive expression' (1990: 9). At this point of the story, the Catholic culture of the time damages Neil's familial relationships, but not his self-image, as he had already achieved by then a sense of self-confidence with regard to his sexuality.

Religious culture alone cannot explain the existence of sexual prejudice since homophobia has also operated as an 'organizing principle of our cultural definition of manhood' (Kimmel 1994: 214). *When Love Comes to Town*, like McNicholl's and Hogan's novels, illustrates how, in certain environments, homophobic behaviour – in its manifestation of aggressiveness and repudiation of softness in other men – becomes normative among young men. 'Homophobic harassment,' Tristan Bridges and C. J. Pascoe point out, 'has as much to do with failing at masculine tasks of competence, heterosexual prowess, or in any way revealing weakness as it does with sexual identity' (2016: 416). In *When Love Comes to Town*, Neil, a 'rugby hero' (28), also faces the pressures to fit in, so he readily uses homophobic slurs, and joins the other boys' banter about 'the sexual availability of the female talent' (15). To confirm his public image as a heterosexual, Neil once has drunken sex with a girl, Yvonne Lawlor, which solves the problem of 'the lack of romance in his life' (31). His cruel rejection of Yvonne, though, makes him feel uneasy. In a way, Neil's 'straight-acting' behaviour becomes both a blessing – he avoids harassment – and a curse, as his popularity depends on maintaining an image of masculinity, sustained by sexist and homophobic attitudes.

Far from being a 'natural' behaviour, Neil's performance of hegemonic masculinity connects with gender anxieties. Neil constantly regulates himself – 'there isn't the slightest hint of effeminacy about him' (32) – and looks down on other gays who look more effeminate than him: '[Eddie] was such an effeminate-looking bloke, not just physically, but in mannerisms, facial expressions and speech. And that awful, clipped accent couldn't possibly be the way he really spoke' (72). Among gays, gender performance marks distinctions and hierarchies, but what is relevant here is how Neil's obsession with his masculinity diminishes through the course of the story. When he walks into the gay bar, he experiences a sense of relief: 'All his normal self-consciousness left him. There was nothing to worry about here. Nobody cared. He felt himself being submerged into the sexual sea of graceful movement' (81). As he distances himself from the gaze of his family and straight friends, Neil evolves into a more self-reliant individual.

Lennon inserts in his novel another typical element of the coming-out narrative, which is his character's transformation thanks to his entry into a gay subculture, which helps him unlearn homophobic stereotypes of the time, like the view that gay men 'prey on vulnerable people',[13] and that they cannot have 'lasting, caring relationships' (Irish Council of Civil Liberties, 1990: 27). Initially, Neil associates gay life with a dark sexual underworld, but these prejudices disappear as he befriends other gays (one of them, he is surprised to find, is in a long-term relationship), who help him understand that there are different options and lifestyles available to everybody. Furthermore, if at the beginning of the story Neil presumed that being gay entailed serious renunciations – like family, straight friends, and a stable love life –, he finally learns that it is the others' decision to accept him as he is. As he tells his friend Gary: 'I'm still your friend if you want me to be' (178).

In short, Lennon's *When Love Comes to Town* recreates a time when popular ideas about gay sexuality were highly influenced by religious doctrine, heterosexist assumptions, and the gender anxieties of masculinity. This is precisely the culture that shaped Neil, who, in the earlier chapters, features as a dislikeable character who reproduces the moralistic views of the society around him. Even though Lennon's protagonist gains maturity and a new self-image as a homosexual in the course of the story, *When Love Comes to Town* suggests that early 1990s Ireland was far from achieving equality and recognition for gays.

JARLATH GREGORY'S SNAPSHOTS

As indicated above, Lennon's book adheres to 1990s gay and lesbian identity politics, as the protagonist's coming-out to family and friends features as a central act of self-affirmation and liberation. A stark contrast is provided by Jarlath Gregory's *Snapshots*, where one of the protagonists, Oisín, declares that 'it feels right saying you're gay, and it's a relief, but it also ties you down' (6). The second protagonist, Jude, is similarly sceptical about the benefits of being out, and prefers to pass unnoticed so that nobody 'bother[s] [him]' (84). None of them struggles with (in)authenticity, and they are sure that, in certain contexts, closetedness is a better option than being openly gay. Gregory's gay protagonists therefore live partly in the closet (they come out to people they confide in); and feel no urge to make a homosexual identity public.

Gregory, as Cronin remarks, dispenses in *Snapshots* with clichés of the coming-out story, as 'neither coming out nor the promise of romance bring resolution or catarsis', for the simple reason that 'being closeted about one's sexuality is not the primary problem' (2020: 574). The story alternates between the first-person narratives of Oisín and Jude, interspersed with very short third-person chapters, called 'snapshots', which provide external perspectives on life in post-ceasefire Crossmaglen, Northern Ireland (County Armagh), which is, in Gregory's words, 'a famous little IRA town, not the best environment for being ostentatiously gay' (Kelly, 2005: 41). Gregory's style here, as in his follow-up *G.A.A.Y.*, is chatty and fast-paced, coloured by dialect and yoof slang, all this infused with a 'darkly camp tone' (Cronin, 2020: 574). His story not only breaks with previous models of the coming-out narrative, but also captures the voice and experience of a younger generation which sets itself apart from the world of adults.

Gregory became a fresh voice in Northern Irish writing when *Snapshots* appeared in 2001, a time when 'there were few, if any, gay voices in Ulster fiction' (Bradley, 2001: 18). *Snapshots* develops within a conservative milieu, but the writer produces here a gay narrative which refuses victimhood, as Oisín and Jude manage to overcome personal and social barriers to be together. Such social barriers were hard to surmount in the context of early-2000s Northern Ireland, since there was a high level of 'self-regulation in terms of space, visibility and behaviour' among the Northern Irish LGBTI+ population, especially those living in rural areas (Duggan, 2012: 42). A relevant factor affecting the lives of LGBTI+ people has been the 'provincialism' of small towns, which is 'related to political parties in Northern Ireland being interwoven with Christian fundamentalism' (Schubotz and McNamee, 2009: 202). In *Snapshots*, Gregory portrays a similar world of Northern Irish provincialism, in a place like Crossmaglen, where, as Oisín says, 'everybody knows your life' (6). This frustration is shared by all young characters in the story, gay or straight, in a small town where great pressures exist to conform.[14]

Like McNicholl's novel, *Snapshots* recreates a rural Northern Irish scenario of entrenched homophobia,[15] the crucial difference being that in Gregory's text the younger generations generally display more tolerant attitudes than adults (both Oisín and Jude have accepting friends). Here, generational divides are tainted by conflict and disaffection, especially within the family, where parents become 'uncomprehending of the dilemmas faced by [young people]' (Hand, 2001: 68). Confrontations at times become too violent and bitter; Oisín's final scene with the mother, after she discovers his sexual relationship with Jude, is one of unleashed fury. Jude, on his part, suffers his mother's recriminations after she finds a gay magazine under his bed, and cannot help feeling angered when he finds her crying: 'He stared at his mother's worried face and despised her' (125). Homophobia is also present at school, and Jude surprises himself by timidly defying a teacher's notion that gays are genetically imbalanced. This language of homosexuality as a shameful condition and disease,[16] as is made clear in the story, only belongs to the adult world of family and education.

Even though Jude and Oísín are similar in the sense that their narratives of formation involve their alienation from dominant values, they feature as 'polar opposites' (Hughes, 2019: 91), which allows Gregory to explore notions of sameness and difference surrounding homosexual lives. Oísín is, arguably, a more complex character because he is a traumatised individual. Famous for being the younger brother of an IRA martyr, Seán, Oísín behaves as an 'angry' queer (114), who wears eyeliner to Seán's televised funeral, and whose drawings of Jude – 'his head's split open like a crocus' (27) – express both his erotic obsession with him and his trauma about his brother's death, which he witnessed. His gender non-conformity or queerness, far from relating solely to his homosexuality, works as a rebellion against the values of his community and his parents, proud as they are of Seán's memory and the masculine ideal the elder brother embodied. Throughout the story, Oísín clings to his queerness, provoking the open repulsion of many people, who 'give [him] looks that show surprise that [he] belong[s] to the real world' (26), and the unacknowledged fascination of some others, like Jude. Seeing him wearing his eye-liner, Jude tells Oísín:

> 'You just want to be different,' he said.
> 'Well you just want to be the same!' I called, but he ignored me. (27)

As an angry queer, Oísín reverses the expected behaviour of gender self-policing for males. Jude, on the contrary, attempts to blend in by displaying more conventional attitudes, but grows increasingly uncomfortable with himself (at one point, he outs another boy to protect his closetedness within his family), consummating his rebellion the moment he accepts his attraction to Oísín.

The topic of sameness and difference is further explored in the terrain of sexual identity and desire. As a social category, homosexuality, David M. Halperin reminds us, is 'more than conscious erotic same-sex preference'; it functions as 'an overriding principle of sexual and social difference' and thus adds another dimension into 'the social construction of the self' (2013: 280). Thus, it transpires that having same-sex desires – and acting on them – does not necessarily translate into feelings of difference from the mainstream values of heterosexual masculinity. In *Snapshots*, Gregory makes readers reflect on the aforementioned distinctions between homosexuality and same-sex desires. His novel includes two self-identified heterosexual characters, Mike and Neil, who seek Jude and Oísín respectively for casual sex. Mike uses sexist banter – 'Shena has the best set of tits on her!' (94) – and homophobic slurs – '"Oisín" Mike said and spat [. . .] "Faggot" he said' (96) – to assert his heterosexual masculinity, but then invites Jude into his bed for sex. Likewise, IRA member Neil brags that 'he'd fuck the barmaid' (61), but then makes sexual advances on Oisín. Unsurprisingly, both Mike and Neil enforce silence and denial on their same-sex desires and relationships: 'It never happened,' Neil warns Oisín (134). Gregory hence dramatises in *Snapshots* how, while gay sex may be a common occurrence in highly repressive environments, the real transgression is to oppose mainstream values of heterosexual masculinity, by means of embracing a homosexual identity or expressing same-sex love in an open way, just as Oisín and Jude would like to do.

Same-sex love goes against everything that Jude and Oisín were taught, yet they manage to break free from the constraints of masculinity, politics, and religion. If at the beginning the boys communicate their mutual attraction through indirect signs, they eventually evolve into close friends and, when they finally kiss, 'they shoot each other full of the bullets of a mutual but mirrored love' (177). Gay love, though fulfilling, still feels violent and forbidden in this context – 'Love is war', Oisín tells us (196). The two boys' heroic act, though, is to have resisted their numerous pressures to keep their love hidden from one another.

JARLATH GREGORY'S G.A.A.Y.: ONE HUNDRED WAYS TO LOVE A BEAUTIFUL LOSER

Gregory's follow-up, *G.A.A.Y.: One Hundred Ways to Love a Beautiful Loser* (2005), takes readers to a radically different scenario, the gay youth culture of 2000s Dublin. The protagonist, the twenty-year-old Anthony Broderick, feels at ease with his homosexuality, and has a wide group of gay friends. The novel teems with references to gay culture and, as an early reviewer points out, Gregory offers here fresh insights into Dublin life, as *G.A.A.Y.* depicts a side of the city 'the straight world never sees' (Leonard, 2005: 95). The writing style is similar to that of *Snapshots*, and the novel, Cronin notes, offers 'bitterly comic dissections of modern youth' (Cronin, 2008–09). The story is told in one hundred short chapters – some of them no longer than two pages –, which construct a mosaic of Anto's life, not only through his voice, but also from the viewpoint of others. Some episodes – which focus on online dating and the gay scene – give an idea of a gay culture of increased freedoms, but somehow limited to confined spaces and pre-established behaviours. At some point, Anto self-mockingly admits that his romantic life lacks 'chemistry', and that he is suffering from 'gay fatigue' (144).

Set in the Celtic Tiger years, *G.A.A.Y.* reflects the emergence of a modern Ireland where gay men became more visible within mainstream culture. This situation, though, had its shortcomings, as it relied on an oversimplification of gay men's lives and experiences. Susannah Bowyer has studied this phenomenon, observing that in the late 1990s and early 2000s there was a 'liberal urge' to project an Irish 'gay brand' of progress and modernity, which celebrated the erstwhile demeaned figure of the effeminate homosexual, focusing on his 'camp performance' as if this was his only and most important personal trait (2010: 810). In an interview, Gregory explained that he was aware of this new stereotype of gay identity, which inspired him to create his protagonist:

> I was trying to deliberately create a character who was the typical gay best friend in the romantic comedies happening at the time. I wanted to get that character a voice and an inner life, because, in all the previous incarnations, characters like that were becoming more prevalent, but they were flat and always the same type. They were there just to deliver sassy one-liners and help the girl get the right guy. (Carregal-Romero, 2019: 202)

Gregory's Anto thrives in this liberal culture and defines himself as a 'gay cliché' (15) who has 'learned how to brand [him]self as a sorted, happy gay boy whom you'd love to buy a pint for' (95). Anto is also portrayed as a character that voices principles that belong to the language of gay and lesbian identity politics, where coming-out means being authentic: 'To be out is to say that love and sex are natural, are no more complicated than they should be, are happening no matter how someone else wants to suppress you' (30). Aware of the unnecessary pain some people inflict on themselves,[17] Anto also tells us that 'the fear of stigma is greater than stigma itself' (42). In some ways, in *G.A.A.Y.* (but not in *Snapshots*) Gregory inherits the educative approach of previous 1990s novels, like Lennon's *When Love Comes to Town*, Emma Donoghue's *Stir-fry* (1994), and Colm Tóibín's *The Blackwater Lightship* (1999).

Though educative, *G.A.A.Y.* is also a modern, Celtic Tiger text where Gregory dramatises how the liberalism of the late 1990s and early 2000s period swiftly transformed the sexual culture of the younger generations. In this scenario, sex becomes part of everyday conversation, and not a subject which requires discretion. Anto and a gay friend, for example, joke about an American rapper, allegedly a homophobe:

> 'Have you ever sucked cock to Eminem?' I asked
> 'No way! That's a disgrace. That's sleeping with the enemy. I'd suck his cock, though'
> 'I find it empowering.' (emphasis in the original, 117)

Sexual gratification becomes an end in itself, even if one ends up 'sleeping with the enemy'. The traditional sexual morality of Catholic Ireland – pervasive in the other novels analysed in this chapter – is nowhere to be seen in *G.A.A.Y.*

This 'sexual revolution' of Celtic Tiger Ireland, as Tom Inglis observes in *Lessons in Irish Sexuality* (1998), was capitalised by the liberal market, which, through the mass media, motivated young people to be sexually attractive and adventurous as a means to achieve popularity and success. Though celebrating sexual freedom, these messages also served the interests of consumer capitalism, in the form of beauty products, fashion clothes and so on (see Inglis, 1998: 101–24). This situation, as shown in Gregory's novel, led to a growing concern about physical appearance and investment in the body as symbolic capital. Anto, for instance, writes a guide to one of his gay friends, to help him become more attractive: 'A fashionable haircut shows that you're an up-to-speed gay-boy, i.e. that you're in the know. Being in the know makes you one of us, and therefore means that you're on the same wavelength, which in turn makes you shaggable' (118). Image and style, Anto implies, become central elements of Dublin's gay youth culture. This veneer of glamour, though, exerts strong pressures on people to have the 'right' kind of body image. A 2000s study on the experiences of young gay Dubliners, from the ages of 16 to 25, reveals that the 'gay body' can easily be 'denigrated for being the wrong shape, inappropriately dressed, or insufficiently attractive in the domains of leisure and pleasure that constitute the gay scene' (Barron and Bradford, 2007: 234). *G.A.A.Y.* does not engage with this reality of body-shaming, promoted by a consumerist culture which the novel reflects but never problematises.

In many other ways, *G.A.A.Y.* is a tale of queer empowerment which dispenses with well-known conventions of the gay fiction that had been produced until then, which foregrounded topics like the pain of growing up homosexual and familial rejection (Anto has a difficult relationship with his father, though this is not a central topic). Free from tragedy and trauma, *G.A.A.Y.* displays a keen sense of gay affirmation, even though a past of suffering does shape Anto's militant queerness, as he had gone through 'a phase of trying to be a man' just before he quit the GAA team, 'devastated that all the slurs people threw at [him] were true' (32). Some years later, as an empowered queer subject, the protagonist regards sports like GAA – an icon of Irish masculinity – as a ritual some men perform to be able to touch one another: 'Fags are great at all sorts, but we have the decency to leave group sports to heteros who need their man-groping fix' (47). Here, Gregory's protagonist disparages what he sees as 'typical straight male awkwardness' (51), which discourages emotional and physical intimacy among men. Much as Anto sees himself as a product of the gay culture of his time, he also views heterosexual masculinity as a social construct. Yet, symptomatic of a social order which eroticises power and gender difference, Anto feels attracted to the straight acting and homosexually repressed GAA footballers Cathal (with whom he had a previous affair) and Khalid (a Muslim immigrant from England).

G.A.A.Y. not only reconfigures the temporality of coming-out stories by presenting the protagonist's coming-out as situated in the past, but also frustrates the narrative expectations of the genre, since much of the plot revolves around Anto's failed attempts to help Khalid and Cathal to come out as gay. Influenced by his white, liberal, and post-Catholic values on gay life, Anto quickly dismisses Khalid's particular struggles and primary identi-fication as Muslim. Thus, instead of trying to help him reconcile his religion with his (presumed) same-sex desires, Anto attacks the homophobia of Islam, provoking Khalid's hostile reaction: 'Don't disrespect my religion, man' (100). If Khalid's main barrier is religion, Cathal, the protagonist's other romantic obsession, remains more clearly trapped by the gender anxieties of heterosexual masculinity. When, in response to his bullying, Anto publicly calls him 'a closet-case loser' (178), an infuriated Cathal punches him in the face. Despite this moment of violence, the novel finishes on a positive note in a scene where Cathal suddenly overcomes his personal limitations and visits Anto asking for forgiveness, just to end up kissing him on the street, 'surrounded by [. . .] smiling passers-by' (208). Like Khalid, Cathal never comes out or declares his attraction to Anto, but this optimistic ending suggests that he will eventually do so.

Gregory's *G.A.A.Y.* does not fit into most of the formal characteristics of coming-out narratives but as suggested earlier, the novel largely endorses the gay politics of the genre, with its educative approach and emphasis on coming-out as an act of self-acceptance. Amidst the liberal glow of 2000s Dublin, Gregory dramatises how, when it came to being gay, there was still too much negativity and fear of emotional intimacy. As a gay boy who is comfortable with his sexuality, the protagonist has some valuable advice for his 'closet cases': 'The biggest challenge of being lesbian, gay or bisexual is rising above the idiocy of people who won't accept you for yourself' (162).

CONCLUSION

The novels included in this chapter explore how the dominant language of masculinity increases the vulnerability and damages the emotional development of the young gay protagonists in areas such as personal identity (the compliance with or rebellion against gender expectations); mental health (internalised homophobia, suicidal ideation and so on); and social life (exclusion and discrimination within the family and the school). If characters like Lennon's Neil and Gregory's Cathal (in *G.A.A.Y.*) adhere to masculine norms at the cost of self-suppression and emotional distress, other characters like McNicholl's Gabriel and Gregory's Oisín face the humiliation of being feminised in the eyes of others. Hegemonic masculinity is in these texts exposed as sustaining heteropatriarchy and unequal power relations. This language of masculinity is, for example, linked to political strife and the paramilitary in *Snapshots*, and is enacted by a gang who bashes Neil when he exits a gay bar in *When Love Comes to Town*. In Hogan's *The Ikon Maker*, the influence of toxic masculinity explains Diarmaid's sense of emasculation, which leads to great emotional turmoil and violence against his lovers, male and female.

Read together, these novels portray the changing sexual morality of Ireland and Northern Ireland, from the 1970s to the early 2000s. Religious homophobia is highly destructive in *The Ikon Maker* and *A Son Called Gabriel*, which recreate contexts of silence and Catholic sexual guilt, capturing the protagonists' sense of identity confusion as they come to terms with their same-sex desires. There is no possibility, in Hogan's and McNicholl's novels, for the young characters to develop a healthy identity as homo-sexuals within their Irish context – thus, whereas Diarmaid exiles himself, Gabriel chooses to study in England against his family's expectations that he join the priesthood. If in the 1970s there were no social outlets for gay men, in the early 1990s there was a gay scene in cities like Dublin, and this makes all the difference to Lennon's protagonist; Neil, whose entry into a gay subculture proves crucial. In Lennon's novel, which, as observed, adopts most of the conventions of the coming-out narrative, Neil already recognises himself as gay, but his task is to unlearn a language of hetero-patriarchal masculinity. Like Lennon's Neil, Oisín and Jude in Gregory's *Snapshots* confront familial homophobia and the pressures of a suffocating masculinist culture. Yet Gregory portrays hope for change in the younger generations, as both Jude and Oisín find friends who are more accepting than the adult world of the family. Set in Celtic Tiger Dublin, Gregory's *G.A.A.Y.* depicts a more open universe where the old sexual morality becomes replaced by a new culture of individualism and sexual freedom. A self-assured gay boy, the protagonist escaped his old self when he left the GAA team and stopped worrying about being a 'man' (32). Taken together, these coming-out novels promote a language of resilience, foregrounding their central characters' need to escape from received notions of masculinity, while they establish their own emotional truths and love relationships away from social and familial expectations. These novels tell the evolving story of LGBTI+ social liberation from silence to assurance, and everything in between.

FIVE

The Only Real Way to Fight Evil
is to Hold Someone's Hand

The Cultural Narratives of AIDS in Irish Fiction

In a 1993 article, journalist and writer Nuala O'Faolain praised the Irish gay community for the ways in which they had confronted the silence and misinformation about HIV/AIDS in Ireland. Gay activists, O' Faolain points out, helped raise awareness about the disease, because, at the beginning, many people 'thought HIV infection was just an American thing, and you wouldn't get it if you stayed away from Americans' (1993). AIDS first appeared in Ireland in 1982, with the diagnoses of two men who had had gay relationships abroad, a fact which helped create the popular notion that AIDS was a foreign disease. Even when scientific knowledge of the virus and its prevention advanced, misconceptions and stereotypes remained entrenched in Ireland, due the dominant conservative culture of the time, which impeded the emergence of a public language of sexual health[1] in a country which had, by then, 'poorly developed diagnostic and treatment services for sexually transmitted infections' (Nolan and Larkan, 2016: 255). As the popular association between gay sex and the virus grew, public authorities in Ireland saw an opportunity to reinforce Catholic sexual morality.

In the mid-1980s, while international institutions like the World Health Organization (WHO) 'emphasized safer sex rather than abstinence and harm reduction rather than prohibition' to tackle the AIDS crises (Nolan, 2018: 106), the Irish political class and the Catholic Church still stressed the importance of sexual abstinence and heterosexual monogamy as preventative measures, strengthening, if only indirectly, the cultural linkages between gay sex, abjection, and the disease. In their 1987 booklet about HIV/AIDS, the Health Education Bureau (HEB) omitted references to safe sex practices and classified gay and bisexual men as a 'high risk group' (6), stating that 'condoms cannot offer 100% protection' (9) and that, 'to avoid AIDS, the most effective way of all is to stay with one faithful partner' (8). Opposing the HEB's approach, the association Gay Health Action (GHA) judged these messages as 'simplistic, ineffective, moralising, more concerned with reinforcing traditional moral values than combatting the spread of AIDS' (1987).[2] A predominant culture of sexual prudery and compulsory heterosexuality, epitomised by the HEB's booklet, imposed taboos and shameful silences, which impeded knowledge on safe sex and hindered self-empowerment in the face of the epidemic.

In spite of this enforced sexual ignorance, in comparison to the US and Britain, Ireland had a low incidence of HIV infection among gay men – the highest incidence was among the (also denigrated) population of drug users (O'Connor, 1995). Nonetheless, as David Conaty warned in a 1989 article for *The Irish Times*, 'the lack of education Irish people ha[d] about AIDS' became a high-risk factor when they arrived in foreign lands, as there were numerous HIV-positive Irish people living in London, 'whom people in Ireland [did] not know about'. Thus, just as numerous Irish homosexuals left Ireland, AIDS was spreading rapidly in many British and American cities, a situation that proved 'tragically relevant' for many of these gay migrants (Casey, 2018: 230). This largely ignored reality of gay migration and vulnerability in the face of AIDS shall be further explored in some of the texts analysed in this chapter.

Moreover, as also occurred in many other Western countries in the course of the 1980s and 1990s, Irish society adopted transnational discourses of HIV/AIDS not only as 'gay plague',[3] but also as a disease that was easily transmitted to 'innocent' people through casual infection, which led to social blaming and irrational fears.[4] In his *Prejudice in Ireland* (1997), Micheál Mac Gréil defined AIDS stigma as 'potent a mixture of fear, blame and anger' towards people who were perceived to have brought the disease upon themselves, as if they deserved their infection (352). These 'extremely negative' attitudes, Mac Greil opined, were only intensified by the public association between the disease and homosexuality/drug injection (451). For homosexuals, AIDS stigma was, and remains, linked to notions of gay promiscuity. Because of this homophobic prejudice, for many Irish people the virus emerged almost as a natural consequence of gay sex, thus fostering among many homosexuals 'fatalism about the avoidance of infection', as well as 'feelings of guilt' (Smyth, 1998: 671).

In twenty-first-century Ireland, discrimination against HIV-positives persists, but is no longer sustained by the same fatalism as before, thanks to the 1996 development of the antiretroviral therapy ART, which inaugurated a 'post-AIDS' era where HIV could be experienced as less threatening, and as a chronic condition instead of a death sentence. The virus and its negative cultural associations still circulate, though. Cormac O'Brien reminds us that today's post-AIDS discourses provide the general population with a sense of 'false security', a 'cultural amnesia' which lessens the urgency of HIV awareness and prevention, and invisibilises the persistent stigma attached to the disease (2020: 128). HIV stigma, O'Brien explains in a 2013 article, still 'manifests in many ways', exemplified by legal cases undertaken by the Dublin AIDS Alliance, where HIV-positives protested that they were denied services to which they were entitled, under the excuse that they should visit HIV-related medical practitioners instead (76).

Even within the gay community, HIV stigma has a strong presence. If in more conservative times society's homophobia was inextricable from AIDS stigma, in today's Ireland the 'normal', respectable gay individual has gained acceptability at the expense of the 'deviant' one, for instance, the seropositive homosexual – a situation which exemplifies the presumably homonormative nature of today's gay culture. Among Irish HIV-positives 'protective non-disclosure' remains prevalent not just because of personal choice, but due to the persistence of 'anachronistic discourses of depravity and infectiousness', endorsed by the wider population and non-infected gays alike (Murphy et al., 2016: 1468). Gay seropositives no longer experience 'the kind of support that typified gay community responses to HIV in the early years of the epidemic' (1468), at a time when HIV-infections in Ireland rate higher than in the years of the AIDS crises.

In what follows, the present chapter offers analyses of novels and short-stories – Micheál Ó Conghaile 'Lost in Connemara' (2012), Keith Ridgway's 'Andy Warhol' (2018), Anne Enright's *The Green Road* (2015), Desmond Hogan's *A Farewell to Prague* (1995) and Colm Tóibín's *The Blackwater Lightship* (1999) – which, while describing times prior to the introduction of ART therapy, also illustrate contemporary circumstances. These works of fiction shall be read in light of the aforementioned cultural narratives of AIDS, also considering the literary tropes identified by Cormac O'Brien in his study of Irish theatre. One of these is the 'punishment paradox' – present in plays like Declan Hughes' *Halloween Night* (1997) and Loughlin Deegan's *The Queen and the Peacock* (2000), which, while presenting AIDS characters as deserving empathy, relies on politically disempowering messages of 'hidden-ness, suffering, victimhood and death', promulgating (if only indirectly) the idea of AIDS as the unwanted consequence of operating 'outside normative sexual paradigms' (O'Brien, 2020: 129). Whereas the 'punishment paradox' trope usually fits into the realistic narrative mode, with its 'insistence on neat resolutions and cathartic endings' (126), the other category – named by O'Brien as 'positively Irish', present in plays by Neil Watkins – usually takes the form of non-linear, non-realist stories 'rooted in Irish contexts' (127), which are often expressed through monologue, uncovering 'the queer dis-comfort cast upon HIV-positive masculinities' (133). This second approach, O'Brien concludes, proves to be a much more effective way to protest against the silencing and stigma suffered by Irish seropositives.

MICHEÁL Ó CONGHAILE'S 'LOST IN CONNEMARA'

Micheál Ó Conghaile's short story, 'Lost in Connemara'[5], dramatises the death (in the past) of a HIV-positive character, but, in its open challenge against religious repression, deviates from the punishment paradox trope and its engagement with notions of (self)blame and regret in the face of AIDS. 'Lost in Connemara' is the first-person narration of a man who lost his loving partner to AIDS and goes to the Connemara wilderness to scatter his ashes. Ó Conghaile's story dignifies gay love by articulating a language of spirituality and religion, which undermines a public discourse of Catholic condemnation against 'sexual sinners'.

As an AIDS narrative, Ó Conghaile's story refuses to give prominence to the virus: HIV/AIDS is never mentioned, we do not know if the protagonist is infected, and, when he dies, the lover's body, far from being emaciated by disease, looks 'so quiet, so peaceful, so warm, so alive almost' (215). The narrator's most bitter memory is not about the disease, but about the time the Irish-speaking local priest, upon learning that the two men were a couple, cursed them in English, as if exiling them from the community:[6] 'Ye're public disgrace, he yelled. A public disgrace to the village, to Connemara, to this country [. . .] Ye'll pay for this, he said in that hoarse voice of his. Ye'll pay. Glancing sneakily in across the threshold. May the plague not pass ye by' (210-11).[7] The priest's furious words not only connote cruelty and social exclusion, but also reflect the puritanical values that had dominated in a section of Irish society which conveniently imported the cultural association between AIDS, punishment, and gay sexuality, which was often expressed through 'contempt and rejection, smug judgements and lectures, humiliating enquiries, and hasty presumptions' (Hannon, 1990: 104). Despite this general climate of discrimination, Ó Conghaile constructs the priest as the only negative character of the story, as the couple did have supportive friends in the community, 'a warm, caring group, like a family' (216). In this way, the priest alone emerges as a representative of the repressive and dehumanising dogmas of conservative Catholic Ireland.

Tellingly, Ó Conghaile's is not a story against Catholic religion; it rather decries the dogmas that suppress people's desires and emotional needs. As Sorcha de Brún argues, 'Lost in Connemara' links gay and HIV/AIDS discrimination to the subjugation 'felt by other groups in society who were historically marginalized and criminalized' (2017: 28). As a child, the narrator first learnt about the English Penal Laws against Catholics on a school trip to the Connemara wilderness, so, as an adult, he can still picture in his mind crowds of people gathered there in secret, experiencing 'a healing relief at being able to practice and celebrate the forbidden spiritual side of their lives' (209). The Connemara wilderness is precisely the same place where the gay partners celebrated their forbidden love. Ó Conghaile thus establishes a parallel between the Irish Catholics affected by the Penal Laws – 'the twisted, unjust English law' (210) – and the gay men who had to hide from society because of the 1861 Victorian criminalisation of male homosexuality. The connection between both contexts is further suggested by Ó Conghaile's use of religious language to describe gay love and sex, and the lovers' communion with nature:

> We held each other tightly in the yellow twilight of autumn. The red sky a rounded, limitless open roof above us. Grey rocks and green stones under their living crust of lichen, like silent witnesses, participants, all around us. Approving our kisses. We slid down off the stone then, sank into a ready-made bed of wild grass. Where we celebrated the sacrament of our love, drank from the chalices of our bodies. (212)

By connecting gay oppression to the religious oppression of penal times, and by using concepts like 'sacrament' to refer to gay love, Ó Conghaile's protagonist reconciles his religiosity with his homosexuality. The death scene, where the narrator asks his lover's 'soul to stay with [him] for a little while longer' (215), expands on this religious imagery and even becomes reminiscent of the icon of the Sorrowful Mother: 'At least he died at home [. . .] With me holding him. Cradling his head in my hand' (214). As he also does in *Sna Fir* and 'At the Station', in 'Lost in Connemara' Ó Conghaile infuses gay sexuality with a profound sense of spirituality and transcendence. In his tender, moving portrayal of gay love in the face of adversity, sickness, and death, Ó Conghaile draws on Catholic symbols to contest religious homophobia and AIDS stigma.

KEITH RIDGWAY'S 'ANDY WARHOL'

A totally different connection between religion and gay love emerges in Keith Ridgway's 'Andy Warhol', as there is no possibility here for the protagonist to reconcile his Catholic background with his sexuality. Like Ó Conghaile's 'Lost in Connemara', Ridgway's 'Andy Warhol' is a first-person narration which revolves around the protagonist's memories. Ridgway's work, compared to Ó Conghaile's, is more clearly a story of sexual trauma. Trauma, Cormac O'Brien explains (2013), has been used by playwrights like Watkins to 'mobiliz[e] shame to political effect' (81), shifting shame back onto those who stigmatise HIV-positives, in an attempt to find 'post-trauma healing' through storytelling (83). Ridgway's narrator is far from achieving emotional healing, but his voice, rather than merely projecting regret, serves as a powerful denunciation of a Catholic sexual morality which rendered him a damaged individual.

Ridgway's 'Andy Warhol', like other works in this study, reminds us of a recent Irish history of gay migration, of numerous people who left 'a country that was viciously sexually repressed' (Mullally, 2017). In Ridgway's text, while remembering his time in 1980s New York, the narrator waits on his own for his HIV diagnosis at the Gay Men's Health Clinic in Dublin, convinced that he will test positive (the story finishes before he receives the results). The narrative provides no resolution or final catharsis, but dwells on character psychology. Through the internal perspective of his narrator, Ridgway draws attention to the effects of a Catholic sexual morality which, while not being directly mentioned, informs the protagonist's self-per-ceptions, distress and denial surrounding his gay relationships: 'I am closed. I am not gay. I am not queer. I am not anything. I am not Irish [. . .] I am not doing any of the things that I am doing' (340).

This internalisation of a moralistic, homophobic sexual culture – pervasive in other novels, like Hogan's and McNicholl's in Chapter Four – explains the protagonist's dysfunctional behaviour. As a young, inexper-ienced man in search of a new life in the American city, Ridgway's narrator features as an insecure, introvert character, who constantly 'looks at men on the trains' (336), without talking to any of them. He eventually confronts his inhibitions not by socialising with other gays, but by having depersonalised sex in darkrooms and video cabins: 'Glory holes seem like a really good idea [. . .] They are the face I want, most of the time, they are the face of New York. They are a beautiful nothing' (339). Though practiced by a wide variety of people for different reasons, this type of sex, as discussed in Chapter Three, is particularly apt for those who want to evade same-sex intimacy. Ridgway's protagonist, however, cannot free himself from self-judgment. Emotionally crippled and constantly drunk, the narrator manifests an increasing personal unease. The more sex he has, the more self-destructive he becomes, as he eventually loses all sense of agency and behaves as the mere sexual object of strangers:

> Several times, I get scared. A man who stops his car in the middle of nowhere and wants to go into the trees. A man who ties me up and then someone else is there [. . .] Sometimes I find myself crying or cold or unsure of what I've been doing. Sometimes I'm bruised. (340)

The protagonist in this way becomes extremely vulnerable to the AIDS epidemic, due to his disregard of self-care, which grows from his internalised homophobia.

In this bleak portrayal of a young gay Irishman in New York, Ridgway also draws on an Irish culture of sexual ignorance and taboos; early 1990s surveys, for example, indicated that, among Irish homosexuals, 'there [was] a high level of confusion over what constituted safe sex' (Yeates, 1993). Linked to this 'confusion' was a sense of sexual shame that disempowered individuals to acknowledge 'their risk-related behaviour', deterring them from 'taking precautionary actions', as Fiona Smyth remarks (1998: 671). In 'Andy Warhol', the narrator's sexual ignorance further contributes to the lack of self-care he manifests. He has to be warned, for example, by one of his sexual partners about the dangers of unsafe sex: 'No, no man, we have to be careful now you know?' (338). Despite this warning, Ridgway's character continues to witness the AIDS scare as if from a distance, without fully comprehending the panic of others. Even after he learns about the nature of the epidemic, he remains unconcerned about his sexual health, a behaviour that can only be appropriately understood in light of his attitudes of denial and fatalism surrounding his gay sexuality: 'I don't really check or know or care, and sometimes I know full well that they're not using a condom' (340).

Perhaps the most painful consequence of this internalised homophobia is the character's inability to accept his needs for love and connection with other men. In the final part of the story, the narrator engages in a friendly conversation with Paulie, a man in drag, but, as they kiss, his elation gives way to fear: 'And I know, I know completely that what I am doing is something good and right and beautiful and that I am really drunk and if I am not careful I am going to cry' (343). Overwhelmed by terror, the narrator suddenly 'hear[s] shouts start up in [his] mind' (343), and escapes from Paulie. This fear of gay love and intimacy similarly informs the behaviour of Enright's Dan in *The Green Road*. If Ridgway's character has 'a list of fears, and at the top of the list is love' (345), Anne Enright's gay character in *The Green Road*, Dan, believes that 'the word 'love' was so much wrapped up in the impossible and the ideal' (174).

ANNE ENRIGHT'S THE GREEN ROAD

Enright's novel similarly looks at the AIDS crisis in New York in the late 1980s and early 1990s, in the figure of a young Irish man unable to accept his sexuality. Closeted but in a stable homosexual relationship during his time in New York, Enright's Dan is haunted by the memory of Billy, whom he abandoned when he was dying of AIDS. Enright's characterisation of Dan exemplifies the author's evolving fictive concern on the 'frailty of the self' (Barros-del Río, 2018: 44), a vulnerability that connects with 'the challenges posed to Ireland's emergent cultural and national identity by the postmodern condition, cosmopolitanism, the Celtic Tiger economic boom, and its aftermath' (Schneider, 2018: 410). In her fiction, award-winning and critically acclaimed author[8] Enright typically explores social realities, like alcoholism, secularisation, women's issues, emigration, consumerism, and family dysfunction, in relation to 'the personal' (Schneider, 2018: 413). *The Green Road* spans 25 years in the life of a family from rural Co. Clare, the Madigans. The novel contains five main characters (four siblings and their widowed mother), but this analysis shall focus on Dan, whom readers first see from the viewpoint of his sister Hanna, at a family gathering where he announces his intention to become a priest: 'Hanna blamed the Pope. He came to Ireland just after Dan left for college' (8). Whereas in Ridgway's story the influence of Catholic sexual morality is made implicit, in Enright's novel Dan strongly identifies with his Catholic culture. In New York, Dan enters new social circles and befriends gay men, but remains emotionally blocked, like Ridgway's character.

Enright's style has been described as 'brutally honest, cynical and sometimes disturbing' (O'Reilly, 2008), but her usual directness is not part of her character construction of Dan. Part One of *The Green Road*, entitled 'Leaving', contains chapters in the voice of each sibling, except Dan's. In the chapter devoted to him, set in 1991, we find other narrators, specifically a group of New York gay men who are suffering the loss of friends and lovers to AIDS: 'We did not want to be loved when we got sick, because that would be unbearable, and love was all we looked for, in our last days' (37). Physical signs, like the purple bruise of Kaposi's, became a social condemnation,[9] since, 'after the first mother snatches her child from the seat beside you on the subway, it gets hard to leave the house' (37). One of the characters, Greg, takes care of Christian, a former lover dying of AIDS and, later, when Greg is diagnosed, Billy (Dan's lover) vows to stay by his friend. Enright therefore stresses for her contemporary audience an already lost sense of solidarity among gays, who, during the early years of the epidemic, 'provid[ed] social networks for support and campaigning' (Weeks, 1995: 98).

As explained, Dan is in close contact with this gay community, but, throughout the chapter, his innermost feelings remain inaccessible to the reader. He is only observed by others, an external perspective that foregrounds the pain and frustration caused by his behaviour. Arguably, with this stylistic choice, the writer emphasises the contrast between the gay men's social bonding and Dan's self-absorption, lack of empathy and eventual betrayal.

More explicitly than other writers, Enright dramatises in the figure of Dan the traditional 'mind-body split', whereby sexual sin – in this case, gay sex – is experienced as something external to the soul, 'a weakness' and a 'corrupting aspect of our physical lives' (Ley, 2017). Dan, like Ridgway's narrator in 'Andy Warhol', seems to understand gay sex as a base instinct of the body, which can never be allowed to inform one's sense of self. While in New York, Dan has a girlfriend in Boston, Isabelle, a relationship that keeps his heterosexual self-image safe while he 'dabble[s] in guy sex' (61). When he starts a romantic relationship with Billy, Dan still needs to cling to heterosexuality as a state of mind, to the extent that both lovers had to agree on 'the subject of [Dan's] essential and future straightness', even though 'he kissed Billy as though he loved him' (58). Upon Isabelle's return to New York, Dan suddenly becomes emotionally (but not sexually) unavailable to Billy. To highlight the cruelty of his withdrawal, Enright chooses to describe the event from the viewpoint of Billy, who suffers the consequences of Dan's behaviour:

> But it was not Isabelle that did for Billy in the summer of 1991, it was the way he could not reach Dan, no matter how deep he fucked him, as though all the gestures of their love were beautiful and untrue. It was not as if Billy was looking for anything long term, but he was looking for something in that moment. Recognition. The feeling that what they were doing was real to Dan too. (62)

Arguably, this lack of recognition becomes Dan's defence mechanism, as the feelings he developed for Billy disturb the mind-body split that protects his heterosexual self-image at the prospect of his marriage to Isabelle. Like Ridgway's protagonist, Dan is afraid of homosexual intimacy, and his self-suppression crumbles when, after abandoning Billy, he still feels the need to visit him: 'Irish Dan turned up at young Billy's door – ashamed of himself, clearly. They had sex but didn't like each other for it' (66).

Perhaps the most terrible consequence of this mind-body split occurs when Billy develops full-blown PCP (an AIDS-related pneumonia) and dies at hospital in the company of his friends, without Dan by his side. Much to the group of friends' desolation Dan refuses to appear at Billy's deathbed, to comfort him and offer a final gesture of love. His detachment, at this dramatic moment, becomes his most cruel act: 'No one saw Dan for years. We did not blame him. At least, we tried not to blame him' (72). Readers, too, share these characters' frustrations and confusion until, 15 years later in the story, Dan acknowledges that, back then, he was afraid of his feelings for Billy, and consequently behaved as 'a raging blank of a human being' (180).

Just as Enright allow us limited access to Dan's mind, she also frustrates narrative expectations about HIV-disclosure, as we never discover whether Dan had contracted the virus. Her focus is similar to Ridgway's, in the sense that both writers emphasise the pernicious influence of internalised homophobia – an influence that is inextricably linked to their Irish Catholic backgrounds. One feature shared by Enright's and Ridgway's characters is their suppression and denial of their homosexual feelings as they engage in gay sex or have romantic relationships. Their alienation becomes highly damaging, preventing them from adopting attitudes of empathy, understanding and self-care in the context of the AIDS epidemic.

DESMOND HOGAN'S A FAREWELL TO PRAGUE

Sexual trauma is also a central topic in Desmond Hogan's *A Farewell to Prague*, where the author – just as he had done previously in *The Ikon Maker* from the external perspective of Diarmaid's mother – offers a crude depiction of the destructive power of sexual oppression in Ireland, in the figure of Des, a gay exile. Within this scenario of trauma appears the HIV-positive Marek, whose rebelliousness and resilience inspire the protagonist to become stronger. A non-linear and non-realist narrative, *A Farewell to Prague* is devoid of any sense of plot development, since this is a highly experimental novel which reads as a 'postmodernist fragmentary amalgamation of autobiography, fiction, travel-writing and memoir' (Wondrich, 2000: 3). The central motif is the narrator's quest for the meaning of life, which emerges from his two decades of restless migration in Europe and North America. Coping with chronic depression, Des cannot avoid revisiting painful memories, among those: the death of Marek to AIDS; his lost love, Eleanor, and the children they could have had together, and the sexual humiliation that provoked his exile, when a female acquaintance, partner of a Provisional IRA member, threatened to make his homosexuality public. Hogan's 1995 novel fits into several of the characteristics described by Cormac O'Brien in relation to subversive HIV/AIDS theatre productions, as this story dramatises a direct confrontation with 'the sexual and cultural shame that comes with living outside heteronormative paradigms' (2013: 80).

Hogan uses the literary trope of exile, both in the figures of Des and Marek, to deepen his attack against traditional sexual morality (the novel spans the years between the 1970s and early 1990s). In ways that are peculiarly relevant to *A Farewell to Prague*, Edward Said theorises that exiles '[are] always out of place' (2001: 180) and 'feel their difference as a kind of orphanhood' (182). 'What is true of all exile,' Said further argues, 'is not that home and love are lost, but that loss is inherent in the very existence of both' (185). It is because of the 'unhomeliness' of Irish society, Hogan suggests, that his protagonist became an exile, in both a geographical and emotional sense. To highlight this condition of exile, Hogan has his character invoking the memory of other Irish people who, like himself, became victims of cruelty: a rent boy thrown into the Liffey, a widow who is subjected to electroshock, a child whose father beats him up because he has a 'girl's voice' (111), or a single pregnant woman who kills herself, among others. No matter how far he travels, his past experiences in Ireland haunt Des throughout the text. Such obsession not only illustrates Said's association between loss and home, but also Julia Kristeva's formulation of exiles as 'hold[ing] on to what [they] lack, to absence, to some symbol or other' (1991: 5). The exile is free of ties, but, as Kristeva also observes, 'the consummate name of such a freedom is solitude' (1991: 12). This type of solitude is precisely one of the traits of Hogan's Des, who acknowledges that, in his fight to become himself, 'he'd be an exile going between cities of the world, half of the time unwanted' (191). As he drifts from one city to another, Hogan's exilic protagonist experiences much existential solitude, and constantly seeks communion with others.

With its accumulation of seemingly disconnected experiences, the novel's postmodernist form – its highly fragmented, non-linear storyline, filled with impressionistic details and images of suffering and resilience – accurately reflects the protagonist's rootlessness and, at times, his mental collapse. And, whilst *A Farewell to Prague* describes Des's numerous personal encounters in faraway places, 'an AIDS-related death,' Gerry Smith points out, 'appears to be the paradoxical centre of this centreless text' (1997: 155). References to Marek, the AIDS victim, are scattered throughout the text, constructing a life portrait that starts when he and his mother, Eastern European Jews, hitchhiked around Ireland.

In his characterisation of Marek, Hogan adopts anti-stigma strategies, like his use of the 'warrior metaphor' and reluctance to present the HIV body as a 'narrativized other', stylistic choices which promote queer resistance (O'Brien, 2013: 80, 84). Part of the 1980s Berlin's underclass, Marek, Des's friend and ex-lover, contracted HIV as a heroin consumer, and counters his ostracism with scenes of rebellion against society's condemnation: 'Even when they're pushing you into the grave scream, scream a statement' (166). As he dies, rather than succumbing to despair, Hogan's Marek 'keeps fighting for love' (166), and readily shares his philosophy of life with others. The protagonist is one of the several friends that loves and cares for Marek in his last days. Holding Marek's hand, a bereft Des suffers the pain of impending loss, but also experiences a moment of epiphany: 'I feel as if I've been dead all my life. Now I'm only awakening' (119). Marek's death, which amplifies his living example, catalyses a fundamental change in Des, 'leading [him] from one path of search to another' (174).

In this novel about broken lives, Hogan associates the marginalisation of the protagonists, Des, and Marek, with the many other injustices that still pervade present-day societies. In his insightful review of *A Farewell to Prague*, Rob Doyle remarks:

As the memories continue to pass like the landscape outside a train window, [. . .] Desmond gains perspective on his trauma, and on the bitterness that had threatened to consume him. He manages to rescue something small, bright and fragile within himself by forging a faith based on kindness and love. (2013)

The forging of such 'faith' would have not been possible without Marek, who, even on his deathbed, talked 'about forgiveness and gratitude' (135). Inspired by Marek's struggle with AIDS, Hogan's protagonist learns that 'the only real way to fight evil [. . .] is to hold someone's hand' (157). Des's final discovery is that, in the face of cruelty, love can still provide an antidote to depression and despair.

COLM TÓIBÍN'S THE BLACKWATER LIGHTSHIP

Whereas in *A Farewell to Prague* Hogan's HIV-positive character has a distinctive, dissenting voice, in *The Blackwater Lightship* Colm Tóibín's Declan is characterised by silence. Published in 1999, Colm Tóibín's widely acclaimed *The Blackwater Lightship* is one of the first novels to explore the impact of HIV and AIDS in Ireland, doing so in a rural setting rather than in an urban or metropolitan one.[10] In the story, Declan, who is in his twenties, reveals himself to his family as gay man dying with the virus. His impending death catalyses his reunification with his sister, mother, and grandmother at their old family house in Cush, Co. Wexford. Such reunification is made possible thanks to Declan's gay friends, Paul and Larry, who behaved as his alternative family during his earlier stages of AIDS, accompanying him to hospital, taking care of his medical treatment, and offering him accommodation.[11] Because Tóibín subverts common 1990s stereotypes of male homosexuality as anti-social, pathological and sex-driven, Robinson Murphy praises *The Blackwater Lightship* for its reworking of 'an oppressive framework so as to allow for the formerly excluded to participate and celebrate their non-heteronormativity, or queerness' (2009: 487). However, for some critics, Declan's characterisation as an HIV-positive is problematic, due to his distancing within the narrative (the story is told from the sister's perspective) and his shameful silence about his illness and sexual past.

A leading voice in Irish fiction since the early 1990s until the present moment, Colm Tóibín has become famous for his reticent prose, for making silences 'speak' and reveal new layers of meaning (Delaney, 2008: 18). In his gay fiction, Tóibín dramatises the exposure of hidden traumas in the figures of characters that, though having come to terms with their sexuality, still struggle with a sense of uneasiness and duplicity when it comes to their most intimate relationships. Social change may facilitate sexual freedom, but Tóibín's gay characters often confront impediments to fully free themselves from a burdensome past. Many of his stories revolve around the acknow-ledgment of an emotional pain in need of expression and readjustment. With regard to Tóibín's style, it has been further observed that the writer 'avoids the temptation to the rhetorical or the sentimental', creating instead characters who are 'continually forced into self-reflective postures' (Mahony, 1998: 256) – a self-reflective posture that, in *The Blackwater Lightship*, is not adopted by Declan, but by his sister Helen, the protagonist of the story. In his fiction, Tóibín casts no judgment on his characters' actions, but allows the reader to consider their dilemmas in the broader scenario of their time and place.

Given the socio-cultural context of *The Blackwater Lightship*, set in the early 1990s, any consideration of Declan as a gay AIDS victim must engage with the general silence surrounding homosexuality at the time. As the author explains in an interview, AIDS forced many gay victims to come out to their families in the final stages of their disease:

> When AIDS arrived in Ireland, it was an absolute disaster, because the fact of being gay was not ever mentioned. It was a situation in which people –and I knew many of them– in the same night had to tell their parents that they were a) gay, and b) dying of AIDS. Their parents were worried about the neighbours and what was in the papers, what it would look like to the outside world. Even on an intimate level, this affected large families in small towns, and it all took on an element of almost unbearable pain. (Ehrhardt, 2013)

The scenario here described by Tóibín attunes to his characterisation of Declan. On his visits to Cush, Declan enjoyed the company of his mother, Lily, and grandmother, Dora, but 'never told [them] anything about himself' (142). Unlike Dora and Lily, Helen was aware of her brother's homosexual-ity, but she did not know where he lived, and 'it was years since she had met any of Declan's friends' (30). When Paul informs her about Declan's HIV status, Helen admits to herself that her brother 'had replaced his family with his friends' (34), which becomes 'a powerful statement on the incompre-hension that many gays have experienced, their need to seek support outside their families, the stigma of their sexuality, and the shameful condition of AIDS victims in Irish society' (Carregal-Romero, 2016: 360).

Significantly, once his family learns about his HIV-status, Tóibín's character remains unable to open up emotionally, and continues to be silent about his personal life. This silence contrasts with the outspokenness of his non-HIV-infected friends, who share with Declan's family their personal histories of resilience and self-fulfilment, to the extent that these two characters come to represent 'gay suffering and gay triumph' (Persson, 2007: 150). In this way, unlike Declan, Paul and Larry emerge as symbols of a new, more liberal Ireland which embraces sexual diversity.

As previously indicated, whereas critics generally agree that Tóibín's is a progressive gay narrative that redefines heterosexist definitions of family and community,[12] there is a lack of consensus on the implications of Declan's characterisation as an AIDS victim. Jennifer Jeffers, for example, considers Declan's illness as a punishment for his sexual behaviour, because, through one of the friends (Paul, who is in a monogamous relationship), we learn that Declan had multiple lovers. This sense of punishment is reinforced, Jeffers argues, by this character's (shameful) silence: 'Declan never speaks; he is spoken for' (2002: 117). José Yebra takes the view that, because readers witness his physical deterioration, 'Declan's body is devoid of sexual connotations,' so it is symbolised as 'the site of Irish Catholic morality and repression' (2014: 99). Eibhear Walshe, on his part, offers a more balanced view and explains that 'the novel's strengths as an AIDS narrative come at the expense of the representation of the homoerotic and of a contemporary Irish gay subjectivity,' since Declan 'has no gay subjectivity beyond his bodily frailty: no boyfriend, no lover, no named sexual partners, no erotic past' (2006: 129). Other analyses connect Declan's silence with the character's previous experience of family estrangement (Costello-Sullivan, 2012), or the lack of relevance his sexual past has in the context of his terminal condition (Carregal-Romero, 2016). It is worth noting that Declan's silence applies only to his illness, his emotions about it, and his sexual past. Though he never speaks about his gay relationships, Declan does have a voice, and goes against family expectations when he demands his friends' presence in Cush.

Declan's silence about his sexual past may well be regarded as a dramatisation of AIDS self-stigma, an aspect that was neglected in previous analyses of the novel. In their recent study on AIDS self-stigma in Ireland, Nadine Ferris France and others argue that, despite the visibility of an HIV/AIDS public discourse on sexual health, 'a culture of silence emerged where HIV was never discussed' within the family, or on interpersonal levels (2015: 4). In addition, self-sigma has been discovered to be 'not just an internalisation of the prevalent social stigma, but a distortion and ampli-fication of it' (France et al., 2015: 2). In *The Blackwater Lightship*, Tóibín seems to foreground Declan's self-stigma – his 'distortion and amplification' of social prejudice – by removing any possible instances of recrimination throughout story. His family and friends, for example, feature as loving, generous, and non-judgmental. When informed of Declan's situation, Dora, the grandmother, intuitively compares AIDS to cancer, thus dispelling the shameful connotations of the illness: 'Nothing can be done. It was the same years ago with your father's cancer. There was nothing the doctors could do.

And poor Declan's only starting his life' (47). Given her rural Catholic background and religiosity,[13] Dora's is a surprisingly open-minded attitude.

This enlightened attitude also extends to the ways in which family and friends avoid the contagion paranoia of the time, when there was much fear about being physically close to AIDS victims. In *The Blackwater Lightship*, Tóibín has Declan's friends and family holding his hand, embracing him, or touching him when he sweats profusely or soils himself. Whereas at the time the AIDS-ridden body was too often relegated to abjection, in Tóibín's novel Declan is 'never deprived of his dignity' (Carregal-Romero, 2016: 370). Curiously, as a journalist himself, Tóibín had decried in a 1991 article – almost the same temporal setting of his novel – the ways in which Irish TV panellists exaggerated the danger of HIV infection, giving the impression that 'they did not want to be even touched by people with the AIDS virus' ('Time to be positive about AIDS', 1991). Arguably, even though *The Blackwater Lightship* is set at a time of contagion paranoia, Tóibín's interest here was to produce an educative novel by depicting a society that has learnt to treat HIV-positives with love and respect.[14]

In spite of being accepted and cared by others, Declan fails to abandon his acquired habit of reticence with regard to his personal life. As indicated, in his depiction of Declan's psychology, Tóibín centres on the painful consequences of self-stigma, and how the victim remains trapped by toxic emotions which hinder self-empowerment. Unable to disclose his illness to his family, Declan asked Paul to tell Helen about it. At hospital, Helen tries to engage in a conversation about the conditions surrounding his illness, but Declan is unwilling to talk about it:

> 'This is a real shock, Declan,' she said.
> He closed his eyes and did not reply [. . .]
> 'Hellie, I'm sorry about everything,' Declan said, his eyes still closed. (38)

Helen expresses no moral reproach, but Declan's intuitive reaction is to avoid her gaze, his eyes closed. Far from releasing his emotional pain, Declan manifests self-blame and apologises on account of his AIDS, in a way that could hardly compare with any other disease. Here and throughout the story, Tóibín constantly reminds us that illnesses are experienced not only on a corporeal level, but also on a psychological one. The negative impact of the cultural narratives surrounding HIV/AIDS is therefore shown indirectly through Declan's behaviour.

Aside from suffering the ravages of AIDS, Declan experienced the pain of having anticipated the family's rejection. From the very beginning, readers become aware of Declan's failed attempts at communication, as well as the frustrations caused by his withdrawal from his family. This psychological condition does not simply disappear once he is with his family and receives their support. As she spends time with Helen and Declan's friends, the grandmother recalls the moment she found Declan by surprise, walking on the strand down her house:

> I could see that he had been crying and he was so thin and strange, like as though he didn't want to see me [. . .] And he tried to make up for it when he came into the house. He was all smiles and jokes, but I'll never forget seeing him [. . .] I knew he was in trouble, but AIDS was the last thing I thought of, and I thought of everything. (143)

Here and in other episodes, Tóibín describes Declan's inability to break the silence of his health condition. His voice on this specific matter is only rendered through his friends. One of them, Larry, tells the family how '[Declan] drove to Wexford a few times, to his mother's house, but it was always late and he never went in' (143). The two friends are therefore vital in this new context, as they are the ones who can interpret Declan's silences and emotional needs. When Helen finds her mother 'smothering' Declan with attentions in his room, she wonders whether her brother might be uncomfortable about it, but Paul tells her:

> 'He was so afraid that your mother would refuse to see him or something,' Paul said. 'I think he desperately wanted her to know and help him and yet he couldn't tell her, and now he has her there and she's trying to help him'
> 'It might be better in small doses,' Helen said drily
> 'It might also be exactly what he wants,' Paul said. 'He talked about it so much.'
> (161)

Paul voices here his friend's desires to come closer to his mother, and later makes it clear to her that her son 'wants [her] approval' (223). Declan had been estranged from his family for years, and this distance is now presented as one of the consequences of his AIDS self-stigma.

Declan eventually verbalises his long-desired return to his mother in the final part of the novel, when he suffers a health crisis that has him awake all night, crying out loud:

> As Lily wiped his face and forehead and held his hands, and talked to him softly, he began to call out under his breath and, when the next attack came, Helen for the first time understood what he was saying.
> He was saying: 'Mammy, Mammy, help me, Mammy.'

[. . .]
Tears came into [Helen's] eyes
'He's been wanting to say that for a long time,' Paul said, 'or something like it. It'll be a big relief for him.' (259)

This union with his mother becomes a highly emotive moment of both extreme pain and relief. As Paul notes, this is the first and only time Declan abandons his reticence and opens up emotionally, and the assumption is that he has now started to transcend the silence of his AIDS self-stigma. Declan's future, unfortunately, will soon be destroyed by the virus (his rapid bodily deterioration in the course of the story constantly reminds us that he is approaching death).

Because it avoids recrimination and insists on how Declan 'can and should be loved' (Wiesenfarth, 2009: 18), Tóibín's is a sympathetic AIDS narrative, but the novel somehow foreshadows some of the contradictions and shortcomings of the more liberal, tolerant, and gay-friendly Ireland of today. Readers are invited to celebrate the achievements of non-seropositive gay men like Paul and Larry, but Declan remains distanced for much of the story and has, in Walshe's words, no 'gay subjectivity' (2006: 129). *The Blackwater Lightship* thus seems to conform to the most relevant features of the punishment paradox trope, illustrated by Declan's wasted body, his status as a 'narrativized other' (O'Brien, 2013: 84), as well as by the images of 'hiddenness, suffering, victimhood and death' that Tóibín uses to create his HIV-positive character (O'Brien, 2020: 129).

Drawing on Cormac O'Brien's conceptualisation of post-AIDS Ireland, one may also argue that, in his late 1990s novel, Tóibín dramatises the emergence of a culture of homonormativity, where white, middle-class gay men achieve cultural prominence only by emulating 'heterosexual lifestyle paradigms' (2020: 125) – this sense of the homonormative in Tóibín's text is exemplified by Paul, who shares the romantic story of his non-official Catholic wedding to his soulmate, François. Homonormativity, O'Brien further explains, is a neoliberal ideology which also privileges youth and an athletic physique, which explains the current post-AIDS situation: 'Homonormativity d[oes] not create any spaces for HIV-positive masculinities, [. . .] [as] less-than-perfect health is disavowed and shamed in this culture of the ideal lifestyle and body' (2020: 125). In this respect, one may note how, in *The Blackwater Lightship*, Tóibín fails to create a 'space for HIV-positive masculinity', since, as already explained, Declan (unlike his friends) never narrates his personal story and remains unable to voice his most intimate feelings.

Yet, set prior to the development of the antiretroviral therapy ART, Tóibín's novel should not, perhaps, be simply classified as a politically disabling post-AIDS narrative promoting homonormativity, as the story is grounded in a context of greater homophobia and fear surrounding HIV/AIDS. The question remains, however, whether Declan's shameful silences could be read as a moral punishment for his sexual past, or as a careful rendition of a character's damaged psychology. Because Tóibín foregrounds Declan's failed attempts at communication, this analysis supports the latter option. Through Declan's silence and distress, Tóibín explores some of the toxic emotions involved in AIDS self-stigma, like self-blaming, isolation, and fear of rejection.

CONCLUSION

Novels like Tóibín's are still relevant to today's audiences, since AIDS (self)-stigma remains one of the 'great[est] barrier[s] to those living with HIV' (O'Brien, 2013: 76). Recent figures of HIV infection indicate that Ireland is failing to make progress in 'ending the HIV crisis' (Donohoe, 2019). Despite people's wider access to sexual health services and the availability of PrEP (a medication that prevents the contraction of the disease), in 2018 HIV diagnoses 'increased by 8% over the number of diagnoses in 2017 and are 6% higher than the previous high of 502 diagnoses in 2016' (Donohoe, 2019). This trend remained steady in the course of 2019, and it 'almost double[d] the European average' (Dunne, 2019). To raise awareness about these alarming rates, representatives from associations like HIV Ireland and ACT UP came to the forefront of the 2019 Dublin Pride Parade, 'in response to the steady rise in new HIV diagnoses in Ireland, and the persistent and pernicious silence and stigma that continues to surround HIV' (Donohoe, 2019b). It appears that, despite today's visibility of non-moralising discourses of sexual health, and the existence of a culture of sexual freedom and gay affirmation, homosexual HIV-positives remain marginalised, which provokes their self-stigma and non-disclosure of their disease on interpersonal levels. As explained, this post-AIDS situation may originate from a neoliberal homonormative language which repudiates the 'imperfect', aged and/or diseased body. Therefore, in this post-AIDS era the recent high rates of HIV infection seem to point to problems other than social awareness of the disease.[15]

Although the novels and short stories analysed here are set in the 1980s and 1990s, when the disease was much more destructive, these narratives can nonetheless be read in light of present-day conditions. Even if religious condemnation has now been largely replaced by the strictures of neoliberal homonormativity, the discrimination suffered by Ó Conghaile's protagonists in 'Lost in Connemara' does not differ much from current discourses of 'depravity and infectiousness' (Murphy et al., 2016: 1468). Desmond Hogan's

A Farewell to Prague, on its part, centres on the still existent social exclusion of drug addicts, in the figure of the HIV-positive Marek. The ostracism and cruelty Marek suffers contrasts with his kindness and vitality, personal traits that the Irish exile Des, friend, and former lover of Marek's, comes to recognise and admire. In Tóibín's *The Blackwater Lightship*, Declan counts on his gay friends' support but, for years, hides his seropositive status from his family, afraid as he is of their reaction. Declan's non-disclosure, however, caused him much distress. His silence on his illness and sexual past, rather than being perceived as a moral punishment, has been read here as a manifestation of his AIDS self-stigma. Similarly damaged by toxic emotions, the gay characters in Enright's *The Green Road* and Ridgway's 'Andy Warhol' migrate to 1980s New York, having no clear recognition or acceptance of their same-sex desires. During their time in New York, both characters develop feelings of denial with regard to their gay experiences. Their internalised homophobia, as explained, prevents them from adopting attitudes of empathy and self-care in the face of the AIDS epidemic. Overall, the narratives in this chapter address the consequences of a culture of sexual shame and HIV/AIDS stigma, just to promote a deeper and more nuanced understanding of the social and personal conditions affecting HIV-positives, past and present.

SIX

The Room Feels Warmer When You're in it

Lesbian Relationships in Emma Donoghue's
Contemporary-Set Novels

In her twenties, Emma Donoghue was already known as one of the most famous lesbians in 1990s Ireland, after her publications of *Stir-fry* (1994) and *Hood* (1995), two novels that achieved international acclaim, 'earn[ing] her translations into several languages' (Fantaccini and Grassi, 2011: 398). At the young age of 25, Donoghue talked of her lesbianism on Gay Byrne's The Late Late Show, where 'she did all right', despite the fact that 'someone did ring up and say she should be stoned to death' (Grant, 1995: 8). This TV appearance was not her only public statement as an Irish lesbian. In academic interviews and popular media, Donoghue readily shared her experiences of growing up lesbian in the 1980s, when, as she said, 'there was a kind of an active silence around [homosexuality]' (Bensyl, 2000: 79). Literature, for Donoghue, became a way of escaping from this silence. As an adolescent, she enjoyed the lesbian novels published by American and British feminist presses, but she could hardly reconcile her sexuality with her Irishness: '"Irish lesbian" still had the ring of a contradiction in terms: how was I to conceive myself as a practising Catholic and a furious lesbian feminist, a sweet colleen and a salty sinner?' (Donoghue, 1995b: 159). As Donoghue suggests here, role models for women were severely limited in Catholic Ireland, a situation that the novels in Chapter One address in further detail.

As a young lesbian, a milestone novel for Donoghue was Maura Richards's *Interlude* (1982), with its graphic, passionate descriptions of lesbian sex 'occurring within [Irish] borders' (Donoghue, 1995b: 165). But, while Richards's text felt like a sexual liberation for a teenage Donoghue, Mary Dorcey's lesbian poetry and short stories, as well as her public persona, became her most profound inspiration: '[Dorcey] very much stood there and said, "Yes, I'm a lesbian and I'm a writer, here's my work"' (Bensyl, 2000: 75). Following Dorcey's lead, Donoghue began her prolific literary career with her historical lesbian play, *I Know my Own Heart* (1993),[1] and has again demonstrated her interest in the lesbian past[2] with the 2004 publication of *Life Mask*, analysed in Chapter Eight. In other historical novels, like *Slammerkin* (2000), *The Sealed Letter* (2008) and *Frog Music* (2014), Donoghue similarly explores and rewrites the often silenced and/or misinterpreted stories of women who suffered the discrimination of having transgressed gender expectations. Her more recent *The Wonder* (2016) and *The Pull of the Stars* (2020) delve further into the patriarchal oppression exerted by male-dominated institutions, like the religious and medical ones, in the contexts of nineteenth-century, post-famine Ireland (*The Wonder*) and the 1918 Great Flu pandemic in Dublin (*The Pull of the Stars*). Donoghue also became a widely known, best-seller author thanks to *Room* (2010), which recalls the 2008 terrible case of Elisabeth Fritzl, who had been abused and kept captive by her father for 24 years.

This chapter concentrates on Donoghue's contemporary-set novels *Stir-fry*, *Hood* and *Landing* (2007), and how they explore lesbian life in 1990s and 2000s Ireland. Unlike Dorcey, who had an extremely difficult time in 1970s and 1980s Ireland, Donoghue became a noted author and public intellectual at a moment when homosexual rights were on the political agenda (e.g., gay decriminalisation in 1993), which facilitated the emergence of new gay and lesbian voices in Ireland. In interviews, Donoghue acknowledged that the 1990s was a relatively tolerant decade but was also careful to point out that social acceptance for lesbians may also be a matter of social class and personal independence. Being the daughter of a prominent academic, Donoghue herself recognises the relative ease with which she could publicly identify as a lesbian: 'If I were working-class or even something like a lesbian mother, I'd be in more trouble' (Grant, 1995: 8). Donoghue therefore considers her coming-out experiences as non-representative of a 1990s Irish context where, as she remarked, many homosexuals still lived partly in the closet, 'living in two worlds' (Bensyl, 2000: 76), as some of her characters in her 1990s *Stir-fry* and *Hood* do.

Aside from exploring notions of silence and (in)visibility surrounding lesbian life, this chapter also addresses Donoghue's aforementioned three novels from the viewpoint of gender identities and the tensions between feminism and liberalism as reflected in her fictional lesbian relationships. *Stir-fry* and *Hood* dramatise how, with the advent of liberalism, feminism began to be judged as outdated. In this 1990s scenario, as some Irish lesbian activists pointed out, 'feminism is seen to be for older lesbians who lived through the 1970s and is regarded as almost irrelevant by a lot of younger lesbians' (Gibney et al., 1995: 164).[3] If in *Stir-fry* the liberal Jael constantly mocks Ruth's feminism, in *Hood* the young lesbians of the community adopt a liberal attitude that focuses on individualism, disregarding notions of woman bonding and solidarity. The culture of liberalism is omnipresent in Donoghue's 2007 novel, *Landing*, which features a hyper-feminine lesbian,

Síle, whose characterisation epitomises Debbie Ging's concept of 'gender repolarisation' in Celtic Tiger Ireland:

> The shift towards neoliberal government and its concurrent commercialisation of the media-scape have been key drivers in facilitating the discursive and representational repolarisation of gender [. . .] This model addresses consumers in increasingly gender-reductive ways. This is particularly evident in the growth of gender-specific cultural genres such as chick-lit, chick-flicks and lad mags. (2009: 55–6)

This gender repolarisation, Ging adds, is 'so blatant and so passé' that it re-stereotypes women as 'obsessive shoppers or shoe fetishists' (53) – such description, as shall be observed, perfectly fits Donoghue's protagonist in *Landing*. Of course, this repolarisation of gender identities has a clear impact on non-heterosexuals as well. In the Western world, as Kay Siebler explains:

> Contemporary definitions of LGBT are put forth by the capitalist consumerist culture to sell LGBT consumption, relying on marketing versions of uncomplicated sex, gender, and sexuality binaries. Marketers need us to either be male or female; masculine or feminine; and a specific version of gay, lesbian, or trans to sell a product. (2017: 6)

Thus, even though gay and lesbian liberation initially meant an open challenge to gender norms, there is today a sense of homonormativity,[4] expressed along the lines of gender stereotypes and consumerism, which affects the identity formation of non-heterosexuals. The analysis of *Landing* addresses the implications of gender repolarisation in Donoghue's characterisation of Síle and her relationship with the Canadian Jude.

Set in an almost completely different Ireland than the one portrayed in *Landing*, Donoghue's first novels, *Stir-fry* and *Hood*, originate in a context where there was an urge to make the long-hidden experiences of lesbians public. Both *Stir-fry* and *Hood* adopt characteristics of the coming-out story (*Stir-fry* more obviously so) and use first- and third-person narratives that focalise on the consciousness and 'subjective coherence' of highly sympathetic protagonists, who progress towards a new sense of self thanks to their self-exploration of love and desire (Cronin, 2020: 572).

STIR-FRY

Donoghue's debut novel, *Stir-fry*, is the coming-out story of the seventeen-year-old Maria, who moves from rural Ireland to Dublin to study at university. She shares a flat with the older Jael and Ruth, who initially remain silent on their lesbian relationship. Maria, who enters the flat as an unquestioning heterosexual, eventually develops romantic and sexual feelings for one of her flatmates. Like some gay narratives of the 1990s, such as Tóibín's *The Blackwater Lightship*, *Stir-fry* privileges an educational approach rather than one of outright condemnation of society's prejudices. Donoghue herself remarks that: '[*Stir-fry*] has rather too many of those let-me-explain speeches for my taste – but they seemed more necessary (for both straight and lesbian readers) in 1994 when it was published, when questions like "why do you hate men?" had more currency' (Thompson, 2003c: 173). Donoghue was therefore acutely aware of her novel's place and time, and the social impact she wanted to create.

In her introduction to David Marcus's 1994 edited collection of short-stories *Alternative Loves*, LGBTI+ scholar and activist Ailbhe Smyth emphasised the need to promote a '[public] language which can give shape and substance to our unnameable, and thus unnamed, longings' (vii). Undoubtedly, Donoghue's *Stir-fry* took part of this cultural project to 'give shape and substance' to lesbian experience, as demonstrated by Maria's maturation and discovery of her same-sex desires. The protagonist's initial ignorance about lesbianism partly originates from her Catholic education at school, where nuns talked of 'active homosexuals' as though they were evil figures, 'mortal sinners' (77). Other than this, Maria had no solid notions of homosexuality, so, for her, 'it was never real' (69). Because of this 'unreality' of lesbianism, Maria cannot perceive that Jael and Ruth may be partners, even though she notes that they share a bed. Maria's agnosia in *Stir-fry* is similar to the one manifested by the male characters in Dorcey's 'A Country Dance', who could not see lesbianism until it was made blatantly obvious.

In her analysis, Paulina Palmer makes no use of the concept of agnosia, but nonetheless calls attention to Maria's blindness with regard to lesbianism, and observes that in *Stir-fry* Donoghue reverses the structure of conventional coming-out stories, since, 'whereas examples of the genre generally open by foregrounding the queer protagonist's isolation and alienation and conclude on a positive note with her locating some form of supportive same-sex community, *Stir-fry* operates the other way round' (2012: 30). Unlike other protagonists of coming-out stories like Lennon's Neil in *When Love Comes to Town*, Donoghue's Maria does not struggle with a sense of loneliness and inauthenticity, having to hide her 'real' lesbian self. For Maria, lesbianism is initially inconceivable, but she gradually recognises her same-sex desires in the company of her flatmates. Donoghue may, in this way, reflect how the general non-recognition of lesbianism hampered her character's lesbian awakening.

If such discovery is difficult, it is because Maria initially lacks 'the language to articulate her same-sex desires to herself,' so 'she is unable to explore them, let alone express how she feels' (Peach, 2004: 112). Given her Catholic upbringing, Maria is understandably shocked when she accidentally finds Jael and Ruth kissing passionately in their kitchen. For days, she retreats into silence and barely talks with her friends, as she feels awkward and threatened by the proximity of lesbianism: 'All she wanted was not to be afraid and embarrassed [. . .] A kiss on a kitchen table, that was all she had to go on. Somewhere between private and public, terrible and tender' (73). Rather than a reaction of total rejection, Maria's fear relates to the secret allure of lesbianism. The strangeness she feels at this stage fades and turns into growing affection and sexual attraction towards her two friends as the story progresses.[5] Thanks to her flatmates, Maria undergoes a process of learning (the same one Donoghue wanted her readers to experience), acquainting herself with her two friends' lesbian culture, so she discovers the 'queer' meaning of the colour purple (159) and new terms like 'squirming' (143). As also occurs in other coming-out stores, this entry into a sexual subculture proves crucial to the protagonist's self-knowledge and facilitates her politicisation as a feminist as the story evolves.

Maria's gradual acquisition of this new language requires the unlearning of popular stereotypes about lesbians: short hair, moustaches, boilersuits, lack of personal hygiene, aggressive behaviour and so on. To understand injurious language, as Judith Butler explains in *Excitable Speech*, one should consider the sources where 'hateful, racist, misogynistic, homophobic speech' originate (1997: 50). Donoghue considers such sources through the character of Yvonne – Maria's closest friend at college – who voices the aforementioned stereotypes and clearly features as a (rather humorous) caricature of heterosexual femininity. The reader acquires this impression because, for instance, Yvonne is obsessed about dating boys, constantly worries about her looks and voices the clichés of heterosexuality: 'I don't think women and men can be friends' (53). As Maria grows closer to Jael and Ruth and begins to displace her, a hurt Yvonne complains: 'Are normal people just too boring for you nowadays, is that it?' (208). Stereotyped as she is, Yvonne comes to represent the entrenched prejudice of a heterosexual culture that judged homosexuality as its deviant contrasting image.

In Donoghue's text, Maria's distancing from the dominant heterosexist culture goes hand in hand with her progressive familiarisation with feminism and queer activism under Ruth's tutelage.[6] Thanks to Ruth's influence, Donoghue's protagonist for example learns to see through the artifice of stereotypical female behaviour, asking Yvonne: 'Don't you ever get sick of girls? The way they – we – talk, smile to soften any harsh remark, and nod devoutly' (132). Maria joins the Women's Group at campus, but among her peers feminism provokes much derision; one of Maria's classmates calls Ruth a 'raving loony feminist' (126). If the Women's Group arises much hostility, the same is true about the GaySoc to which Ruth belongs.[7] After giving her speech for the GaySoc, Ruth becomes demoralised by her audience's homophobia. To comfort her, Maria makes a rather oblique declaration of love: 'The room feels warmer when you're in it, you know?' (172). This is but one of the numerous scenes that portray the growing intimacy and special closeness between Ruth and Maria, while they spend time together cooking, swapping anecdotes about childhood, family, school days and other personal aspects.

This affinity between Ruth and Maria contrasts with Jael's friendly but brash and selfish behaviour. In the course of the story, Jael emerges as an exploitative (and also unfaithful) partner[8], so, paradoxically, the committed feminist Ruth finds herself in a relationship that reproduces the conventional gender binaries of hetero-patriarchy, as she adopts a subservient role as Jael's lover. In an interview, Donoghue reconciles these contradictions by hinting at the complex nature of human relationships, describing herself as an author who 'writes stories, not utopian manifestoes' (Thompson, 2003c: 177).

Unlike Dorcey's middle-aged protagonists, who form relationships characterised by sameness and mutuality, Donoghue's characters are younger lesbians who display much more conservative attitudes. Whereas Dorcey's writing in *A Noise from the Woodshed* and *Biography of Desire* is clearly inspired by the feminist and lesbian movements of the 1970s and 1980s, Donoghue's *Stir-fry* and *Hood* are recognisably 1990s-set and reflect a moment of transformation in Ireland, when ideas of liberalism and individualism mixed with, or contradicted, other discourses like feminism. The apolitical Jael, for example, behaves as a modern, liberated woman when she reclaims her sexual freedom, but her behaviour towards Ruth betrays basic principles of feminism, like equality and sisterhood. When Ruth and Jael break up, Maria realises that she actually loves Ruth, so the novel closes with her decision to come out as lesbian to her. With this ending, Donoghue appears to intervene in the aforementioned 'debate' between feminism and liberalism by having the young Maria choose the feminist Ruth as her love object and, symbolically, as her lesbian 'mentor'.

HOOD

Hood, Donoghue's follow-up novel, is similar to *Stir-fry* in the ways in which it also features an unequal lesbian relationship, where one of the women,

Cara Wall, behaves as the exploitative lover of the other, Pen O'Grady. Whereas *Stir-fry* follows the maturation and lesbian awakening of Maria, *Hood* describes the six days after the death of Cara in a car accident, from the perspective of the bereaved Pen. Rather than following a linear storyline like *Stir-fry*, *Hood* alternates between past and present events, and offers a more nuanced portrayal of the protagonist's psychology as she copes with loss and her situation as a closeted lesbian. *Hood* is not a story of sexual discovery like *Stir-fry*, but Pen's various acts of coming-out as a lesbian widow bring her some sense of liberation and relief in the midst of grief.

An early reviewer of *Hood* underlines that 'the issues [Donoghue] tackles are not just gay ones' and that '*Hood* is much a book about grief as anything else' (Grant, 1995: 8). Grief, it must be said, is a culturally-mediated experience; Pen's grieving process is inseparable from her situation as a closeted lesbian, so, as Antoinette Quinn rightly notes, Donoghue locates lesbian mourning in a 'continuum of human suffering' and, by doing so, her readers not only learn 'the secrets of the closet but vicariously undergo the experience of being closeted' (2000: 155). Implicit in Quinn's observation is the novel's educational value, as it attempts to make the general public aware of the pain caused by the lack of recognition of queer kinship in contexts of grief.

While the protagonist's grief is invisible to others, Donoghue allows her readers access to Pen's private grieving and most intimate memories of her beloved Cara, which show an in-your-face aesthetics with graphic descriptions of lesbian desire, female sexual organs and bodily fluids.[9] Pen's heightened lust is a common reaction, albeit often silenced, that some bereaved people experience, as Donoghue herself outlines: 'I was struck by some discussions of sexual feelings in studies of the bereaved that I read; I had assumed they'd be numb to feel any desire' (Thompson, 2003c: 177). In *Hood*, Pen soon realises that Cara's death signifies the loss of a cherished sexual life. With Cara, Pen became 'a creature of pleasure', but she now lies on their bed all alone, 'dull and dry' (153). When the protagonist has her period, she remembers how Cara enjoyed the taste of her menstrual blood, which provokes a sudden sexual arousal. When Pen closes her eyes, she visualises 'the most beautiful thing'; Cara's 'cherry-red clitoris' (257). Drawing on scenes like this one, Tammy Clewell concludes that Pen takes refuge in her sexual memories to counter the public invisibility of her grief, arguing that 'Donoghue's text makes a strong case for the merits of private grieving' (2009: 145)

Yet, while Donoghue does foreground the merits of her character's private grieving, Pen still feels pained by her isolation and social non-recognition of her loss, and much of the story concerns her gradual reclamation of her widowhood. One of the consequences of her closeted lesbianism is that Pen bears the burden of a 'disenfranchised' type of grief. Kenneth J. Doka defines disenfranchised grief as 'the grief experienced by those who incur a loss that is not, or cannot be, openly acknowledged, publicly mourned or socially supported' (1999: 37). For those suffering disenfranchised grief, their attachment to the deceased person becomes socially invalidated or diminished,[10] as 'there is no recognised role in which mourners can assert the right to mourn and thus receive support; grief may have to remain private' (Doka, 38). Because identities are culturally mediated by the languages available, Donoghue's protagonist finds it difficult to reclaim her status as a primary mourner and a widow, the latter concept being associated with marriage and heterosexuality.

Donoghue therefore addresses the connections between society's hetero-sexism and Pen's disenfranchised grief, but instead of offering a picture of blatant oppression, *Hood* provides readers with a nuanced rendition of the social practices and conventions that render lesbianism unspoken. Pen and Cara themselves decided to hide their relationship while living together with Mr Wall, Cara's father. Even though Mr Wall never questions Pen's newly acquired position within their family, Pen presumes that he would behave as a homophobic bigot were he told about their relationship. Because of her prejudices, Pen does not reach out to Mr Wall after Cara's death, even though on several occasions he implicitly declares his knowledge of the real bond between the two women.[11] Some of Pen's apprehensions, like her distrust of Mr Wall, prove wrong as the story unfolds, but as is also made clear, the protagonist's fears originate in a social climate of suppression and non-recognition of lesbianism.

Public mourning rituals, *Hood* shows, can also heighten the individual's experience of disenfranchised grief. Studies from numerous Western countries have demonstrated that conventional grief care arrangements have been construed as a 'concern for those considered to be part of the deceased's heterosexual nuclear family', therefore 'affirm[ing] that institution as the most essential societal bond, both for the deceased and for society in general' (Reimers, 2011: 252).[12] In *Hood*, conventional mourning rituals obstruct the recognition of lesbian relationships due to their heterosexist nature. At the church funeral, Pen observes how the unmarried Cara – a 'pussyeater', as she called herself (135) – is assumed to be a spinster, surrounded as she is by white, virginal flowers which mock her fierce opposition to Catholic sexual morality. Pen attends the funeral as a friend, but dislikes herself for her self-imposed discretion: 'When these people looked at me they could have no idea that I was anything to their missing relative; that I had let her dip her biscuits in my tea, on and off, for thirteen years' (132). Back at home, Cara's sister confides to Pen that she looked 'weighty' and 'responsible', 'like widowed' (150). Deeply moved, Pen confirms her widowed status, and this gives both women a chance to come closer and speak warmly about the person they have lost. In all instances, coming-out as a lesbian widow has curative effects, helping Pen alleviate the added burden of disenfranchised grief.

As the story progresses, readers learn that Pen, because she is a Catholic school teacher, has a good reason to remain closeted, since, as noted in Chapter Two, Section 37.1 threatened the professional security of LGBTI+ teachers. Despite this threat, Pen courageously comes out to one of her colleagues, Robbie. In her conversation with him, Pen is overwhelmed by an anger directed at the wider society:

> 'I suppose,' he said [. . .], 'it must be like when a husband or wife dies. Only less. . . official.'
> I nodded. My throat was full of angry words, but they weren't for him. (182)

Tellingly, Pen's silent rage increases as she grows aware of the injustice of her situation. When talking to her boss, Pen can only timidly present Cara's death as the loss of a beloved friend and housemate. Her frustration surfaces some days later when she returns to school and realises that she cannot grieve as an official, heterosexual, widow: 'What galled me most was that if it had been a husband, Sister Dominic would have given me two weeks off' (248). But, most importantly, Pen now feels that it makes a difference to her whether she speaks of Cara as a lost friend or a lover:

> I did not want to disown Cara by diluting her into my 'housemate'. Of course I had done that very thing over and over while she was alive, but it seemed wrong now that there was no longer any possibility of calling off the lie, now that there was no chance that I would ever bring her on my arm to a staff Christmas party and say, this is my beloved, in whom I am well pleased. (175)

Because of her disenfranchised grief, Pen grows increasingly uncomfortable with her closeted lesbianism. Nowhere is this clearer than at the end of the story, when Pen decides to come out to her mother and tell her about her past with Cara. A deluge of tears is announced, and they hold the promise of emotional cleansing: 'The first drop touched the skin under my eye as the sky opened and sent down the rain' (309). By asserting herself as the widow of the late Cara, Pen struggles against the disenfranchised grief that threatens to aggravate her mourning.

To make her novel richer in its cultural analysis, Donoghue also looks at Pen's disenfranchised grief as being provoked not only by the larger society, but also by her contemporary lesbian subculture, in the figures of Cara's friends. According to Vicky Whipple, who writes in an American context, lesbian subcultures have tended to focus on issues such as civil rights, feminism or sexual freedom, but generally lacked a language of support for the bereaved – consequently, there is a 'lack of an appropriate grief model' (2006b: 71). *Hood* dramatises how the developing lesbian subculture and community of 1990s Dublin can create solutions for the social injuries inflicted on lesbians, but fails to accommodate different types of sensibilities, like Pen's as she battles with grief. If the Catholic funeral made Pen feel invisible, the alternative lesbian wake becomes a much more humiliating experience. One of the purposes of funerals is to give the community the opportunity to offer signs of caring for primary mourners, but far from feeling comforted, Pen is irritated: 'What really enraged me, as I sat listening to them praise a woman I barely recognized, was that I didn't figure' (294). Hurt and offended, Pen leaves the house the moment Sherry encourages Jo to read a poem for Cara, as 'she was the last one [sexually] involved with her' (299). Donoghue portrays this lesbian community as alienating and insensitive toward Pen's suffering, and thus 'refu[ses] to construct a monument to gay pride or to gay victimization' (Quinn, 2000: 164). Donoghue achieves this effect by producing a novel that addresses the exclusions within the lesbian community she creates in the novel.

Tellingly, if the lesbian communities in Dorcey's fiction involve themselves in feminist activism and women's rights, the one in Donoghue's *Hood* embraces the liberal, post-feminist model that developed in Britain and America in the mid-1980s. In her analysis, Clewell identifies the foreign influences on Cara's lesbianism, and regards the lesbian fiction Cara bought in Britain and the United States as 'an example of an oppositional discourse that circumscribes the possibilities for lesbian self-realization' (141). As a self-declared lesbian feminist, Donoghue appears to be uncomfortable with the 'libertarian models'[13] of lesbianism in Ireland, which endorsed an 'adventurous approach to sex' as a means of self-fulfilment (Palmer, 1993: 23), and went hand-in-hand with the advent of values of individualism and consumerism in 1990s Ireland. In some ways, the libertarian model entails a reversal of traditional sexual ethics.[14] However, those freedoms do not apply to Pen, who becomes an outsider to the lesbian community because she does not (and cannot) fit into their lifestyle. Even though the women of the community, including Cara, enjoy wearing political T-shirts with shocking messages, their activism is limited to their own sexual freedom – not the freedom, wellbeing, or emancipation of other, more oppressed, bisexual, and lesbian women like Pen, who, as a teacher, is affected by Section 37.1.

Neither were Pen and Cara equal partners, and this is arguably where Donoghue's criticism of the libertarian model becomes most salient. If lesbian feminists defined 'lesbian relationships from the viewpoint of camaraderie and woman bonding,' the libertarians saw gendered difference 'as the pivot of desire' (Palmer, 1993: 14, 23). Cara chooses Pen as her life-partner precisely because she represents stability, but her libertarian approach to the relationship is based on the abuse and exploitation of Pen's devotion. When describing what Pen's love means to her, Cara becomes brutally sincere and unnecessarily cruel: 'I know what it's like, it's like the free milk cartons we used to get at school. Sometimes I want it and sometimes I don't want it but it's just sitting there every morning, so sometimes I stamp on it' (222). This scene contains masochistic overtones, as Cara responds to her partner's tears of humiliation by embracing and kissing her whilst Pen says nothing 'for fear of provoking her' (222). Difference – the power she had over her partner – is how Cara sustained her erotic attraction to Pen. This sense of difference is, as previously noted, a gendered one, since in *Stir-fry* and *Hood* Ruth and Pen act as 'the masquerading heterosexual "wifey" washing up as her man/ husband/ butch/ woman reclines on the sofa' (Jeffers, 2003: 4). But, whereas in *Stir-fry* Ruth is a feminist, Pen cannot be defined as such; she is a closeted lesbian, afraid that the wrong people would discover her sexuality. Throughout *Hood*, Donoghue insists on the unequal nature of the protagonists' relationship; Pen learnt to tolerate Cara's exploitative behaviour not because she accepted her libertarian views, but because of her vulnerability and emotional dependence on her.[15]

Within the community, the only person who offers Pen her sincere support is the older lesbian Jo, who started as a feminist back in the 1970s. That Cara was abusive of Pen's devotion is not to deny that she loved and cared for her. Jo, for example, readily intimates that: 'You two had something really special going there, Pen. I could tell how much she cared about you' (49). At the end of the novel, the possibility is open for the development of a close friendship, or even a romance, between Pen and Jo. As in *Stir-fry*, when she has Maria choose Ruth instead of Jael, Donoghue favours the feminist model over the libertarian one by portraying Jo as the only positive character of the lesbian community.

In *Hood*, the Irish heterosexist culture, the lesbian community's hedonism, and Pen's closeted homosexuality oppress the protagonist in different ways. Aware that silence and invisibility had made her life easier in the past, Pen starts grieving privately, but gradually reveals herself as a lesbian widow, reaching out to others (e.g., Cara's sister, Jo, her mother, her colleague) in an attempt to find human communion in the face of bereavement. To a large extent, Pen's struggle against her disenfranchised grief liberates her, leading her toward self-renewal and a more open life as a lesbian.

LANDING

Donoghue's 2007 novel, *Landing*, recreates a radically different scenario than *Stir-fry* and *Hood*. While in the two previous novels Catholicism still affected some of the characters' worldview and assumptions, in *Landing* the old conservative morality becomes replaced by the new 'religion' of the liberal and brashly consumerist Celtic Tiger Ireland. Similarly, notions of coming-out, so important in Donoghue's early novels, are no longer relevant in *Landing*. The novel describes the transnational, long-distance lesbian relationship between the Canadian Jude Turner and the Irish Síle O'Shaughnessy. On first appearance, Donoghue's *Landing* is only an idealised romantic story, but, progressively, the novel creates relevant connections between sexuality and 'themes of economic and social class difference, national identities, and the obstacles to migration' (Casey, 2011: 67). Set in Dublin and small-town Canada, *Landing* alternates between the voices and perspectives of Síle and Jude. The style – which shows how the lovers communicate via e-mail, voicemail, and instant messaging – reflects the novel's modern setting, as also does its foregrounding of 'hybrid ethnicities' (Síle is of Indian and Irish origins) and 'displaced national boundaries' (O'Toole, 2013: 137), due to the increased mobility propelled by globalisation.

Landing has been analysed from the perspectives of cosmopolitanism (Charczun, 2020) and queer migration (O'Toole, 2013), but this reading shall focus on how Donoghue writes here about non-heterosexual identities in Ireland and Canada. Unlike the lesbian couples in *Hood* and *Stir-fry*, Síle and Jude are faithful and genuinely devoted to one another, and these romantic feelings keep them together against all odds. Their union transcends geographical and cultural barriers, surviving long periods of no physical and sexual intimacy, so, when Síle felt lonely, 'she conjured up Jude, or rather her absence, a hot ghost for Síle to wrap her body around' (151). In several ways, their characterisation resembles well-known cultural narratives of ideal heterosexuality, and thus contains traces of the homonormative. This impression is reinforced by the fact that Síle's two non-heterosexual friends – who behave as clichés of bisexuality and gay sexuality respectively – share no such romantic qualities, and their relationships are less than perfect.

One of Síle's friends is the bisexual Jael – the same Jael of *Stir-fry*, but ten years older –, who fits into widespread stereotypes about bisexuals (male and female) as being 'obsessed with sex', 'immature' and 'less trustworthy and loyal [. . .] as romantic partners or friends' (Morrison et al., 2010: 212). Portrayed precisely in this way, as 'immature' and 'untrustworthy,' Jael – who 'ha[s] the sexual ethics of a bonobo chimpazee' (177) – attempts to kiss Jude behind Síle's back, just to 'take [Jude's] measure' (176). Donoghue's Jael also boasts her modern views when she complains about 'the whole straight-slash-queer thing' (229) yet keeps her bisexual life occluded thanks to her heterosexual marriage and secret lesbian relationships. Ironically, Jael's liberal behaviour represents no significant change from more conservative times when people constantly resorted to secrecy and duplicity to avoid moral judgment.

If Jael features as a stereotype, the same can be said about Marcus, who, as he proudly proclaims, has 'already slept with all the Dublin guys [he]'d ever had any interest in' (85). Tired of casual sex, Marcus enters into a relationship with Pedro, a love affair that is described in mainly sexual terms, as their reported romantic activity is to spend whole weekends at home having sex. Though they 'exchange garlands and vows' in a marriage-like ceremony and start living together (230), their sentimental union quickly dissolves because, as Marcus tells us, 'Pedro's never been faithful to one man in his life' (307). In the figures of Jael, Marcus and Pedro, stereotypes of bisexuals and gay men become reaffirmed and unchallenged. Arguably, by making this contrast between the friends' unromantic lives and the lesbian couple's noble feelings for each other, *Landing* implicitly endorses a homonormative view on non-heterosexual relationships.

The transnational romance between Jude and Síle also serves Donoghue's purpose to reflect on socio-cultural differences between Canada and Celtic Tiger Ireland, the latter being characterised as a 'less-than-ideal state' (Casey, 74). Donoghue's *Landing* shows how discriminatory behaviours like homophobia and racism remained palpable in the cosmopolitan Dublin of the early 2000s (there are, for example, several references to the 2004 Referendum, which denied Irish citizenship to children born to immigrant parents).[16] The Irish-born but racialised Síle, whose mother was Indian, encounters xenophobia and misogyny on the streets of Dublin. She gets told: 'Go home, Paki bitch!' (35), but, when she is in Toronto, she feels 'visually unremarkable, and the effect [becomes] oddly relaxing' (250). On the issue of Irish intolerance, Donoghue, having lived in London (Ontario, Canada) for several years, explains in an interview that:

> I do find Canada on a whole to be a few decades ahead of Ireland when it comes to women and queer people, because it's been having that civil-rights conversation for longer, and it is not as invested in Catholicism. Also, it's got such a vague sense of identity – which allows it to truly include immigrants – whereas Ireland still wrestles with its lingering sense that there are the real Irish (white Catholics) and then everybody else. (Donoghue and Palko, 2017)

According to Donoghue, because in Canada there has been a longer tradition of civil-rights conversation, Canadians generally adopt a more flexible and carefree attitude with regard to racial and sexual issues.

In *Landing* this contrast between Canadian and Irish attitudes, to which Donoghue referred in the interview above, is thoroughly explored through the main characters. When, via email, Síle talks of her 'somewhat traumatic' act of coming out of the closet, Jude responds: 'I'm not sure whether I was ever in. I wasn't too concerned about being normal' (71). Later in the story, on a visit to Canada Síle becomes infuriated when she realises that Jude and Rizla – Jude's male ex-partner and best friend – remained occasional sexual partners after their break-up. Jude tells her that their sex was about 'company' (138), but an insecure and frustrated Síle tries to make sense of the situation by applying the conventional categories of sexual identity:

> 'I thought you were a dyke. So you're still bi, is that what you're telling me?'
> 'Those are your words,' said Jude thickly. (137)

While Jude understands sexual relationships as a matter of emotional and physical intimacy, Síle feels disoriented by her partner's acknowledged sexual fluidity and irreverence towards sexual categories (her reaction also denotes bisexual negativity). Síle's insecurities, as Zusanna Sanches argues, relate to 'the fallacy of normativism of queer communities,' which establishes fixed gender and sexual categories (2011: 301). As illustrated by this and other scenes, Síle needs to transcend this rigid way of thinking in order to embrace a more flexible understanding of human relationships and desires.

Connected to Síle's 'inflexibility', *Landing* also addresses the ways in which the 'sexual revolution' introduced by the liberal, market-oriented culture of the Celtic Tiger era promoted a somewhat dogmatic and conventional approach to sexual and gender identities (a situation which exemplifies Ging's concept of 'gender repolarisation', which, in turn, connects with today's homonormative culture). In this respect, Donoghue's text reflects Fintan Walsh's finding that, in Ireland, there has been a proliferation of LGBTI+ 'identity categories', stimulated by the production of markets that 'provide the means by which imagined selves can be purchased into being' (2016: 8). In *Landing*, Síle features as a *femme* lesbian who spends much of her salary in expensive stylish heels, fashion clothes, jewellery, make-up, and other beauty products. Síle, in fact, resembles the *femme*, post feminist and consumerist protagonists of Linda Cullen's *The Kiss* (1990), characters that Donoghue herself had disliked in her review of the novel (see Chapter One). References abound as to Síle's obsession with her feminine looks, which may also relate to the pressures of her feminised profession as a flight attendant. When she buys a €800 plane ticket for Jude, Síle comments: 'It cost me no more than a couple of pairs of good shoes, and god knows I don't need any more shoes' (226). The Canadian Jude, on the contrary, is no participant of such a consumerist culture (she grows her own food, does not own a credit card, refuses to request a bank loan). Neither does she 'buy into' any identity categories, even if Jude knows that her romantic and sexual preferences are for women: 'In my case – in a bunch of cases – labels don't fit' (154). Jude, who assures Síle that 'labels don't fit,' is nonetheless described as masculine, or butch, on several occasions, but, as Kaarina Mikalson perceptively notes, 'this reading of Jude's gender comes mostly from Síle – perhaps as a femme, Síle is invested in using the term butch and so building a recognizably queer partnership' (2018: 56).

As noted earlier in the chapter, this is not the first time Donoghue creates in her fiction gendered roles for lesbians, but the key difference now is that, unlike *Stir-fry*'s Ruth and *Hood*'s Pen, Síle behaves as hyper-feminine and self-consciously *femme*, and proudly so, as the following passage in Canada seems to illustrate:

> 'That sure is a nice accent you've got. I thought Rizla here must be pulling my leg, because you don't look Irish.'
> Jude stiffened.
> Síle beamed back at him. 'And the funny thing is, Dave, I've been told I don't look like a lesbian, either.' (131)

In response to the Canadian man's tactless remark on her non-white Irishness, Síle chooses to bring another 'anomaly' to attention: she looks like a straight woman, but she is actually a lesbian. Whereas Tina O'Toole reads these lines as an affirmation of Irish cultural hybridity, an interaction that 'splices received ideas about Irish identity, sexuality, and ethnicity, constructing Síle as an avatar of contemporary Irish society' (2013: 138), the same passage can be interpreted in light of this character's constant and unambiguous reclamation of her *femme* lesbianism. Implicit in Síle's remark is that most lesbians, unlike her, are visibly masculine. Síle's behaviour is therefore more conservative than she may dare to admit, as demonstrated by her internalisation of traditional gender roles. Surprised by Jude's supposedly feminine culinary abilities, Síle says: 'For a tomboy, Jude, you're turning out to have weirdly housewifely traits such as the cooking everything from scratch' (70). Though Mikalson opines that Síle is oppressed by *femme* invisibility because '[she] has to come out regularly' (57), one may also argue that, since this character consciously adheres to the gender dichotomies of her liberal culture, her *femme* identity may well provide her with a sense of social and symbolic capital.

Given that in the last chapters Síle makes the vital decision to migrate to Canada out of her love for Jude, a final topic to consider could be LBGT migration. *Landing* explores a new scenario where neither economic necessity nor sexual liberation becomes the reason for leaving Ireland. If in Donoghue's

'Going Home' (1994), included in *Alternative Loves,* two queer diasporans had escaped Irish homophobia in London, in *Landing* the English Marcus and Spaniard Pedro enjoy an easy life in Dublin, and then find acceptance as a gay couple when they move to small-town Ireland (this reverses long-established patterns of homosexual migration from rural areas to cities). Yet, despite this generally positive rendition of twenty-first century LGBTI+ migration, some of the obstacles of today's liberal cultures and economies come to the forefront when Síle prepares her migration to Canada.[17] As she browses the Canadian Government's immigration website, Síle encounters all kinds of impediments to migrate there sponsored by Jude, as they are neither 'conjugal partners', 'common-laws' nor 'in a mutually interdependent (marriage-like) relationship' with 'joint bank accounts, wills [and] credit cards' (278) – some of these being categories that establish connections between affects and economy. Síle now finds that 'labels don't fit' (154), that personal relationships and experiences do not neatly fall into identity categories, no matter how modern and liberating these categories seem to be: 'Some days this emigration project made Síle feel like a smuggler' (291). After all their tribulations, Jude and Síle remain together, now in Canada, as committed partners. In *Landing*, Donoghue celebrates lesbian love and romanticism while addressing the complexities of contemporary life and the limitations of identity categories.

CONCLUSION

In an interview, Donoghue reflects on gender identities when she explains that she 'come[s] from a feminist background which explains gender as a pure social construction,' but that, to her surprise, '[her] boy and girl [have] emerge[d] pretty hard-wired in their passion for cars and baby-dolls respectively' (Ue, 2012: 104). For Donoghue, the problem is that, even if some boys and girls do manifest 'inborn preferences,' society 'does everything it can to exaggerate, harden and police those differences' (Ue, 2012: 104). Some innate behaviours thus become stereotyped as either masculine or feminine. In *Stir-fry* and *Hood*, the two lesbian couples inadvertently adopt roles that bear more resemblance to heterosexual conventions than to feminist principles of mutuality and equality. As previously discussed, Donoghue has the liberal (and masculinised) Jael and Cara behaving as exploitative lovers of the feminist Ruth and the 'wifey' Pen, which may be interpreted as a critique of the 'libertarian model' of lesbianism (using Palmer's term). If in *Stir-fry* and *Hood* none of the lovers identifies herself or the other as masculine or feminine, the opposite is true in *Landing*. In this novel, references abound as to Síle's obsessive investment in her *femme* identity, both in psychological and economic terms. As has been suggested, her hyper-femininity and appreciations of Jude's perceived masculinity bespeak this character's internalisation of Celtic Tiger Ireland's homonormativity and 'repolarisation of gender' (Ging, 2009: 55). The Canadian Jude, on her part, does not 'buy into' this type of liberal culture, and features as a somewhat wiser character than Síle.

Hence, as made obvious in the analyses of the three novels, Donoghue rejects idealised portrayals of Irish lesbianism. As she had already explained in the context of her publication of *Stir-fry* and *Hood*, LGBTI+ writers should not succumb to simplistic images of queer affirmation; they should not be afraid to 'name the negatives' of their respective communities (1995b: 168). By 'naming the negatives,' Donoghue insists, 'we queer folk [. . .] pass crucial advice from one generation to the next' (1995b: 169). In her writings, Donoghue not only deals with some of the negative aspects of her contemporary queer culture, but she also gives 'shape and substance' to lesbian experience in Ireland (Smyth, 1994: vii). It is in this way how, at the beginning of her career, Donoghue already became a potent literary voice, a writer who 'g[a]ve voice to what ha[d] been censored' (Fantaccini and Grassi, 2011: 404). This chapter has attempted to foreground how, in her contemporary-set lesbian novels, Donoghue produces a nuanced depiction of lesbian experience in 1990s and 2000s Dublin, breaking previous social silences on the female body and sexuality, the disenfranchised grief of lesbian widows, the tensions between the feminist and liberal ideologies within a lesbian subculture, the fraught position of homosexual teachers in Ireland, as well as some of the exclusions within the lesbian community.

SEVEN

He Did Not Fit the Bill as a Gay Man

Narratives of Gay Life and Identity in Celtic Tiger Ireland

In *The Contemporary Irish Novel* (2004), Linden Peach explains that, in the last years of the twentieth century, Irish fiction became a vehicle for the investigation of previously neglected spaces and identities, offering an unprecedented analysis of Irish society. At the time, Peach argues, Irish fiction underwent a cultural shift whereby authors began to dramatise the 'shock of what was hidden for so long' (17), exposing the 'wider consequences' of the marginalisation many individuals suffered (21). This desire to tell alternative stories inevitably involves the emergence of voices and experiences that had been silenced by Irish society's rigidity in the past. Nonetheless, this critical approach to the past does not translate itself into a complacent celebration of present conditions. Unlike liberal discourses that draw a sharp distinction between tradition/oppression and modernity/ freedom, Irish authors usually 'submit the whole concept of modernization to scrutiny' (Peach, 11). Expanding on Peach's analysis, in *Irish Literature in the Celtic Tiger Years* (2011) Susan Cahill calls attention to the important topic of memory in this cultural scenario. For Cahill, Celtic Tiger fiction usually manifests a dynamic connection between past and present, and the way in which these works engage with memory often articulates 'the occlusions and absences of Celtic Tiger culture' with regard to the body and sexuality (6).

The present chapter draws on the above to analyse a number of works: Tom Lennon's *Crazy Love* (1999); Belinda McKeon's *Tender* (2015); Colm Tóibín's 'The Pearl Fishers' (2010); Ridgway's *The Long Falling* (1998), 'Angelo' (2001) and *The Parts* (2003), and Frank McGuinness's 'Chocolate and Oranges' (2018). The texts chosen challenge the celebratory, modern icon of gay life, and address the prejudices and shortcomings of the liberal economy and culture, with its excessive focus on individualism and consumerism. In these works, as in many others from previous chapters, silence – in the shape of shameful, unspeakable secrets, silencing, inarticulacy, the discretion required between speakers, and so on – features as a narrative element which makes visible for the reader hidden realities of Irish society. In this way, these stories provide a language for previously silenced issues and identities, contest and revise conventional frames of reference in terms of margins and centre, and effectively explore the relationship between dominant discourses and situations of concealment and discrimination.

If the topic of silence (present in previous chapters as well) is also foregrounded here, it is because the Celtic Tiger period – which spans the years between the early 1990s and 2008 – was expected to put an end to the censorious culture of Catholic Ireland, with its imposition of shameful silences on the body and sexuality. In 1990, the election of Mary Robinson as President of the Irish Republic symbolised the emergence of a society that no longer defined itself as essentially Catholic and traditional. The newly elected President, a reformist lawyer and an advocate of women's liberation, had been known for her work to legalise contraception in the 1970s and male homosexuality in the 1980s (together with Senator David Norris). From the early 1990s onwards, Ireland has transformed itself into a much more secular and liberal nation. This trajectory towards liberalism has been accompanied by major debates involving vital issues such as women's role in society, the wider availability of contraceptives, support for unmarried mothers, the exposure of a silenced history of abuse against women and children in Catholic institutions, divorce legislation, and the social accept-ability of homosexuals.

Yet, despite this fight for equality and new civil rights, the gap between the rich and the poor widened during the 1990s and 2000s, as the Celtic Tiger was characterised by an aggressive implementation of neo-liberal and free-market policies. Public discourse during the economic boom 'emphasised certain features and elided others'; that is why, though there was a growing inequality in access to housing, education and healthcare, the Celtic Tiger evoked 'an euphoric sense of self-congratulation' (Kirby, 2010: 68). Before the 2008 collapse of the Irish economy, critics of the Irish experience of globalisation had already warned that 'the benefits of the "Celtic Tiger" [were] largely illusory, and a focus on conventional economic indicators conceal[ed] a picture of increased inequality, erosion of employ-ment security, and marginalization' (Whelan and Maître, 2007: 139–40). In the Celtic Tiger years, social class oppression not only increased, but, in general, remained silenced by a discourse of prosperity and modernity. In some cases, though, class issues did become blatant in public discourse, and served to reinforce regulations in terms of gender, sexuality, and ethnicity, as illustrated by the 2004 Citizenship Referendum.

With regard to women's and LGBTI+ issues, Diarmaid Ferriter argues that, due to the political and ideological dominance of the Irish Catholic Church until the end of the twentieth century, 'a sexual liberalism based on individual rights experienced elsewhere in the West in the 1960s and 1970s was delayed in coming to Ireland' (2009: 10). This culture of 'sexual liberalism' became identified with the advent of the neo-liberal policies of the Celtic Tiger economy. In 1990s and 2000s Ireland, discourses of national progress and justice concentrated on the equality of social identities; for example, the increased visibility, recognition and protection of gay identity, with no intersectionality about issues of social class. New representations of gay men in Celtic Tiger Ireland promoted a notion of social progress that was connected with the lifestyle principles of liberal capitalism.

Because gay identity was associated with Irish modernity and sexual freedom, gay men began to be 'represented as the epitome of an urban, metropolitan, consumerist lifestyle' (Cronin, 2004: 255). A new, excessively optimistic stereotype of gay life served to celebrate a modern and progressive Ireland, positioned as a stark contrast to the conservative, Church-dominated version of the nation. Building on this idea, Susannah Bowyer argues that in Ireland this modern view of gay life relies on the identification and pursuit of pleasure, so characteristic of consumerism. 'The libidinal overtones identified as significant in postmodern culture', Bowyer explains, 'coalesce in the global gay brand's association with a covetable sense of sexual ease and enjoyment and the queer frisson of transgression' (2010: 805). Though this liberal culture endorsed progressive values that benefitted homosexuals, the same ideology also used this 'global gay brand', by default white and middle-class, to re-stereotype homosexual life while setting aside socio-economic disparities. This modern view of gay life – which excludes gay men who are non-white, older, rural, or working-class – had an impact on the identity formation of many young gay men, but hardly represented the actual experiences of numerous homosexuals, who continued to suffer 'marginalisation, harassment, violence and exclusion in education, work, and social life' (O'Donnell, 2008: 3).

Ireland's 2008 economic collapse prompted a critique of the 'hyper-individualism' of the Celtic Tiger ideology, with its focus on the 'individual primarily as worker and consumer' (Share, Corcoran and Conway, 2012: 185). Despite this critique, in the present post-Catholic[1] and post-Celtic Tiger moment, some of the old prejudices, constraints and social injustices remain intact. Apparently, the post-crash Ireland of the 2010s has reinforced 'the inculcation of norms of individual accountability' (Kiersey, 2014: 356), making the individual responsible for her or his self-empowerment, as if no structural oppression existed for a significant part of the population. Set in the early 2000s, Keith Ridgway's *The Parts*, which dramatises the often-hidden reality of gay male prostitution, reminds us of the still existent marginalisation and exploitation of the underclass. For instance, a recent study found that situations of 'unstable family backgrounds, homelessness and drug abuse' are still evident amongst many of the men who enter the sex industry in Dublin (Ryan, 2016: 1717).

Though of a very different nature, another example of this persistence of sexual inequalities concerns the social illegitimacy of gay fatherhood, which Tom Lennon describes in his 1999 novel, *Crazy Love*, where the protagonist places his hopes in a near future where 'gay fathers will probably be all the rage' (67). Yet analyses of the 2015 referendum indicate that 'concerns about children were the soft underbelly of the marriage issue' (Healy, Sheehan, and Whelan, 2016: 43), and that is why, as Emer O'Toole observes, 'the Yes side avoided posters representing gay couples and families, such as men holding hands, women kissing, and children with same-sex parents' (2017: 116).

TOM LENNON'S CRAZY LOVE

The silence of gay fatherhood, as shall be explained, is one important topic in *Crazy Love*. Lennon's second and last novel (the author died in 2002) is the story of Paul Cullen, a successful executive who feels depressed because he is a gay man married to a woman. As he did in *When Love Comes to Town*, Lennon adopts here well-known conventions of the coming-out story, as disclosure of sexual identity is portrayed as the required step towards authenticity and emotional healing. *Crazy Love* is narrated in the protagonist's own voice, and Lennon effectively introduces here the stylistic device of second-person narration, which, in a series of inner conversations, emphasises a sense of a split personality between the "real" gay Paul, and the Paul of social appearances. As he tells his straight, public self, Paul got married simply because "everyone else *you* knew was doing it" (emphasis supplied, 22).

Whilst Lennon's 1993 debut recreates a time when Catholic values and morality had a considerable social influence, *Crazy Love* is set amidst the liberal culture of Celtic Tiger Ireland, and adds a new dimension to the representation of heterosexual masculinity, since, in those years, 'Irish masculinity became increasingly defined by the acquisition and display of affluence; though still bound up with aggressive risk-taking and bravado, such energies were to be channelled into the pursuit of wealth and the accumulation of consumer goods' (Woods, 2014: 29). Though uneasy about pretending being heterosexual, Lennon's Paul is highly invested in the masculine culture of his time: 'Fifty-five K and a brand new 520i with alloy wheels and tinted windows at the age of twenty-eight. That's success' (17). If owning an expensive car boosts his male ego, Paul manifests the same proprietorial pride in the company of Johnny, his gorgeous assistant and eventual lover: 'You get that surge of pride heterosexual men get when they have a beautiful woman by their side' (41). His obsession to 'possess' Johnny leads to all kinds of disruptive behaviours; Paul constantly pursues encounters with him, bends work ethics, and displays an aggressive bravado when he sees Johnny with Derek, his boyfriend: 'You roar out of the car park like someone with a deathwish' (160). Affected by the constraints of his masculine culture, Paul initially fails to control his emotions and make peace with himself.

The fundamental change for Paul – his final crisis of heterosexual masculinity – occurs due to a mental breakdown that compels him to come out at work. Because his anxieties prove illusory and Paul suffers no exclusion,[2] Michael G. Cronin argues that Lennon projects an uncritical view of the supposedly tolerant and progressive values of the middle-class liberalism of Celtic Tiger Ireland. Such impression is reinforced, Cronin adds, by Lennon's stereotypically negative portrayal of Catholic Ireland – here represented by Family Solidarity members protesting outside government buildings – and the working-class, in the figures of two men who harass a gay couple in a restaurant, while Paul, who witnesses the scene, remains silent and ashamed (2004: 258). Whereas *Crazy Love* contains characteristics of a clichéd narrative, there are some visible cracks in Lennon's positive rendition of liberal Ireland, which relate to the issue of gay fatherhood.

After his coming-out, Paul tries to find ways to reconcile his fatherhood with an open homosexual life, but this proves impossible.[3] A situation like the one described by Lennon is by no means rare. In contemporary Ireland, popular notions of 'gay men as "risks" to children' persist (Ó Súilleabháin, 2014: 174), which explains why gay parenting 'continues to provoke strong anxieties' (Ó Súilleabháin, 2017: 500).[4] This was presumably worse in the 1990s, the time *Crazy Love* is set. To highlight the protagonist's role as a loving father, Lennon's text repeatedly shows Paul's adoration for his baby girl, Lia,[5] but this close attachment to the daughter becomes threatened when Anne – now pregnant with their second child – discovers his affair with Johnny (not with a woman, as she had suspected), which only magnifies her disgust: 'She's screaming about catching AIDS' (210).

Lennon dramatises how, in a liberal yet heterosexist society, same-sex parenthood – because it involves not just individual rights, but the education of children – presents numerous challenges, as it goes beyond the Celtic Tiger's principles of sexual liberation. The final chapter, set two years later, shows Johnny and Paul cosy at their own home, delightfully engaging in parenting practices with Lia and the new baby. This picture of domesticity is then contrasted with the silence and disapproval surrounding gay fatherhood. When the girl, Lia, mentions that she knows Johnny, Anne – determined that her ex-husband's gay life remains hidden from their children – bitterly complains: 'What sort of example is it?' (237). Due to their social pressures, Paul and Johnny have internalised a need for silence and discretion. It is no coincidence that Johnny's family knows Paul only as his friend, and that Paul claims no recognition of Johnny as a co-parent. Nonetheless, by foregrounding the wellbeing of the children in the company of Paul and Johnny, Lennon's 1999 novel makes a case for the legitimacy of gay parenting.

Lennon's *Crazy Love* locates gay identity within a liberal culture that allows for new freedoms and self-affirmation. Paul, though, cannot lead an open life as a gay father, and even lacks a language to articulate this situation of discrimination (he simply adopts strategies of concealment). Therefore, as the novel closes, some of the 'wounds' of homophobia remain open. Nowhere is this clearer than in the case of Anne; she initially features as an open-minded, tolerant woman that criticises the blatant homophobia of Catholic associations like Family Solidarity, but her reaction of horror at discovering Paul's sexuality demonstrates the lingering and sometimes silenced prejudices against gays in Celtic Tiger Ireland. *Crazy Love* thus depicts a liberal world where discriminatory attitudes persist below a veneer of progress and modernity.

BELINDA MCKEON'S TENDER

Set in late 1990s Dublin like Lennon's *Crazy Love*, Belinda McKeon's *Tender* also concerns itself with a young gay man's self-acceptance and various acts of coming-out, but her novel offers a more thorough exploration of the contradictions of liberal Ireland, this time from the perspective of a young straight woman, the gay character's closest friend. A journalist and playwright under commission to the Abbey Theatre, McKeon made her debut as a novelist with *Solace* (2011), which, like *Tender*, focuses on the experiences of young characters moving from rural Ireland to Dublin. *Tender* is the coming-of-age story of Catherine Reilly, who starts a life in Dublin as a Trinity College student and develops an intense friendship with James Flynn, the first gay person she ever meets. Told entirely in Catherine's voice, *Tender* captures the 'youthful expression' of emotions through its use of 'raw'[6] language (Ryan, 2016: 137). Structurally, *Tender* has five sections, stylistically different, that reflect Catherine's consciousness and evolving maturation. Particularly, the third section, with its broken yet powerful prose, represents 'Catherine's crisis – in fact, James's crisis as well' (Tierney, 2015). McKeon, as shall be explained, makes use of this crisis (and the circumstances surrounding it) to dramatise how the sexual oppression of 'traditional' Ireland, rather than disappearing altogether, adopted new expressions (and silencing practices) in the youth culture of Celtic Tiger Dublin.

On first impression, in *Tender* this youth urban culture appears as nothing but oppositional to the moral values of previous generations. McKeon's novel, for example, suggests that friendships between straight women and gay men proliferated in the Celtic Tiger years, when an increasing number of youngsters, like Catherine, wanted to distance themselves from conservative Catholic Ireland. It is therefore no surprise that Catherine's conflicts with her parents, back in her town, concern her personal independence and her friendship with James.[7] In one of these conflicts, to dispel her parents' suspicions that their relationship is a sexual one, Catherine feels forced to tell them that James is gay. While the mother accuses James of being 'troubled', the father exhorts: 'I don't want you associating with the likes of that fellow' (99). Patriarchal and homophobic oppressions become linked here; if Catherine's parents become afraid of their daughter's potential sexual liaison with James, their fear only increases when they are informed he is a gay person, a negative influence. These intergenerational conflicts reassert Catherine's modern identity and strengthen her attachment to James, to the point that she adopts a protective role: 'It is my job to look after him' (220). By taking care of him, Catherine asserts her resistance against her parents' patriarchal control of her life.[8]

Tender thus depicts a 1990s scenario when women and gays reclaimed new freedoms, and how their friendships acquired positive connotations of social progress and solidarity. McKeon, however, characterises Catherine's friendship with James as highly oppressive in the end. Patrick Mullen rightly notes that *Tender* 'reveals Catherine as rightly opposed to homophobia but yet more invested in sexual repression than she may like to admit,' thus 'expos[ing] the false optimism of the Celtic Tiger and reveal[ing] the violence of a reassembled repression' (2017: 91). *Tender* teems with references to the protagonist's possessiveness towards James as a gay person; she now has 'one of her own' (79) and feels 'a surge of pride [. . .] when she talked or thought about James, about how close she was to him' (111). This proprietorial pride boosts Catherine's self-confidence as a modern, open-minded woman, but does not contribute to a mutually supportive friendship with James.

As is made clear as the story progresses, Catherine's idea of this friendship is influenced by a liberal context which promoted an excessively optimistic, problem-free icon of gay life and identity. Catherine not only idealises this friendship – she talks of her 'precious gay friend' (110)–, but also has clear expectations from it:

> She wanted him back to herself. Not the dark, quiet version, not the version she had been with all day, the James who had worried her and exhausted her [. . .] She wanted the brilliant, funny, vibrant James, lit up with enjoyment, teeming with it, and she wanted him to be only her friend. (180)

In the story, when Catherine hears James complain about his pain and isolation as a gay person, her reaction is to dismiss his problems or silence him,[9] as it is only the optimistic, happy and carefree version of James that Catherine wants. Catherine regards herself as James's protector and best friend, but without realising it, represses his need for an emotionally honest relationship. Her behaviour may therefore symbolise the contradictions of a liberal culture that celebrates the presence of gay men but refuses to engage with the presumably unpalatable aspects of their existence, like the homophobia they still suffer, their loneliness and mental health problems.

Another contradiction is revealed when Catherine, who supposedly welcomes James's sexuality, feels repulsed by his gay desires. In one of the scenes, the protagonist becomes ashamed when she finds James staring at an attractive man in a bookshop: 'She felt it like nausea [. . .] What had she imagined? Body pressed to body, mouth to mouth, crotch pressed to crotch, in the poetry section of Hodges bloody Figgis?' (148). James's public and unapologetic display of his gay desires challenges Catherine's tolerance. One of the ironies of the novel is that, even if Catherine loves and cares for James, her role as protector conceals her own selfishness and determination to establish the terms and conditions of their relationship. As discussed, Catherine's obsessions lead to the destruction of their friendship, and, contradictorily, re-enact the familiar patterns of surveillance and repression of her traditional, Catholic background.

Even though Catherine, as McKeon puts it, features a 'neurotic' (Tierney, 2015), James is no hapless victim of her obsessions. When the two friends start having sex, Catherine realises that they had arranged a 'deal', which means that she will comply with James's desire to keep their affair secret (265). In a series of reversals, McKeon transfers sexual stigma from the gay man to the straight woman and characterises this heterosexual relationship as being in the 'closet', with Catherine experiencing the silence and non-recognition of illegitimate love. This situation has shameful implications for Catherine, who is seen by others to behave, inappropriately, as James's 'mother' (270) and 'wife' (218). When their final crisis erupts, both Catherine and James resort to their familiar languages of homophobia and sexism. James withdraws from her to start a relationship with Liam, so a jealous Catherine tries to separate them by informing the boyfriend that James is 'troubled' (421), mimicking her own mother's words about him. James, on his part, adopts a well-known practice of patriarchal societies: the public shaming of women on the basis of their sexual behaviour. Shouting at her for others to hear, James ridicules her desires for him while denying their sexual relationships: 'It was laughable, *laughable*, what she had done, what she had tried to do – as though he would want to touch her' (emphasis in the original, 376). Exiled from the group of friends, Catherine faces her peers' moral judgment. If anything, their final crisis demonstrates that deeply regressive attitudes still persisted in the youthful, modern, and liberal culture of late 1990s Ireland. *Tender* therefore dramatises how the crisis between the protagonists connects with a falsely optimistic Celtic Tiger culture of tolerance and sexual freedom.

COLM TÓIBÍN'S 'THE PEARL FISHERS'

Like McKeon's novel, Colm Tóibín's short story 'The Pearl Fishers', included in *The Empty Family* (2010), portrays silenced sexual realities (secret, shameful relationships) which contradict Celtic Tiger's ideas of sexual liberation.[10] 'The Pearl Fishers' brings together the married couple Gráinne and Donnacha, two upper-class members of the Catholic laity, and a middle-aged homosexual man, the unnamed first-person narrator. As they share dinner, Gráinne announces her intention to publish a book detailing her sexual abuse by Father Moorehouse when he was their teacher. Gráinne's husband, Donnacha, is the man with whom the narrator had a passionate love affair during their adolescence and early adulthood. Donnacha enforces silence on this issue, so their past relationship remains consigned to secrecy. More than any of the other stories in this chapter, Tóibín's text, as Cahill explains in relation to general trends in Celtic Tiger fiction, delves into 'Ireland's not so distant past [to] complicate any linear, progressive paradigm of modernity' (6).

Tóibín's 'The Pearl Fishers' (the title comes from an opera whose homoeroticism inspired the protagonist but left Donnacha indifferent when they watched it together as students) is set at an unspecified time during the Church scandals, when, from the 1990s onwards, reporting of clerical abuse became widespread. In recent decades, the legal prosecution of clerics has replaced the traditional Irish reticence concerning the sexual abuse of minors. Yet child abuse had also been taking place within families and communities, and, for much of the twentieth century, 'the excessive focus on suppression and containment diverted attention from the fact that there was already substantial public and judicial awareness of sexual crimes against children' (Ferriter, 330). While liberals regarded Church representatives as witting accomplices of child abuse, conservative sectors of the Church blamed gay priests for these sexual crimes, and their response was to develop 'strategies to exclude homosexual men from religious life and on purging seminaries of "gay subcultures"' (Bowyer, 814).

As a public intellectual, Tóibín argued that many gay men of his generation (he was born in the 1950s) did enter the priesthood because '[homosexuality] was not allowed for as a possibility' (2002: 275). None-theless, Tóibín insists, to blame gay priests for these crimes is not only inaccurate but cruel: 'For the many gay priests in the Church it is deeply disturbing and indeed frightening that their sexuality can be so easily associated with rape, sexual cruelty and the abuse of minors' (2010b). Sexual transgressions in Catholic institutions cannot be attributed to the mere presence of gay priests, since these sex scandals 'involved both paternity cases and the sexual and psychological abuse of children by priests, brothers, nuns and bishops' (Donnelly and Inglis, 2010: 8).

In his story, Tóibín locates these controversial cases within a cultural tradition of silence that favoured the concealment of abuse. Typical of Tóibín's fiction, 'The Pearl Fishers' is characterised by the central character's moral ambiguity, emotional injuries and careful reflection on the past to make sense of the present. Very little happens in the present time of the story, as the plot revolves around the protagonist's memories and what he refuses to say or acknowledge. Here, silence is both a personal and social issue, and as also happens in *The Blackwater Lightship*, becomes a central narrative feature.

According to Foucault, 'silence itself – the thing one declines to say, or is forbidden to name, the discretion that is required between different speakers – is less the absolute limit of discourse [. . .] than an element that functions alongside the things said, with them and in relation to them' ([1976] 1998: 27). In precisely this way, Tóibín dramatises how silence impedes knowledge, but creates its own cultural codes, affecting individuals' assumptions, perceptions, and worldview (as shall be argued later, a similar approach to silence is taken by Ridgway in his fictive account of male prostitution). These considerations on silence become particularly relevant in light of the narrator's newly acquired knowledge that Father O'Neill (another priest in the story) had abused some of his male students:

> The idea of a priest wanting to get naked with one of the boy's at St. Aidan's and stuff his penis up the boy's bottom was so unimaginable that it might have happened while I was in the next room and I might have mistaken the grunts and yelps they made for a sound coming from the television. Or I might have mistaken the silence they maintained for real silence. (70)

As a young man, the narrator was influenced by a variety of silence that enforced ignorance about sexual realities that, for him, belonged to the realm of the unimaginable. Similarly, prior to the breaking of silence on this issue, clerical abuse was almost unthinkable. Many victims themselves either lacked the language to denounce their situation or were simply not heard. Connected to this social silencing of abuse are both Gráinne's belated revelation and the narrator's disbelief. At sixteen, she and the narrator used to meet with the priest to discuss poetry and prayer. Gráinne wants to make the narrator a witness of those private meetings, in which she claims that Father Moorehouse 'had [them] in his thrall' (70). The narrator – perhaps, due to his past agnosia, or 'inability to understand the significance of what is being seen' (Pine, 2013: 6) – suggests that their sexual relationship, if it existed, was consensual: 'There was nothing, not a single detail, not a blush, for example, on either of their faces, not a thing unusually out of place' (79). The narrator distrusts and dislikes Gráinne, and judges her as opportunistic and eager for attention. Paradoxically for the reader, there is no way to verify his opinion; whether or not Gráinne became a victim, the narrator could have hardly perceived anything due to an agnosia derived from the social silencing of clerical abuse in the past.

Like Gráinne's sexual past with the priest, the narrator's and Donnacha's secret relationship fell outside the realm of the acceptable or even the imaginable. This secrecy was also required because at the time Donnacha had already begun his relationship with Gráinne. But, unlike Lennon's protagonist in *Crazy Love*, Paul, whose marriage to a woman makes him feel inauthentic, Tóibín's Donnacha seems to have never faced such dilemma. Donnacha's characterisation may remind us that notions of sexual identity do not necessarily align with the individual's sexual preferences and experiences.[11] As Alan Sinfield explains in *Gay and After* (1998), people who regularly engage in gay or lesbian relationships but identify as heterosexual represent a 'disturbance' from the viewpoint of gay identity politics (11). Sinfield underlines that, contrary to the liberal impulse to 'separate the straights and the gays', many people see 'no inevitable contradiction between occasional or secondary gay experience and a heterosexual self-image and lifestyle' (12).

In Tóibín's story, Donnacha's heterosexual self-image and lifestyle connect with his cultural affiliations as a militant Catholic, for whom (heterosexual) marriage becomes a compulsory ritual for his public role as a family man. In ways that are relevant to the story, Judith Butler theorises that 'sexuality is regulated through the policing and shaming of gender,' hence 'the homophobic terror over performing homosexual acts [. . .] is often also a terror over losing proper gender' (2000: 164). In Tóibín's story, Donnacha's silence on his 'homosexual acts' and his choice of 'proper gender' may be viewed not only as his adherence to the Church's moral teachings, but also as being connected to questions of social and symbolic capital. The middle-aged Donnacha belongs to a generation in which 'the Catholic Church still ha[d] considerable influence not just in the religious field, but in the character of Irish social life,' since 'being a good Catholic helped get contracts and jobs, be elected, be educated, be well known and liked' (Inglis, 1998b: 13, 11). Curiously, Donnacha features as a successful hospital administrator who gives radio interviews and has meetings with the Health Minister and the Taoiseach.

One of the ironies is that Donnacha remains a highly elusive character. All his past and present actions are reported and interpreted by the narrator, who is hurt by Donnacha's decision to conform to a 'normal' life and relegate their past relationship to silence – he offers 'not even the smallest hint of recognition' (88). Through the figure of the narrator, who complies with Donnacha's silence, Tóibín resists stereotypes of gay liberation while reflecting on the traditional but still existent suppression of homosexual experience. Tóibín's 'The Pearl Fishers' accounts for the complex legacies of silence in a society whose approach to sexuality continues to be affected by a past of denial and secrecy.

KEITH RIDGWAY'S THE LONG FALLING

While Tóibín's 'The Pearl Fishers' develops during the time of the Church scandals, Keith Ridgway's *The Long Falling* is set in 1992 against the background of the 'X' case.[12] Both texts compare gay experience with the changing sexual morality of Celtic Tiger Ireland and the exposure of hidden realities of abuse. In his debut novel, Ridgway places his two protagonists, Grace and her gay son Martin, within a milieu where there is hope for change, yet they fail to free themselves from the constraints of the past. Formally, *The Long Falling* alternates between the perspectives of several characters, major and secondary ones. In this way, readers not only gain access to the protagonists' self-perceptions, but also how others interpret the main characters' actions and behaviour. This multiplicity of perspectives becomes especially relevant in the case of Martin; while his internal view-point offers a somewhat sympathetic approach to his past struggles and present needs, the external perspectives on him depict him as a rather cruel, unstable, and self-centred individual.

The Long Falling tells the story of a battered wife, Grace Quinn, who escapes her town in Monaghan, after killing her brutal husband. As her gay son did when he left home, Grace wants to establish a new life in Dublin, away from her painful past and the constraints of country life. In a 1998 interview, Ridgway commented how the different geographies and places people belong to irremediably influence notions of personal identity and agency. These interrelationships between place and identity, Ridgway argued, became extremely relevant at the time:

[The Long Falling] is about different cultures, perspectives, generation gaps, urban and rural divides, which is kind of universal. But in Ireland in the last ten years it's become very sharp and very apparent and there is this tension between the new kind of Ireland which we're all patting ourselves on the back about, which is very liberal and so on, but there are still people in Ireland who are trapped in a kind of older version, the girl in the 'X' case and Grace are examples of that. (quoted in Madden, 2010: 23)

The Long Falling, as suggested, calls attention to the realities of pain and isolation of a battered wife, who finds herself trapped in this 'older version' of Ireland. Grace is only able to denounce her oppression and reclaim her victimhood when, in Dublin, she learns of the 'X' case and identifies with the girl.[13] Whereas she remained silent in Monaghan, in Dublin Grace feels empowered to share her story of abuse with Sean (a friend of Martin's) and Mrs Talbot (a new friend she makes), but remains unable to explain her crime to Martin: 'She had no language for telling him. Had no place, no setting, no words to begin it, no words to end it' (205).

Grace's lack of a language – and her past inability to identify herself as a victim of her husband – stems from the traditional silencing of domestic violence. This social silence was first broken in Ireland by feminist activists who, in the 1970s, insisted that 'women were battered, that rape within marriage was a reality' (Beale, 1986: 64). From the mid-1980s onwards, investigative journalism also proved influential in the shaping of public opinion. Following highly publicised cases such as Ann Lovett's,[14] journalists brought to light many other dark aspects of Irish society, including stories about 'clandestine childbirth, clumsy self-abortion, brutal husbands or incestuous fathers' (Ferriter, 525). This type of journalism, as *The Long Falling* shows, became associated with the advent of liberal ideas in Ireland. A spiteful Martin degrades his mother when he evicts her, telling her to ask Sean, his journalist friend, 'to make a story' of her crime, since 'everybody loves a battered wife' (227). Though he now identifies with his retrograde father, Martin shares with Grace a common history of suffering. This becomes evident the time he came out, when the father unleashed his fury against the two, blaming Grace for his son's homosexuality. After Martin's departure, Grace's situation worsened, as the husband 'began to beat [her] very badly, drunk or sober' (152). The vital difference between the two is that, whereas Martin could escape and remake his life, Grace remained trapped in an abusive marriage.

In the figure of the father/husband, Ridgway weaves homophobic and patriarchal violence together. Yet, as Ed Madden observes, the 'divisions Ridgway represents in this novel as generational and geographical are also gendered: it is women who are left behind in the "new" Ireland of the early

1990s' (2010: 30). Grace is certainly 'left behind' by her son, which leads Madden to conclude that *The Long Falling* effectively 'unravel[s] any easy correlation of gay and feminist politics' (30). This anti-feminism, though, is embodied by Martin, and not by the other gay characters. Martin's anti-feminism features as a pernicious influence from the father, and his self-absorbed, self-destructive behaviour may well reflect the repercussions of the homophobia he suffered. The stigma gays experience during their youth, Gerard Rodgers relates,[15] often has irreversible consequences in their adulthood: 'Habituated residues can still be present in current thoughts, moods, and feelings,' as these men remain 'vulnerable to enacting the social feedbacks of stigma in unconscious ways' (2018: 143, 166). This psychological condition seems to shed light on Ridgway's nuanced construction of his gay protagonist.[16]

Having experienced fear and violence in Monaghan, Martin begins in Dublin a new life that is tainted by the moral considerations, insecurities and anxieties provoked by the previous one. For example, he regards the gay sauna as a degrading place where everybody is 'rotten in some way' (122), but he went there 'three times a week sometimes, in his first days in Dublin' (114), and continues to visit it when his boyfriend is absent. Jonathan Butler argues that the boyfriend's absence (Henry is in Paris for much of the story) obsesses Martin because he is the 'anchor [to] his Dublin identity' (2008: 66). However, when his boyfriend returns, Martin describes their sex in a way that renders Henry a prop of his sexual needs:

> Making love. For Martin it was loaded. It was heavy with a weight that he thought peculiar to himself. He suspected that it did not mean as much to other people. That no one but he felt defined by it. It was what he was. The circumstances of his life had flowed from the way he wished to make love. From that clumsy declaration. I am what I want. I am this. (221)

Ridgway characterises the sexually liberated Martin as having an unhealthy relationship with his sexuality, since he places an exaggerated significance on sex as a means of self-affirmation, and the language he uses – 'I am what I want' – points to problems of emotional intimacy and an inability to bond with others. As explained, Martin suffered the father's violent homophobia, and his damaged psychology may well reflect the consequences of a past where he was taught to regard gay sex as 'not natural' (184), as something which not even 'the animals in the fields [do]' (188).

The residues of this toxic past account for his numerous anxieties in the present time of the novel. After several years in Dublin, Martin shows no signs of psychological recovery, as Grace's mere presence in his flat makes the 'shadows of his growing up' lengthen (108). He also grows paranoid the moment he finds Grace at home after he makes love with Henry: 'And now this. As if she had waited in the street for the right moment' (224). Some critics, like Jonathan Butler (2008) and Magdalena Stepien (2013), suggest that, in the final part of the story, Martin reports on Grace in order to repudiate her and assert an urban gay identity, but such notion is problematic. Martin's behaviour is nothing but self-destructive; not only does he metaphorically turn into his father, whom he 'hated' (239), but his betrayal of his mother is also condemned by his gay friends and boyfriend, who decides to abandon him: 'Jesus, Martin. You're so fucking stupid. Your father's son' (293). This unhappy ending, where he alienates himself from those who love him, only reinforces the impression that Martin remains trapped by a past of emotional turbulence.

In *The Long Falling*, Ridgway complicates the liberal icon of gay identity, making it clear that a culture of individualism and sexual freedom cannot cauterise the psychic damage caused by the protagonist's upbringing within a devastatingly homophobic environment. The novel also suggests that, while liberal Ireland can accommodate the sexual liberation of young homosexuals by providing them with an urban centre and a gay scene, such economic-driven solution hardly promotes notions of equality and solidarity among the socially oppressed, here represented by Grace as a battered wife.

KEITH RIDGWAY'S 'ANGELO' AND THE PARTS

Issues of social class and their connection with possibilities of self-realisation reappear in Ridgway's later work. Whereas *The Long Falling* describes the generational, geographical and gender divides of the early 1990s Ireland, 'Angelo' (*Standard Time*, 2001) and *The Parts* (2003) emphasise the social class divisions of Dublin,[17] a city which, according to the author, 'became a parody of gross commercialism and consumerism' in the 2000s (Gleeson, 2012). Both 'Angelo' and *The Parts*, as shall be explained in what follows, connect this critique of liberalism to the portrayal of a failed relationship between a young gay man, who is part of Dublin's gay scene, and a rent boy, who remains trapped in a much more marginal world.[18]

Ridgway in this way contrasts the experiences of middle-class young men with those of rent boys, underclass and young (often teenage) prostitutes who usually provide sexual services for older males. As also appears to be the case today,[19] rent boys have remained relatively invisible in the 1990s and early 2000s,[20] in which Ridgway's texts are set.[21] In *Rent* (2000), Evanna Kearins notes that, in the 1990s, there was a 'perceived growth in male prostitution', but 'little public concern has been expressed about it' due to the 'lack of recognition of this subculture' (20). Kearins adds that most rent boys themselves would not admit involvement in prostitution 'for fear of legal and social recrimination' (2000: 122); the 1993 Sexual Offences Act made it illegal to solicit or loiter on the street for the purposes of prostitution, but failed to tackle the class oppression and socio-affective problems affecting prostitutes. Such problems are far from being solved; a 2011 study found that among Dublin rent boys the 'average age for leaving school was 14 years, just below the legal age of 15 [. . .] [Most] participants left home before they were aged 18. This was mainly because of stealing, drug use, or sexual or physical violence' (McCabe et al, 2011: 1008). Instead of criminalising street prostitution, there is a need to implement policies to help rent boys (many of them minors) out of prostitution.

For some of the commentators on Kearins's *Rent*, her finding that married men count as the rent boys' main clientele became a salient issue. Kathryn Holmquist opened her review by underlining that these married men 'suppress their true sexuality at great psychological cost' and that, 'when it all becomes too much to contain, they seek a brief sexual encounter with a male prostitute' (2000: 13). Like Holmquist, Jim Clarke established a connection between a homosexual underworld and male prostitution, as he defined the latter as 'a potent combination of homosexuality, vice, abuse and shame' (2002). Though it seems true that most clients lead double lives, the idea that they should be considered repressed homosexuals (or bisexuals) struggling with shame is debatable, since, as previously discussed, numerous heterosexual men engage in secondary gay experiences with no inner conflict regarding their sexual identity.[22]

As we also learn in Kearins's book and in Liam McGrath's short documentary *Boys for Rent* (1993), many of these clients want to fulfil their most hidden sexual fantasies specifically with teenage boys, and not with adult men[23] – they thus have ephebophilic desires. Ephebophilia does not necessarily align with abuse, but the key factor is that, because of the rent boys' perceived vulnerability, this sex may easily involve violence. This is a situation that, according to Kearins, some rent boys accept as part of their work, as they become 'prepared to oblige sadomasochists' (106). As explained in McGrath's documentary, the clients' attraction to boys often translates into a desire for sexual aggression and subjugation of younger males (the documentary is explicit about practices of gang rape, sexual humiliation, non-consented sexual acts and beatings), since '[clients] have this thing about power, that gives them a certain amount of enjoyment [. . .] Most of the guys are into violence; they are older than you, they dictate you' (1993). It is therefore not hard to conclude that, because most rent boys suffer violence and severe social disadvantages, concerns about illicit sex or the clients' 'true' sexuality should be sidelined in favour of analyses that focus exclusively on the prostitutes' experiences of class oppression and exploitation.

This necessary cultural analysis is carried out by Keith Ridgway in two works, which approach the underworld of rent boy prostitution from different angles. While *The Parts* Ridgway exposes the unpalatable realities of male prostitution while describing the psychological and sociocultural world of the rent boy character, in 'Angelo' prostitution features as a secret that the unnamed narrator, who was Angelo's friend and lover, fails to discover. 'Angelo', like many other short-stories by Ridgway, concerns itself with the 'malfunctioning of the mind and with the mind's way of perceiving the world' (McCourt, 2014: 230). As a young middle-class gay man, the narrator passes judgment on Angelo's appearance:

> He did not *fit the bill* as a gay man really. His clothes were random, occasionally awful, he was lazy about his appearance so that it was not uncommon to see him turn up with greasy hair and unattractive stubble, and it annoyed me greatly that he could often be seen in places like The George or The Front Lounge, carrying an old plastic bag from Dunnes. (emphasis supplied, 201)

The narrator conforms to the modern image of urban gay life, yet Angelo is cast as an outsider even if he is also gay. Ridgway's economic metaphor – 'to fit the bill' – brilliantly captures the idea that, to be regarded as a standard gay man, one should care about his physical attractiveness and be, or at least look like, a middle-class consumer. The narrator reaffirms this link between consumerism and gay identity when he remarks: '[Angelo] did not wear aftershave, did not belong to a gym, did not go to the theatre or the cinema or seem to do anything that involved any kind of expenditure at all' (210). Influenced by mainstream discourses that silence the realities of the socially oppressed, the narrator cannot 'see' Angelo beyond his own social class values and conventions.

In the story, Ridgway describes the narrator's sex with Angelo – a poor immigrant whom he fetishises as an exotic foreigner – in the language of consumerism and sexual commodification, an attitude which prevents him from developing a more profound relationship with his lover: 'I enjoyed him, and it was enjoyment without clutter, without notions of permanence or exclusivity or special treatment' (208). Tired of being the narrator's 'occasional shag' (206), Angelo accuses him of practicing 'McDonald's sex' (217). Ridgway's fast-food metaphor may well indicate that this model of sexual behaviour (of instant gratification but little emotional attachment) is an import from a gay male global culture. The author adopts a somewhat sarcastic tone when, confused by Angelo's attentions after their first sexual relationship, the narrator remarks: 'It was right to exchange blow jobs but pleasantries like this were something of an invasion' (198). In a darker tone, the narrator expresses no real concern when, as they have sex, he realises that Angelo 'had a scar, horribly pinkish white, on his lower back, ending in his left buttock, which he claimed was from a stabbing in London, which was one of those version stories, it changed over time' (196). Along the narrative, Ridgway offers clues indicating that Angelo is vulnerable and that he is involved in some kind of dark underworld, but the narrator continually fails (or refuses) to read the signs.

To dramatise the two characters' social differences, Ridgway contrasts the narrator's misperceptions with Angelo's evasions and distortions of his actual experiences. Through the narrator, we learn that Angelo made up stories about his past, remained silent about his personal life, and that none of his friends knew where he lived. Because the reader is deliberately left unsure as to the extent of the narrator's self-deception, Ridgway effectively captures the ambiguities between knowing and unknowing, between innocence and wilful blindness. After some months together, the narrator is already aware that Angelo has a double life, as he informs us that he often ran out of money and disappeared without explanation, just to return some days later and take him out 'for wildly expensive meals' (210). Despite all the strange circumstances, the narrator suspects nothing when an unknown, older man – later revealed as Mr Duncan, who had taken a teenage Angelo under his wing – phones him to ask about Angelo, with a 'posh, wealthy, clear, business-like' voice (218). When he informs Angelo about this call, the narrator senses his awkwardness and fear, but then assumes that his friend is only embarrassed because he is 'being tracked down by a jealous former sugar daddy who wants him back' (224). Some days after, Angelo disappears, leaving no trace behind.

Significantly, even though prostitution features as a silenced reality, a subtext of sexual exploitation explains the enigmatic ending of the story. While Angelo remained silent about his situation because of the stigma of prostitution, the narrator's attitude – his blindness, ignorance, and middle-class complacency – seems to be a consequence of the social silencing of male prostitution.

Contrary to the indirect handling of prostitution in 'Angelo', in *The Parts* Ridgway deals with this underworld in a direct, "in-your-face" way. Ridgway's portrayal of Celtic Tiger Dublin in *The Parts* is a complex and original one, as it 'strongly convey[s] the idea of multiple cities existing in the same space at the same time' (Lawson, 2003). To reinforce this notion of coexisting 'multiple cities', the novel employs postmodernist techniques like polyphony, fragmentation, shifting perspectives, a pastiche of narrative styles (third-person omniscient, third-person subjective, first-person and stream of consciousness), and widely varying forms of texts, among them letters and e-mails, chat room conversations, Dublin listings and event guides, and male escort advertisements.[24] Tellingly, this multi-layered form serves to explore the various layers of ignorance and social silence concerning rent boy prostitution: for example, one of the characters expresses his surprise when discovering the rent boy trade in the Phoenix Park: 'Who could tell that this was going on, right here, just here, right in the middle of town [. . .] It's like one city inside another. Parallel cities' (367).

As a polyphonic novel, *The Parts* contains a cast of six main characters and numerous short sections focusing alternatively on each of them. The characters' storylines become connected by the 17-year-old Kevin, or Kez, who traverses the diverse social spheres of Dublin life due to his work as a rent boy. In the course of the story, Kevin emerges as 'the moral centre on which the novel turns' (O'Donnell, 2013: 191). Kevin's storyline often interrupts the others' narratives, and he is the only character to have stream of consciousness sections, describing his hopes, fears and anxieties. Through this character's tribulations and vulnerability, Ridgway examines notions of class oppression, sexual exploitation, and the silencing of prostitution.

Kevin is first seen through the eyes of Kitty Flood (one of the main characters) as he is having sex with an aggressive client in a rich Dublin district. Looking through her window, Kitty spots a naked boy in a neighbour's house and observes how an older man reaches for him, 'his hands mov[ing] the boy, straightening him out, tilting his head back, opening his mouth' (9). Though the teenager's distress is evident to her, Kitty expresses a disbelief similar to that of the narrator in 'Angelo', and cannot (or does not want to) comprehend that she is witnessing a scene of abuse: 'It's impossible to believe, and if Kitty is seeing this then she's probably laughing' (10).

Through Kitty's agnosia, Ridgway seemingly depicts a kind of social indifference to, or non-recognition of, class oppression and sexual exploitation. After all, there was in Celtic Tiger Ireland a social discourse that suggested that the 'selling of sex has become accepted by society', and that prostitution 'is now an industry based on choice' (McGurren, 2014: 83). In *The Parts*, Ridgway by no means offers such sanitised view on prostitution, as his rent boy character – who hails from a dysfunctional family and an economically disadvantaged background[25] – is haunted by his unspoken fear that 'someone would take him to the country and cut his throat' (68). In a series of stream-of-consciousness sections, readers also learn about one traumatising memory concerning a client who beat him up: 'Sometimes still he thought that his jaw hurt. It ached, like it was remembering' (139). This attack went unreported, because Kevin is convinced that nobody would help him: 'He told nobody. It would be a hard thing to tell –it would bring questions and long looks, and maybe it would make people laugh and they would talk about him as if he wasn't there' (140). Ridgway suggests here that, where there is social silence about a specific type of abuse, victims, if they choose to speak out about their suffering, may encounter other people's agnosia, disbelief and moral judgment. Like Angelo's in the short story, Kevin's silence also has strong implications as to the stigma of prostitution.

An opportunity for Kevin to escape the underworld of prostitution opens up when he meets Barry, but theirs turns out be a failed romantic story. Again, this failure originates from the clash between two different social worlds, but, unlike the narrator in 'Angelo', Barry shares his frustrations about his gay culture. In one of the episodes, set in a gay club amusingly called "Penetration", Barry is rejected by a potential lover who had asked him whether he was 'top' or 'bottom': 'What a stupid bloody question anyway *–are you active or passive, do you take it or give it, are you this or that?* The cheek of him, asking that, reducing everyone to that, as if it was set in stone, as if all that mattered was which one you were, fucker or fucked' (emphasis in the original, 44). Barry protests against this 'conceivably heterosexual view of sex' (44), which promotes fixed gender roles and sexual attitudes as something natural and desirable among gay men.[26]

Ridgway's novel accurately reflects a situation which has only exacerbated in recent years, due to the increasing dominance of a digital culture that, as Kay Siebler explains, reduces gay identity to an index of sexual behaviours and body types (e.g., in dating websites and mobile phone applications). As discussed in Chapter Six in the analysis of Donoghue's *Landing*, contemporary LGBTI+ culture reinforces 'binaries of sex, sexuality, and gender' and creates 'archetypes' that have a strong influence on the identity formation of non-heterosexuals (Siebler, 2017: 80, 99). This commercialisation of gay identities positions sex and body image as central elements.[27] Tellingly, in Ridgway's account of gay life in the early 2000s, the gay character's insecurities do not stem from the possible impact of homophobia, but from his need to look physically attractive. And, although he has several sexual partners, Barry cannot bond with any of them and thus feels 'unloved, loveless' (119). When he goes on a date with another man, the two of them complain about the gay scene, but they end up having sex the same day, never to see each other again.

Though critical of Dublin's gay scene, Barry is highly invested in his liberal culture, which partly explains why his relationship with Kevin fails. Barry – who works for a Dublin journalist – looks for rent boys to interview and, when he meets Kevin, develops a sexual but paternalistic interest in him, romanticising himself as the boy's possible saviour. As they share dinner one evening, they find themselves in pleasant company, but the romanticism is broken the moment Kevin announces he must leave:

'I have to go'

'Where?'

Kevin frowned, and seemed to hunt around for an answer

'Oh,' said Barry, 'I mean, really? So early? That's a pity'

[. . .]

He found it suddenly appalling

'Do you have to?' he asked

'Go? Yeah, sorry'

No, he tried to say, I mean do you have to fuck for money? But he nodded. (303)

Communicated through indirection and silent gestures, their distinct sensibilities incapacitate them to bridge the gap created by their social class differences, provoking 'the first uneasy silence of the evening' (303). Kevin cannot mention the reason for his sudden departure; he has to go and meet a punter, an encounter he cannot miss because it was organised by his pimp. Even though he presumably accepts what his friend does for a living, Barry fails to see beyond the social silencing of the lives of boys like Kevin, for whom prostitution is not a simple matter of choice.

Frustrated because of Kevin's sudden departure, Barry reverts to his usual fast-food sex life and goes to the sauna to 'chas[e] ass' (318). Part of the gay scene, the sauna in Ridgway's fiction emerges as a symbol of homosexual life 'under capitalism' (Cronin, 2004: 262), a system that inevitably affects the ways gay sex is often expressed and understood in terms of the principles of consumerism. Barry describes his sex in the sauna as meaningless and 'waste' (318), and he is consumed by sexual guilt when he discovers that Kevin, kidnapped by his client, had phoned him asking for help.[28] As he previously did in 'Angelo', Ridgway does not openly criticise the lifestyle promoted by modern gay culture, but he shows how it may damage personal relationships, creating obstacles to intermale intimacy.

In 'Angelo' and *The Parts*, Ridgway vividly portrays the glitter and grime of the materialistic Dublin of the Celtic Tiger years. Both texts abound with references to a new liberal culture of sexual freedom, individualism, and consumerism. However, the rent boy characters, because they belong to a lower social stratum, remain trapped in a marginal and restricted world. Ridgway foregrounds this clash of cultures in his depiction of failed relationships between a male prostitute and young gay man, whose agnosia, middle-class complacency, and prejudices originate from the social silencing of the gruesome conditions surrounding prostitution. By so doing, Ridgway also challenges the celebratory modern icon of gay life, exposing the ways it contributes to the negative outcome of these homosexual relationships. This last aspect is, perhaps, more salient in the short story, where the narrator cannot 'see' Angelo beyond his own social class values and conventions. In

The Parts, Ridgway offers readers an unflinching portrayal of the realities of Dublin male street prostitutes. Through Kevin's tribulations and vulnerability, readers not only witness the ugly side of Dublin life, but are also encouraged to grow their awareness of the social class oppression, exploitation, and marginalisation of the 'dispossessed' in the supposedly prosperous Celtic Tiger Ireland.

FRANK MCGUINNESS'S 'CHOCOLATE AND ORANGES'

Another text that foregrounds issues of social class for gay men is Frank McGuiness's short story 'Chocolate and Oranges' (*Paprika*, 2018). A widely acclaimed playwright, McGuinness became in his early career a pioneer in his renditions of gay identity on the Irish stage – in his 1985 production, *Observe the Sons of Ulster*, the kiss between two male characters, Pyper and Craig, became 'the first overt representation of gay physical action on the stage at National Theatre in Dublin' (Cregan, 2004: 674). Before McGuinness, Cormac O'Brien notes, homosexuals had only been represented in Irish drama as 'sinister, troubled antagonists' (2020: 125).

In 'Chocolate and Oranges', McGuinness depicts the world of the immigrant underclass through the figure of Ion, a gay Romanian who works as a hotel cleaner. As Fintan Walsh argues, there is a great scarcity of work 'exploring the experiences of LGBTQ immigrants', and this is a cultural analysis which needs to be done, as Ireland is 'far from a readily welcoming place' (2016: 11). As former BeLonG To[29] activist Michael Barron explains, in some environments, like Direct Provision centres, LGBTI+ individuals confront a double oppression: they not only suffer 'continuous fears' about being outed and discriminated against by other inmates, but they also (like other racialised immigrants) face the racism and prejudice of the white LGBTI+ community (O'Rourke et al., 2013: 27).

Though the gay protagonist in 'Chocolate and Oranges' is no asylum seeker under Direct Provision, he is a similarly powerless and vulnerable individual. McGuinness's story is set before 2007 (the year Romania joined the EU), as it recreates a time when 'there [were] several thousand Romanians in Ireland on work permits, while many more [were] working illegally' (Haughey, 2002). Both Ion and Zoia, the two Romanians in the story, have escaped from a past of political violence; there are references to Nicolae Ceaușescu's dictatorship (1965–89) and its aftermath, and Zoia protests that she 'went without bread' back home (45). The Celtic Tiger economy attracted large numbers of Eastern Europeans, but many of them were exploited at work. This is the situation in which McGuinness's Ion finds himself, as he faces extreme deprivation in Ireland.

The story is a third-person narrative focussed on Ion, whose sophisticated language and perceptions contradict the popular image of immigrant Romanians as undereducated, and as 'beggars and petty criminals' (Haughey, 2002). Though set in a Dublin hotel, the story features no Irish bosses or entrepreneurs. Zoia functions as their representative, as she does their dirty work by collecting the tips given to the staff: '[She] [was] always ready and willing to do what was best service for those ruthless bastards' (43). As McGuinness suggests in his story, a perverse tactic of liberal economies is to enforce hierarchies among the dispossessed for them to maintain the structures of oppression.

In his works – 'Chocolate and Oranges' being no exception – McGuinness often creates characters that 'find themselves in largely static situations,' often 'immobilized' by 'imprisonment, grief, or authority' – a 'constraint [which] only intensifies the relentless mobility of their thoughts' (FitzPatrick Dean, 1999: 99). This is the situation which Ion encounters, as much of the story describes his bafflement while Zoia bullies him, after he refuses to hand her his tip. Aware of her power, Zoia uses her knowledge of his homosexuality against him, making up a story of Ion 'upsetting guests with [his] queer behaviour' (43), just to add later that 'if he was thinking he could return to Romania and become a teacher of English in a secondary school, she would put paid to such notions –she could see to it as a matter of certainty he would not enter such profession' (43). Abashed, Ion finds a way out of his paralysis by handing her a €10 note, keeping his €50 tip hidden, and his disillusionment about his life in Ireland resurfaces once again when he phones his mother in Romania, 'keep[ing] the dream alive he might soon return' (46). A final irony is that, even though Zoia assumes that he migrated to Ireland because of Romania's homophobia, Ion lacks the freedoms that most Irish gays enjoy, so he would happily return home as a closeted homosexual rather than staying in an Irish society that relegates him to the underclass of the country's booming economy. McGuinness in this way breaks silences on the often invisibilised population of poor immigrants and illegal workers.

CONCLUSION

Overall, this chapter has explored gay narratives that share a desire to tell alternative stories to those sponsored by the dominant discourses of the Celtic Tiger years, which established a dichotomy between Ireland's conservative, backward past and a modern, prosperous, optimistic present for all. Tracing continuities between past and present, the narratives in this chapter refuse to conform to a complacent celebration of liberal Ireland. As observed, one common feature of these texts is their exploration of silence and the effects of social silencing. In this respect, these texts seem to follow a more general trend in Irish fiction. As theorised by Peach, the contemporary Irish novel often dramatises how previously marginalised groups like homosexuals, battered wives, victims of abuse, prostitutes and lower-class immigrants cannot easily cast off the marginalisation and stigmatisation to which they had been subjected, which explains why Irish writers, 'in bringing what has been silenced out of silence', generally dwell on the anxieties and uncertainties of the present moment (Peach, 2004: 221).

The texts in this chapter, as indicated, provide us with multi-layered approaches to gay life, complicating modern stereotypes of gay identity as middle-class, carefree, and sexually liberated. McGuiness's 'Chocolate and Oranges', for instance, features the struggles of an underclass, gay immigrant, whose main source of disempowerment is the social class oppression exerted by Ireland's neo-liberal economy. Issues of social class are also at stake in Ridgway's 'Angelo' and *The Parts*. Here, Ridgway not only foregrounds the vulnerability and grim experiences of his rent boy characters, but, through his gay protagonists' middle-class prejudices and agnosia with regard to prostitution, the author also portrays the effects of the social silencing of class oppression in contemporary Ireland. In Tóibín's 'The Pearl Fishers', the historical silencing of clerical abuse – the shame and subterfuge it involved – is compared with the traditional suppression and stigmatisation of homosexuality. These cultural legacies of silence, as explained in the analysis, reverberate in the present time of Tóibín's short story. Set in the 1990s, the other three novels – McKeon's *Tender*, Lennon's *Crazy Love* and Ridgway's *The Long Falling* – depict a time of rapid and self-conscious social change in Ireland. *Tender* and *Crazy Love* feature protagonists who embrace an imperfect and insecure sense of modernity, where reactionary attitudes of sexism and homophobia persist below appearances of tolerance and modernity. Ridgway's *The Long Falling*, on its part, recreates a scenario where the burdens of class oppression, sexism and homophobia coexist with the rapid emergence of a more liberal but still stratified society, whose values on social justice do not apply to all citizens equally. All in all, against the background of Celtic Tiger Ireland, these texts transcend social silences and articulate a cultural critique of the modern icon of gay life, with its exaggerated optimism, its generational and spatial divides, its correlation between gay identity and consumerism, its focus on individualism as the pretended cure for a past of shame, and its silencing of social class oppression and exploitation.

EIGHT

A Nation of the Heart

Queering the Past in Irish Historical Fiction

In a 2008 article Eibhear Walshe considered how the queer novels of 1990s Ireland were particularly concerned with their immediate context and the demarcation of gay and lesbian issues while, in contrast, the new century saw a renewed interest in historical fiction and the representation of queer culture and sexual dissidence beyond the confines of present-day configurations of gay and lesbian life. 'This return to historical fiction and to times of scrutiny and paranoia around homosexuality', Walshe explains, 'presents [Irish writers] with a metaphorical space in which to debate fixed categories of "gay" and "lesbian" matter in contemporary Irish culture' (2008: 140). Notably, these historical novels' exploration of times of suppression around homosexuality can also provide meaningful commentaries on the contemporary moment, as is the case in the works to be analysed in this chapter.

Gay and lesbian historical fiction, Norman W. Jonas explains, peers through history to find traces of homosexuality in the past, and then 'artistically fill[s] the gaps that evidence cannot supply' (2007: 2). Due to scant and/or largely distorted evidence, there is an inevitable sense of the unknowable in the gay and lesbian past. Nevertheless, as Jonas argues, historical fiction has the power to articulate 'embodied, participatory intuitions of the past' (32), which provide a contemporary vocabulary for conversing with 'history's ghosts' (101). For instance, in *Life Mask* (2004) Emma Donoghue addresses historical erasures regarding the lives of women, since in most cultures lesbian and bisexual women share a 'sense of deprivation at being denied a history' (Palmer, 1999: 207).[1] Moreover, in *Life Mask* the silence of lesbianism in eighteenth-century England somehow mirrors Irish lesbians' relative lack of social power in the early 2000s Ireland, 'a manifestation of which is her invisibility in the mass media' (Morrison et al., 2005: 242). Likewise, in *At Swim, Two Boys* (2001) Jamie O'Neill portrays homosexual comrades participating in the 1916 Rising, dramatizing how, despite being elided from the official narrative of Irish nationalism, 'gay men and lesbian women ha[d] been involved in the struggle for national liberation and independence as long as any other section of [Irish] people' (McClenaghan, 2002: 1062). O'Neill's rewriting of a central episode of Irish nationalism proves to be politically challenging; in the early 2000s, the highest levels of homophobia 'correlated positively with [people's] level of nationalism' and their 'investment in the Republic of Ireland and its hegemonic cultural values' (Morrison et al., 2005: 227).

Given the historical silencing of homosexuality in Ireland and elsewhere, there may be reasons to suspect that gay and lesbian lifestyles are only recent creations, made possible by the advent of liberal values. Nonetheless, for generations gays and lesbians have striven to assert their personal freedom. Significantly, the recovery of a queer past not only breaks the heterosexual consensus that had dominated in Ireland, but can also serve as an act of cultural empowerment, tracing the continuities between past and present while offering alternative renditions of non-heterosexual lives. In his Preface to *Coming Out: Irish Gay Experiences* (2003), a book containing the testimonies of people who grew up homosexual in a staunchly homophobic Ireland, Colm Tóibín explains that:

> Just as Irish identity or Jewish identity would be impossible to imagine without a sense of history, however gnarled and disputed that history might be, so too our past is important. The thin faint line that connects us with those of earlier generations, who lived happily despite everything or suffered in silence for the sin of being themselves, is a line we need to trace with greater definition on our road to liberty. (11)

This 'road to liberty,' as Tóibín relates, requires a profound reflection on the past, one which redresses historical wrongs and highlights examples of resilience. There is, therefore, a need for the public recognition of queer lives and experiences, past and present. As fiction writer, Tóibín himself painstakingly researched Henry James's life for his widely acclaimed *The Master* (2004), where he reclaims the American author's homosexuality and the considerable bearing it had on his work.

If in the early 2000s Tóibín maintained that many Irish gays and lesbians were unable 'to work out the implications of their oppression in their early lives' because they 'gr[ew] up alone; there [was] no history' (2001: 9), in recent years this cultural silence has been clearly undermined, the most obvious example being the same-sex marriage referendum campaign, which fostered the dissemination of personal testimonies within communities and in the mainstream media.[2] Yet the voices of those queer individuals who did not conform to the image of the 'respectable' sexual citizen were not to the forefront. Rachel Asher's analysis of the 2009 Irish Civil Partnership debate can therefore be extrapolated to the 2015 situation: 'The bisexual and transgendered members of the community are invisible and excluded when the debate over partnership rights intensifies, as are the relationships and family formations that exist outside of the romantic, monogamous, long-term, dyadic model' (2009: 483). Arguably, a homonormative model, which resembles ideal heterosexuality, imposed itself in both campaigns and bills.[3]

Opposing the limitations of homonormativity, one of the post-referendum novels in this chapter, Sebastian Barry's *Days Without End* (2016), gives centrality to transgender identity as a source of resistance against hetero-patriarchy. Barry's novel further offers a positive rendition of transgender motherhood, a type of queer kinship that has been marginalised in social debates about LGTBI+ rights. Closer to an Irish context (Barry's novel is set in nineteenth century America) is John Boyne's *The Heart's Invisible Furies* (2017). Published at a time when the country was receiving international praise as a beacon of gay rights,[4] Boyne's novel foregrounds the legacies of a recent history of repression, stigma and violence against Irish homosexuals.

All in all, this last chapter looks at novels which re-imagine the past in an attempt to unearth previously silenced voices, experiences and identities. Drawing on Jonas's study of the genre in the Anglo-American tradition, this analysis shall account for the ways in which Donoghue, Barry, O'Neill, and Boyne reconsider in their novels the characteristic topoi of gay and lesbian historical fiction ('identification', 'transformation' and 'chosen community'). In these texts, the protagonists' sexual identification and subsequent transformation constitute an 'ethical position' and 'a 'fundamental claim to knowledge', allowing them to transcend restrictive, oppressive principles about sexual behaviour (Jonas, 102). Of particular importance is how the protagonists' process of transformation goes hand in hand with their acquisition of a new language of same-sex love and affects.

EMMA DONOGHUE'S LIFE MASK

In *Life Mask*, Donoghue describes the life and times of the celebrated English sculptress Anne Damer in London, between the years 1787 and 1797. Much of Donoghue's novel concerns the protagonist's gradual transformation and identification as woman-loving, a process that ultimately brings self-knowledge and a newly gained ability to reverse a public language of shame, exclusion, and damnation regarding the vilified practice of 'Sapphism'. Set against the background of the French Revolution and the political tensions in England, the novel has been classified as neo-historical, a type of historical novel that creates 'new histories that are "authentic" in that they recognise their own narratives as problematically constructed but continue to function as (fictionalised) narratives that have something to say about the past as well as the present' (Harris, 2017: 194). Being neo-historical, *Life Mask* contains anachronistic terms expressed by British politicians, such as 'weapons of mass destruction' (436), which establish a parallel with 9/11 and the backlash provoked by the subsequent global fight on terrorism. Donoghue's dual temporalities – the late eighteenth century and its imagined connection with the early 2000s – recreate times of intense paranoia, of an increased fear of the other not only in relation to religion, social class and nationality,[5] but also gender and sexuality. It is perhaps no coincidence that, in Donoghue's account, Damer's sexuality comes under fierce public scrutiny precisely at a moment of exceptional 'political unrest' (Bensyl, 2009: 46).

Donoghue's *Life Mask* reconstructs Damer's lesbianism from secondary sources[6] like broadsides and sensationalist tabloids which spread rumours about her, and where she was derogatorily called a Sapphist. The voice of those tabloids is imaginatively incorporated in the novel through the fictitious newspaper *The Beau Monde Inquirer*, a mouthpiece of the English establishment. Fragments from *Beau Monde* feature as introductions to each chapter, offering a wider perspective on the sociocultural climate of the time. Other than that, Donoghue's neo-historical method largely relies on a realist mode – here, an impersonal third-person narrator relating events and experiences chronologically and with precision – which conveys a sense of 'a broadly coherent narrative' (Harris, 194). As shall be argued, the writer's detailed recreation of late eighteenth-century England gives ample evidence of the hetero-patriarchal constraints affecting Anne Damer and other female characters.

To foreground patriarchal oppression, Donoghue has Damer suffer men's sexism long before any intimations of same-sex desire appear. The protagonist flouts feminine norms, and consequently her behaviour is regarded as an affront to male prerogatives. Childless and widowed at a young age, Damer emerges as an unconventional and exceptionally independent woman even within her elitist milieu, where married women who fail to bear a male heir, like Georgiana, are subjected to 'electric shocks and milk baths' (92). Damer devotes herself to sculpture, a 'downright unfeminine' occupation (195), and her prominence is resented by male colleagues who accuse her of using 'ghosts', that is, 'men to help her on the sly' (243). Underlying all those rumours is the patriarchal condemnation of women who step into areas of male privilege and refuse to submit to male authority. Both Damer's independence and gender nonconformism bring accusations against her in the first place.

At that time, Donoghue notes in *Passions Between Women* (1993), lesbian desire was hardly understood as leading towards a new sexual identification but was primarily seen as disrupting 'conventions of femininity', turning same-sex attracted women into 'odd, sinful, unwomanly, even monstruous' in the eyes of society (22). *Life Mask* draws on this social discourse and illustrates how any type of female rebellion could lead to allegations of sexual impropriety, like the practice of Sapphism, of 'man-hating' females who 'haunt their own sex' (208). This lesbophobic insult is inextricable from notions of patriarchal oppression and becomes attached to Damer and the popular actress Elizabeth Farren once their romantic friendship arises the suspicions of the public (Farren, for example, refuses to become engaged to the powerful Lord Derby, thus denying him his patriarchal dividend). At the pinnacle of her friendship with Damer, Farren becomes the victim of a cruel epigram:

> Her little stock of private fame
> Will fall a wreck to public clamour,
> If Farren leagues with one whose name
> Comes near – aye, very near – to DAMN HER[7] (210)

Vulnerable to public opinion, Farren temporarily breaks contact with Damer, not on moral grounds, but because she 'couldn't afford this friendship' (227), as it endangers her career and social position. Both characters had read Mary Wollstonecraft together, and talked about women's need to 'resist oppression' (214), but when Farren is attacked while performing at Drury Lane, 'There was a shout from the pit: "Tommy!"'[8] (453), she is forced to put an end to their friendship. For over 200 pages, Donoghue had detailed the mutual admiration and growing intimacy between Damer and Farren (to the point that lesbian desire is suggested though not enacted), so the actress's self-preservation and abandonment of her friend may well emphasise the interconnections between social structure and agency, when affected by 'the power of homophobia in hetero-patriarchal society' (O'Callaghan, 2012: 143).

Another consequence of this hetero-patriarchal system is Damer's lack of a language and awareness to understand her same-sex desires, a situation which, for much of the story, hampers her identification as woman-loving. Concurrently, Donoghue dramatises how the homophobic discourse of time both denied and recognised the existence of female same-sex desire. In *The Beau Monde Inquirer*, this desire is described as a 'fantastical vice', which, like the liberal ideas of the French Revolution, was 'spreading across Europe' (208). The same *Beau Monde* cautions its readers about the 'impossibilities' that may occur 'whenever two Ladies live too much together', especially if those ladies are 'women [who] demand their Rights' (467). Due to its potential to undermine patriarchy, the feminist resistance arising from female friendships, whether sexual or not, is equated with sexual transgression and a foreign influence to be kept at bay. Yet these contradictory, almost paranoid, messages – Sapphism as an 'impossibility', but a real threat to the system – do create a more visible, albeit damaging, discourse of female same-sex desire, which, as Claire O'Callaghan observes drawing on Foucault (136), has the potential to be appropriated and then reversed by the individual. Damer's process of sexual identification thus begins after her crisis with Farren (when they are publicly condemned as Sapphists) and develops later in her friendship with Mary Anne Berry.

For a long time, Damer can only express her admiration of female beauty through art, but, when the accusations of Sapphism appear, her personal turmoil seems to reveal some repressed truth about herself: 'Truth was knocking in her head like the beak of a chick, cracking the egg from the inside' (287). When she falls in love with Berry, the protagonist's eventual recognition of her Sapphism – 'I am what they call me' (523) – not only signals her sexual identification, but also constitutes Damer's 'fundamental claim to knowledge' (Jonas, 102), making her re-assess and reverse the discourse of homophobia and its lies: 'This was a strange and overwhelming feeling, a sort of whirlwind, but where was the real harm in that?' (559). Berry, though, has not completed the same 'transformation' yet. As their relationship evolves, Berry learns to accept her feelings for Damer, but experiences their desires as unspeakable:

> 'To speak of things changes them,' said Mary, watching Anne like a cat. 'All day I've waiting as if for a storm–'
> 'What kind of storm?'
> 'Guilt, I suppose. Shame. Self-loathing. All that wretchedness.'
> Anne's mouth tightened over each word.
> 'But the storm hasn't come,' Mary assured her. 'Only, I fear it may if we speak.'
> (560)

Berry fears that talking about her love-making with Damer will only bring the shameful connotations of Sapphism into their relationship, so she retreats into self-defensive silence. Donoghue in this way addresses 'the problem of naming' (Jonas, 38), present in much gay and lesbian historical fiction, and has Damer acknowledge that 'she couldn't have named the terms' of their relationship (558). Yet, by this time Damer has fully embraced the mystery of same-sex love, and stakes her ethical claim to build a future together with Berry: 'This wasn't evil, this wasn't debauchery. It was love made flesh' (561). By emphasising the protagonist's transformation and commitment to a new life, Donoghue's *Life Mask*, as Walshe puts it, re-imagines Anne Damer as a historical example of 'an earlier lesbian selfhood' (2008: 145).

As discussed in Chapter One, a lesbian life requires women to be independent from men, a situation that illustrates how sexuality is culturally contingent, and can hardly be disentangled from issues of power, social class, and gender norms. *Life Mask* depicts a time prior to the emergence of lesbianism as a social and political category, which developed at the turn of the twentieth century 'through a series of economic, demographic, and social changes, such as the possibility of women's financial independence' (Stulberg, 2018: 9). This financial independence (as the story closes, Damer inherits Strawberry Hill from her bachelor uncle, Horace Walpole)[9] is what makes the lesbian relationship possible, allowing Damer and Berry a private space away from society's homophobia.

Though set in the eighteenth century, *Life Mask* also speaks to a recent past, to the Ireland where Donoghue grew up as a lesbian. As explained in Chapters One and Two, 1980s Ireland was a staunchly patriarchal and Catholic society where many women either remained subjugated to male authority or suffered the terrible consequences of their transgression. If in 1980s Ireland homosexuality was regarded as anti-Irish and a foreign influence, in Donoghue's depiction of eighteenth-century Britain same-sex desire was similarly considered an 'Oriental vice' (326). Likewise, in both cultural contexts, lesbianism was a largely unknown and, at times, non-viable lifestyle, as 'society ha[d] no structures to protect or accommodate [lesbians]' (Laing, 1985: 17). Even in the late 1990s, a time closer to the publication of *Life Mask*, Irish lesbian activists were still concerned with issues of 'making visible a lesbian identity' (O'Donnell, 2008: 18). This issue of lesbian (in)visibility, past and present, seems to inform Donoghue's rewriting of Anne Damer's biography. In *Life Mask*, Donoghue celebrates Damer's non-conformity and sexual dissidence, thereby reclaiming a lesbian icon of the past and undermining the historical silences on women's lives and sexual passions.

SEBASTIAN BARRY'S DAYS WITHOUT END

Like Donoghue's *Life Mask*, Sebastian Barry's *Days Without End* is set outside Ireland, but also speaks to an Irish context. *Days Without End* portrays the gore and brutality of the nineteenth-century American-Indian wars, from the perspective of the Sligonian Thomas McNulty, who escaped the Ireland of the Great Famine (1845–52).[10] Barry's story, which at times departs from a realist mode and reads like a fantasy tale, transmits the voice and perceptions of the protagonist, in a first-person narration that gives readers direct access to the character's transformation and personal growth.

In the story, Barry's famished protagonist, like many other young men used as instruments of destruction, enters the army because he was 'sick of hungering' (2), but later realises the 'damn foolishness' of war (97), and ends up discovering a connection between the extermination of Native Americans and that of the Irish by British colonisers:[11] 'When that old ancient Cromwell come to Ireland he said he would leave nothing alive. Said the Irish were vermin and devils. Clean out the country for good people to step into' (263). Amidst the atrocities of the American-Indian wars, Barry's protagonist finds self-worth thanks to his chosen community, or queer family, consisting of his 'beau', John Cole, and an orphaned Indian girl, Winona, whom Thomas (or, better said, Thomasina, the character's name in drag) treats as 'a daughter not a daughter but who [she] mother[s] best [she] can' (275). In Barry's follow-up *A Thousand Moons* (2020), an eighteen-year-old Winona, having grown up under the loving care of John and Thomas(ina), takes central stage and becomes ready to retrace her cultural dispossession as a Native American.

Barry, as a playwright and fiction writer, had previously engaged with history from the perspective of marginal individuals, examining gender issues that bring to light forgotten aspects of the past, as in the case of *The Secret Scripture* (2008), which revolves around Roseanne (a member of the McNulty clan, like Thomas), a victim of patriarchal Ireland in the 1920s revolutionary years, who writes her autobiography while locked in a mental hospital. If *The Secret Scripture* was inspired by a dark family secret, *Days Without End* similarly originated from a family revelation, though a much more positive one, when Barry's son, Toby, came out as gay to him. One important lesson Barry learned from his son was that 'gay men from tough backgrounds sometimes used [drag] as a form of empowerment' (Moss, 2017). In the figure of Thomas McNulty in *Days Without End*, Barry historicises the presence of drag and the freedoms it has always offered. As in other places, drag has had a long, albeit silenced, history in Ireland. Jeannine Woods (2018), for instance, documents how, prior to their suppression by the Irish Catholic Church, the games performed at the old wake rituals 'encompass[ed] shifts between genders' (31), and served to 'destabilise fixed gender dichotomies and heteronormative hierarchies' (17).[12]

As shall be explained in what follows, in *Days Without End* drag works as a counter discourse against some of the foundational myths of the American West, that is, 'the national dream of masculinity, conquest, and white power' (Campbell, 2018: 239). Norms of gender and sexuality, and their associated hierarchies of power and authority, become inoperative under the theatricality of drag performance. Even if in the story drag initially appears as a form of entertainment that does not openly challenge people's prejudices, Thomas eventually learns that embodying Thomasina remains the only means by which he can display his sexual love for John publicly:

> They know I am a man because they have read it on the bill. But I am suspecting that everyone of them would like to touch and now John Cole is their ambassador of kisses [. . .] Down down we go under them waters of desire. Every last man, young and old, wants John Cole to touch my face, hold my narrow shoulders, put his mouth against my lips. Handsome John Cole, my beau. Our love in plain sight. (132)

Acting as Thomasina at a saloon, Barry's protagonist arouses the attraction and admiration of rough miners who, for some minutes, 'loved a woman that ain't a real woman' (133), a spell that is broken the moment the performance is over, and the audience crosses the 'borderland of [the] act, the strange frontier' (132). Through Thomas's voice, drag emerges as a liberatory act; momentarily, 'notions are cast off' and the protagonists and their audience enjoy 'a kind of delicious freedom' (133). Drag becomes here a queer performative where same-sex desire is both seen and not seen. Even in its obliqueness, in not making too obvious what it represents (not only the desire between the protagonists, but also the audience's desire for Thomas's feminised male body), drag clearly undermines heteronormative masculinity.

Talking about *Days Without End*, Barry pointed out that, in this heteronormative nineteenth-century America, none of his characters has the vocabulary to identify as gay or trans because 'it wasn't until the 1880s or 1990s when psychiatry was being born that doctors started to put names on these things' (Jordan, 2016). The novel thus takes readers to a time previous to the rise of male homosexuality as a medical problem. Coinciding with the growth of medicine, the final decades of the nineteenth century 'saw the association of "effeminacy" with [male] homosexuality and the demonization of both" (Conrad, 2001: 127). Barry's story works against these associations, which persist today and formed the bases of twentieth century homophobia and transphobia. His protagonist, for example, sees himself as a different 'sort of man', but no less manly than others. When admiring a female friend's beauty, he observes that 'it's like being bathed in flames just looking at her, and I ain't even that sort of man would like to kiss her' (87). Thomas himself crosses gender boundaries relatively easily, and expresses his love for John without any sense of moral conflict. Yet in the America the author recreates there were sodomy laws, which explains the two lovers' need for secrecy and discretion about their sexual acts. The text thus gives almost no space to the protagonists' intimacy as a gay couple,[13] in contrast to the physical affection between the two when Thomas turns into Thomasina.

Because of the freedoms associated with embodying Thomasina, drag offers the protagonist a chance to recognise and embrace a transgender identity, which facilitates the beginning of a new life, together with his chosen community. Similar to what happens in other gay and lesbian historical novels, Thomas's transformation in *Days Without End* brings self-knowledge and a firm ethical decision to resist society's dominant values on gender, sexuality and race.

To complete this transformation, a key influence on Barry's protagonist is his encounter with the Two Spirit people: '[I] spied out the wondrous kind called by the Indians *winkte* or by white men *berdache*, braves dressed in the finery of squaws' (68). If under US settler colonialism Native Americans' general acceptance of 'multiple genders' had marked them all as abject and queer 'by projecting fears of sodomy on them that justified terrorizing violence' (Morgensen, 2010: 109), Barry's protagonist develops a sense of kinship with Indians thanks to the admiration he feels towards the *winkte*, because of how they experience gender fluidity as part of their everyday lives. This newly gained affinity propels his most heroic action in the story, when, as a soldier, Thomas saves the Native American girl, Winona, from being killed, just to re-emerge later as Thomasina and escape with her, behaving as her mother: 'Them Indians in dresses shown my path' (273). This 'path' shown by the two-spirited *winkte*, as the protagonist realises right after saving Winona, is also a path towards self-realisation: 'Maybe I was born a man growing into a woman' (273).

Inspired by the *winkte*'s language on gender fluidity, Thomas(ina)'s rebellions illustrate how drag can work as a philosophy of life and a strategy against social control. When war is over, the exultant John and Thomas decide to 'tie the knot' the only way they can, through drag:

> There's a half-blind preacher in a temple called Bartram House and I don my best dress and me and John Cole go there and we tie the knot. Rev. Hindle he say the lovely words and John Cole kiss the bride and then it's done and who to know. Maybe you could read it in their holy book, John Cole and Thomasina McNulty wed this day of our Lord Dec. 7th 1866. (204)

Notably, although at the saloon Thomasina was only an 'illusion' (9), she now becomes a name 'you could read in [the] holy book.' Marriage thus makes Thomasina's existence official, granting her legitimacy as John's wife. The situation allows Thomas(ina) to explore further options in life, and certainly facilitates the character's adoption of a transgender identity as Winona's loving mother, at least within the privacy of the home.

While Barry's depiction of John's and Thomasina's wedding seems to be informed by current values of homo-inclusion, the writer's queering of the family goes beyond notions of sexual equality to create an alternative value system, one which challenges the ideology of American settler colonialism. In a blatantly racist America, the queerest element of this queer family is Winona. As they ride through Indiana, the family receives the quizzical stares of many people, surprised as they are to see two white men taking care of an Indian girl: 'One big boozy red-faced charlatan soul one place laughing at us and saying looks like we travelling with our whore' (207).[14] The novel portrays how, in a context of savage exploitation of women and dehumanisation of Native Americans, this queer family becomes the girl's only salvation and means to prosper as a human being. After all, as Thomasina reflects about herself and John, 'the point is we living like a family' (135), and, as such, 'half of our pride is in Winona and the other half in our work and in ourselves' (229).

JAMIE O'NEILL'S AT SWIM, TWO BOYS

As indicated above, Barry's *Days Without End* draws on well-known values of modern life (e.g., marriage and romantic monogamy as morally superior), but because it revises received notions of race, class, gender, sexuality, and kinship, emphasising how they work against the dominant ideology, Barry's story seems to stress difference rather than assimilation, or sameness. This contrast between difference and sameness (and its implications) will inform the latter part of the analysis of Jamie O'Neill's *At Swim, Two Boys*, which like Barry's *Days Without End*, revolves around the romantic and egalitarian relationship between the central characters. Same-sex love stories were definitely less common in 2001, the time *At Swim, Two Boys* came out, than they are now. According to John Boyne in his introduction to a 2017 edition of O'Neill's book, the commercial success of *At Swim, Two Boys* increased the visibility of gay love in early 2000s Ireland, a time when gay relationships too often felt 'clandestine' instead of 'perfectly normal' (vi). For some critics, *At Swim, Two Boys* counts as a literary landmark within contemporary Irish fiction, since O'Neill's appropriation of the (by then) 'emphatically heterosexual genre' of historical romance inaugurates a tradition of gay historical fiction in Ireland (Medd, 2007: 23).

Set in the context of the 1916 Rising, *At Swim, Two Boys* centres on the love story between two teenagers, the rebel, working-class Doyler Doyle and the more candid Jim Mack, the son of a shopkeeper. As their friendship deepens and their love grows, so does their commitment to fight for Ireland. Their swimming to the Muglins island, where they raise a green flag and make love for the first time, becomes a cry for freedom and, as the author himself remarks, a 'metaphor for Ireland's struggle and for the boys' own struggle just to be, to find some place to be' (O'Neill, 2015). A third protagonist, the dandyish, Wildean figure Anthony MacMurrough also undergoes his own transformation, as he evolves from being a solitary gay man who exploits youngsters – he prostitutes Doyler – to becoming the two boys' comrade and protector.

Best known for *At Swim, Two Boys*, Jamie O'Neill is also the author of *Disturbance* (1989) and *Kilbrack* (1990), two novels which, while not being historical, are similarly concerned with the male protagonists' quest for their 'true identities' in extraordinarily difficult circumstances (Oliva, 2014: 186). Among its many merits, *At Swim, Two Boys* excels in its poetic language, which, according to Declan Kiberd finds echoes of Joyce's *Ulysses* (1922) and Sean O'Casey's autobiographies. For Kiberd, O'Neill's finest technique here is his use of free indirect discourse and interior monologue, making readers 'see most of the protagonists as they would ideally see themselves' (2001). The story thus deviates from the realist mode by concentrating on the main characters' ideals, hopes and dreams against a background of social and political strife.

Notably, *At Swim, Two Boys* is not just a gay rewriting of the Rising, but it is also rich in cultural, historical, and intertextual references which foreground a 'literary heritage of Irish sexual dissidence' through frequent allusions to figures such as Oscar Wilde, Roger Casement and Pádraig Pearse among others (Valente, 2005: 66). Through his extensive use of intertextuality,[15] O'Neill also constructs a cultural scenario that imagines plausible alternatives to the rigid moral system that became the norm after independence. In this respect, the story's final tragedy – both boys die at war – may well symbolise the eventual emergence of a reactionary state whose 'logic of sexual shame [. . .] confined purportedly vicious young people [like O'Neill's heroes] within Magdalen laundries or industrial schools' (Backus, 2008: 80).

In opposition to this 'logic of sexual shame', gay love takes here the shape of heroic friendship, which David Halperin defines as a homoerotic tradition characterised by 'disinterested love' and a 'readiness to die with or for the other' (2013: 271). Described throughout the text as pure and unbreakable, the boys' friendship predates their same-sex desires. Their sexual awakening grows parallel to their nationalist sentiment, so, when Jim manifests his willingness to join the Citizen Army, this also becomes his love declaration for Doyler: 'I love him. I'm sure of that now. And he's my country' (435). Far from being perverse, shameful or emasculating, gay love in *At Swim, Two Boys* endorses masculine and nationalist ideals like honour, courage, fraternity and self-determination. If nationalisms typically evoked male prowess and comradeship to establish a 'goal – to achieve statehood – and a belief in collective commonality' (Nagel, 1998: 247), O'Neill's protagonists can be seen to embody such ideals, precisely at a time when national identity was under construction. Thus, when Doyler reminds his friend that the English had MacMurrough in jail for his love of another man, and that the Irish would do the same to him, Jim responds: 'Not in my country they won't' (586). Out of his desire to protect his chosen community (Doyler and MacMurrough), Jim makes his ethical claim to fight for a more inclusive and tolerant Ireland.[16]

Drawing on Christopher Nealon's study of pre-Stonewall gay and lesbian writing, Jodie Medd argues that O'Neill makes use of a 'foundling' metaphor (4), whereby homosexual characters escape the isolation and pathologisation imposed on them by the inversion model, just to progress towards a sense of a chosen community with other queer individuals. This situation, as Nealon puts it, allows these characters to 'feel connected to history' on new grounds (2001: 177). Arguably, colonial Ireland experienced a similar process, its own 'foundling' metaphor, since Irish nationalists sought to reverse the 'pathologized racial femininity' foisted on the nation under British rule, in their fight to reclaim a new version of history and Irishness (Valente, 2011: 15).[17] Rejecting this 'racial femininity', Irish nationalism, like other European nationalisms, 'evolved parallel to modern masculinity', to the extent that these movements 'adopted the masculine stereotype as a means of [their] self-representation' (Mosse, 1996: 7). While researching for *At Swim, Two Boys*,[18] O'Neill discovered that, in the nationalist zeal that led to revolution in 1910s Ireland, there was an element of the homoerotic, subsumed into discourses of manly resolution, courage and sacrifice for the nation. Even though Irish nationalism had a distinct gay/homoerotic presence,[19] homosexuality was regarded as anti-Irish for much of the twentieth century. Gay sexuality, on the contrary, emerges as noble, patriotic, and respectable in *At Swim, Two Boys*.

As expected from a story set in the early twentieth century, the novel recreates a time after (not before, as in Barry's *Days Without End*) the emergence of homosexuality as a category of knowledge, when male romantic friendships had already become suspicious of sexual love. The policing of these close friendships, as Foucault theorised,[20] became vital for twentieth-century hegemonic masculinity, with its disavowal of male-to-male tenderness and intimacy, both physical and emotional. In O'Neill's story, the knowledgeable MacMurrough perceives the boys' mutual attraction while observing them swimming in the sea like 'mating ducks' (264), and then begins an interior dialogue with the late Scrotes (his beloved friend and lover, who died of hard labour):

– You know, he said to Scrotes, I remember at my school the monks discouraged particular friendships. Particular friendships they condemned, if not as sin, as occasions gravid with its potential.

– Friendship tending to love may tend to desire, said Scrotes.

– Yes, but desire was there anyway. We all desired. We were riven with it. The monks policed friendship but all they effected was a sexual abandon. Instead of fumbling with love, we fumbled in the dark. (265)

MacMurrough – who had been in prison for 'the love that dare not speak its name'[21] (438) – thus explains that, due to this policing, gay sexuality could no longer be expressed through romantic friendships, so, instead, male lovers had to fumble 'in the dark.' In the course of the story, the boys have to struggle against this enforced 'darkness', and their romantic friendship is constantly put to the test by the Church and the military. When Brother Polycarp tries to convince Jim that he has a religious vocation, the boy soon realises that he cannot separate himself from Doyler, as his friend is his real 'vocation' (135). Doyler, as a soldier, temporarily distances himself from Jim (he almost betrays his promise to swim with him to the island), and begins to internalise a rhetoric of military sacrifice and resolution, but the memory of his friend revives his devotion towards him: 'I try to make him go away, for I'm a soldier now and I'm under orders. But he's always there and I'm desperate to hold him. I doubt I'm a man except he's by me' (498).

As in other gay and lesbian historical fictions (*Days Without End* and *Life Mask* are no exceptions), sexual identification in *At Swim, Two Boys* not only involves a choice to heed the 'call' of same-sex desire, but also the adoption a of new 'spiritual worldview' (Jonas, 114). This second step is fundamental, because, in the cultural context of the novel, homosexuality was 'too shamefully vicious and ignoble to "speak its name"' (Valente, 2005: 74), as illustrated by Jim's growing awareness of the sinfulness of his desires. In one tragicomic scene, a confused old priest hears Jim's confession, but fails (or refuses) to understand that the boy's 'sins of impurity' concern Doyler, not a girl (411). For a time, like Joyce's Stephen in *A Portrait* (1916), Jim bears the burden of shame and religious condemnation, as he believes that 'what he had done was so sinful, so unspeakably so, [. . .] that the Church [. . .] had not thought to provide against its happening' (412).

As is obvious, prior to their transformation, Jim and Doyler need to find a language adequate to the profundity of their emotions. MacMurrough, the adult gay, provides them with such language by sharing stories of ancient Greece. An inner voice, in the image of Scrotes, tells MacMurrough:

Help these boys build a nation of their own. Ransack the histories for clues to their past. Plunder the literatures for words they can speak. And should you encounter an ancient tribe whose customs, however dimly, cast light on their hearts, tell them that tale; and you shall name the unspeakable names of your kind, and in that naming, in each such telling, they will falter a step into the light. (329)

Thanks to MacMurrough, the boys transcend the injurious language of shame attached to gay desire, discovering a sense of a gay history and identity in ancient Greece, which, in turn, helps them 'build a nation of their own.' References to ancient Greece were also common within the early gay liberationist movements and served to counteract gay men's perceived lack of masculinity and respectability. For better or worse, George L. Mosse explains, 'the frequent references to Greece as legitimizing homosexuality led to a strong reaffirmation of the male stereotype' (1996: 149). O'Neill's characters do embody characteristics of the 'male stereotype,' but the main purpose of McMurrough's tales of Greek love is to offer a mirror to the boys' mutual devotion.

O'Neill's MacMurrough, who speaks of the Sacred Band of Thebes, a Greek army of male lovers, is influenced by the cultural movement of Hellenism, which originated from the revalorisation of ancient Greek art in the late nineteenth century.[22] Unsurprisingly, MacMurrough identifies himself (and is identified) with Oscar Wilde (also an Hellenist), an identification that also reminds us how the Wilde's trials in 1895 'created a public image for the homosexual, and a terrifying tale of the dangers that trailed closely behind deviant behavior' (Weeks, cited in Gittins, 1993: 147). In a conversation with an old friend who is involved in the Irish nationalist movement, MacMurrough courageously admits that, when incarcerated in England, he 'was guilty as charged':

> 'Damn it all, MacMurrough, are you telling me you are an unspeakable of the Oscar Wilde sort?'
> 'If you mean am I Irish, the answer is yes.' (309)

Interestingly, MacMurrough, who had been isolated from the national struggle, not only affirms his gay identity here, but also reclaims both his and Wilde's Irishness. For MacMurrough, Wilde emerges as a true patriot, as this writer's irreverence towards Victorian social mores helps him reconcile his homosexuality with his Irishness. As the story closes, MacMurrough equates the rebels' public shaming after the Rising with the one that Wilde suffered after his conviction, 'when Wilde too had been paraded for the crowd' (640). O'Neill therefore effects in his novel a 'nationalizing of Wilde,' reimagining him as an 'empowering queer presence' (Walshe, 2005: 46).

From the viewpoint of contemporary queer politics, *At Swim, Two Boys* might be read as a gay novel that stresses sameness rather than difference, since, in the story, gay love supplements notions of masculinity and nationalism (the opposite happens in *Days Without End*, and, in *Life Mask*, the lesbian couple, though economically empowered, remains on the fringes of society). Read in this light, O'Neill's novel endorses a homonormative culture. In his review, Halperin seems to give no support to such view, as he argues that the novel goes against the grain of an over-sexualised post-liberation gay male culture: 'The turn to romantic friendship and the new emphasis on the tender, loving side of male homosexuality are refreshing' (2003). Michael G. Cronin, on his part, contends that *At Swim, Two Boys* is homonormative, as there is an alliance in the novel between national and sexual identity, and Doyler and Jim fit into the stereotype of the respectable gay citizen of today's Ireland (2020: 578). Yet, whether homonormative or not, O'Neill's immensely popular novel did offer a powerful representation of gay love for its early 2000s readership, less than a decade after decriminalisation, in a still rampantly homophobic Ireland.

In its solidity and mutual devotion, gay love resembles ideal marriage in *At Swim, Two Boys* – and same-sex marriage is usually seen as homo-normative, since this alleged 'heterosexualization of gay culture' further marginalises alternative lifestyles (Ghaziani, 2011: 100). O'Neill's story hints at this marriage-like bond between the boys when, after his sexual relationship with Doyler, Jim asks MacMurrough: 'I never thought of it before and then I wondered, is it this way you'd be with a wife?' (550). As is also suggested in another scene, Jim craves for the domesticity and ordinariness of married life:

> 'I'm just thinking that would be pleasant. To be reading, say, out of a book, and you to come up and touch me – my neck, say, or my knee – and I'd carry on reading, I might let a smile, no more, wouldn't lose my place on the page. It would be pleasant to come to that. We'd come so close, do you see, that I wouldn't be surprised out of myself everytime you touched.' (583)

Even if O'Neill's novel has characteristics of a homonormative narrative, this sameness of gay love does have an undeniable subversive edge in highly homophobic contexts where homosexuality comes to be defined as the abject other of heterosexuality. To enforce this difference, for example, homo-sexual lives had been for long stereotyped as 'inherently tragic' (Woods, 1998: 359), especially after the 1895 downfall of Wilde, so gay love and self-fulfilment became even more transgressive than homosexuality itself.

Though *At Swim Two, Two Boys* ends tragically, much of the story concentrates on the romantic, egalitarian bond between the protagonists, as well their happiness when they are together. O'Neill portrays gay love as heroic rather than tragic, and this heroic nature of homosexuality in the context of the story works against cultural narratives that suppressed and stigmatised gay love in the first place. Ultimately, O'Neill's focus is on a sexual rebellion that blends into a political vision; the boys' desire to found 'a nation of the heart' (329).

JOHN BOYNE'S THE HEART'S INVISIBLE FURIES

Set in the second half of twentieth century up to the 2010s, John Boyne's *The Heart's Invisible Furies* (2017) informs us readers why Jamie O'Neill's gay heroes, Jim and Doyler, would have found it impossible to live as a happy couple in the decades following Irish independence. A prolific author, internationally renowned for his young adult novel *The Boy in the Striped Pyjamas* (2006), Boyne recently decided to speak about his trauma of growing up gay in a Catholic school environment, 'it was not easy', he said, 'to be a young, gay teenager and to be told that you're sick' (Boyne, 2014). In 2014 he published *The History of Loneliness*, a novel told from the perspective of a priest who regrets his previous silences regarding child abuse within the Church. Boyne continues to explore the wrongs of Catholic Ireland in *The Heart's Invisible Furies,* which investigates the recent past through the life story and first-person narration of its central character, Cyril Avery. *The Heart's Invisible Furies* has its genesis in the same-sex marriage referendum, when Boyne watched a RTÉ report where a 90-year-old man, visibly moved, came out of the polling booth, and told a journalist: 'It's too late for me, but not for others' (Leonard, 2017). One of Boyne's intentions, as he relates, was to write 'a condemnation of Ireland for allowing a life like that to happen' (Leonard, 2017).

Even though the narrative occasionally dwells on the tragic, for much of the story Boyne makes use of humour and sarcasm to condemn Catholic Ireland's hypocrisy and double standards. Boyne traces a history of oppression and anti-gay prejudice, but the story is perhaps too dependent on exaggeration, flat characters, implausible coincidences and, at times, excessive melodrama and repetition (to move the story forward, Boyne has several characters die of beatings). In a chapter set in the 1940s, an infuriated, unrepentant man beats up his gay son, causing his death, but 'the jury set him free, finding that his crime had been committed under the extreme provocation of having a mentally disordered son' (56).

In many scenes, as the one above, Boyne stresses for his contemporary readership the effects of homosexual pathologisation in mid twentieth-century Ireland, and how an excessive focus on suppression meant that homosexuality 'was not regularly discussed or acknowledged publicly' (Ferriter, 2009: 391).[23] Such suppression is exemplified in a chapter where a doctor assures the protagonist, Cyril, that 'there are no homosexuals in Ireland' (219).[24] Upon Cyril's insistence that he wants to be cured of his 'disgusting urges' (218), the doctor subjects him to aversion therapy,[25] which only proves to be a deeply hurtful and humiliating experience: 'I stumbled out, barely able to walk and with tears rolling down my cheeks' (223). Though in Boyne's text this medical treatment seems to feature as an ordinary one (Cyril himself asks to be treated), in Ireland aversion therapy did not become as common as it was in other places like Germany and Britain. This exceptionalism, B. D. Kelly suggests (2017), seems to have been caused not so much by Irish psychiatrists' enlightened views, but by their reticence to openly acknowledge the existence of homosexuality.[26]

While describing 1960s/1970s Ireland 'a backward hole of a country' (336), Boyne also dramatises how the relative invisibility of homosexuality allowed certain freedoms, since, for same sex attracted men, 'satisfying [one's] lust wasn't a problem' (211). Like the stories analysed in Chapter Three, Boyne's novel depicts cruising sites as the only social outlet available for gay men in those years. Yet, whereas these short stories highlight moments of empathy and connection within cruising areas, *The Heart's Invisible Furies* feels morally conservative in this respect, as Boyne repeatedly insists on the loneliness and frustrations derived from cruising, a despair which Cyril can only alleviate when he manages to take a man home and have sex with him in a more romantic way: 'I felt warmth and friendship and happiness, and all this for a stranger' (214). Despite his cravings for love, Cyril is always careful not to reveal himself as gay or be open about his life, not even with his sexual partners, for fear of people's aggression, cruelty and rejection.

Similar to some of the works analysed in Chapters Four and Five, Boyne's text explores a recent history of gay exile and migration, of Irish homosexuals who found new freedoms abroad. Though sexual identification is never an issue in *The Heart's Invisible Furies* – in his adolescence, Cyril had already begun 'to come to terms with who [he] was' (176) –, the protagonist's transformation can only start the moment he decides to abandon a life of subterfuge in Ireland (he was going to marry a woman) and migrate to Holland. In Amsterdam, which 'feels more like home [. . .] than Ireland' (330), Cyril at last finds a loving partner, Bastiaan. In these episodes, Boyne underlines the (perhaps idealised) tolerance and openness of the Dutch, and uses Cyril's experience abroad to deepen his attack on a Catholic Ireland where his protagonist remained 'frightened of his sexuality, of sex itself' (Wright, 2017). Another section of the novel takes Bastiaan and Cyril to 1980s New York, where the protagonist witnesses the AIDS crisis, and again confronts Irish narrow-mindedness when his HIV-infected friend from Dublin, Julian, dies at hospital. Ashamed of his 'gay disease' and unable to disclose his illness to his family (377), the heterosexual Julian is obviously affected by the high levels of prejudice, ignorance and misinformation surrounding the virus.[27]

Approximately a third of the story develops outside Ireland, just to have the protagonist return alone to Dublin after gay decriminalisation (Bastiaan is killed in New York by a gang of gay-bashers). As already noted, Cyril's expatriation became fundamental for his transformation, maturation and self-acceptance as a gay man, as it saved him from leading a 'life-time of lying' (299). Back in Ireland, Cyril defends this new ethical position by openly living as a gay man who, when learning of other Irish men's double lives, emphatically refuses to comply with their need for discretion: 'I spent enough of my life lying to people and hiding away. I'm not going down that road again' (483). In the final pages, Boyne does depict the more open-minded attitudes of the 1990s and 2000s, but this portrayal is not excessively optimistic. Habits of deceit and duplicity persist, and the protagonist remains loveless until his death.

As the story of a gay man's life, *The Heart's Invisible Furies* emphasises the historical wrongs and injustices against homosexuals in a very recent past where they were customarily dehumanised and treated as sick, immoral people. As noted above, though, the story at times breaks the principles of verisimilitude due to its heavy dependence on awkward coincidences, clichés and one-dimensional characters. In spite of this, Boyne's novel may work as a warning against present-day complacency, reminding its readers of a not-so-distant past where gays were simply not permitted to live and love as others did.

CONCLUSION

The four novels analysed in this final chapter situate homosexuality and sexual dissidence in a variety of historical, transnational, and political contexts, offering a revisioning of the past that epitomises the growing recognition and valorisation of gay and lesbian experiences in contemporary Ireland. This cultural revision, as Colm Tóibín argues, is fundamental because it constructs a 'sense of history' which traces the 'thin faint line that connects [homosexuals] with those of earlier generations' (2003: 11), in an Ireland where, until recently, gay desire was pathologised and lesbianism was rendered invisible. These historical narratives describe times when there was no public language adequate to the protagonists' same-sex love and passions. The cultural suppression of homosexuality hampers sexual identification, and provokes the protagonists' initial confusion, sense of shame and/ or inability to interpret the nature of their feelings.

This aspect is, perhaps, more salient in Donoghue's *Life Mask* and in O'Neill's *At Swim, Two Boys*. Initially, in *Life Mask* lesbian desire can only manifest itself through art and the aesthetic. In Donoghue's novel, Damer's heroic feat is to reverse a hetero-patriarchal discourse that vilifies the so-called Sapphists, in an eighteenth-century context that denies women their personal freedoms. O'Neill, on his part, unearths a hidden history of same-

sex love and homoeroticism in the nationalist struggle for Irish independence. In *At Swim, Two Boys*, to give shape and meaning to their attachment,
the young protagonists reach far beyond their immediate cultural context,
finding inspiration in heroic tales of ancient Greece. Likewise, in Barry's
Days Without End, the Native American *winkte* provide Thomas with new
possibilities of self-realisation. The *winkte*'s gender fluidity – their view of
transgender identity as a philosophy of life – helps the protagonist establish
a family life and lead a more emotionally fulfilling existence in the company
of his 'beau' and their adopted daughter. In Boyne's *The Heart's Invisible
Furies*, the protagonist grows up alone as a gay person, but, when he exiles
himself, he learns a new language of gay love and self-respect.

A common feature of the four novels is that the central characters find
ways to transcend their social limitations and achieve a renewed sense of
self. They therefore experience radical transformations which not only
erode heteronormativity, but also help them adopt new ethical positions
where same-sex love emerges as positive, even heroic. Ultimately, these
novels open up a space for the recovery and revaluation of queer histories,
traditions and identities, subverting the historical silencing of homosexual
lives.

This silencing seems to be over now. Before gay decriminalisation in
1993, there was no solid gay or lesbian tradition in Irish writing, due to the
political and cultural dominance of a conservative, censorious Catholic ideology
that conflated itself with notions of national identity and social respectability.
In recent decades, the nation transformed itself. Ireland has evolved from
being a staunchly homophobic country to becoming the first nation to
legalise same-sex marriage by popular vote in 2015, after the emergence of a
plethora of voices reclaiming equality. Nonetheless, as observed in this
study, there is today a homonormative culture which threatens to further
invisibilise and stigmatise non-conforming queer individuals.

The present volume, which spans the last four decades, has foregrounded the cultural contribution of writers whose subversive, dissident
voices decidedly challenged the sexual norms and values that have dominated
in Irish society, articulating a new language to explore and understand gay
and lesbian lives and experiences. These authors broke social silences and
foreshadowed debates that would later develop in Ireland, including the
negative effects of cultural invisibility, the dignity of gay and lesbian love, or
the mental health of young homosexuals. The works analysed here further
discuss some other issues that have not received enough public attention yet,
for example: same-sex parenthood, gay prostitution, social class oppression
and poverty among the LGBTI+ population, or the gender and sexual
repolarisation promoted by the liberal ideology of Celtic Tiger Ireland.
Furthermore, from the 2000s onwards, Irish gay and lesbian fiction grew

more confident and, as argued above, the shift towards historical fiction can be seen as a manifestation of the cultural empowerment of gay and lesbian identities in contemporary Ireland.

The novels and short stories analysed in this volume have opened up a cultural space for the exploration of homosexual histories and identities, one which highlights examples of resilience against cultural invisibility and heteronormativity. Taken together, these works not only provide readers with a nuanced rendition of Irish homosexual experience, past and present, but also trace an important evolution for gays and lesbians in Irish society; a cultural shift from silence to recognition.

NOTES

INTRODUCTION

1. I draw here on Frank Sewell's translation.

2. Homosexuality has had a long history of suppression and violence in societies where biblical law became influential. In Ireland, the earliest evidence of negativity towards homosexual activity appears in ecclesiastical texts from the fifth and sixth centuries; allegedly, these Penitentials, instead of representing the sexual attitudes of the Irish population, 'reflect the values of a Christian establishment' (Lacey, 26). In some other European states, the ascendancy of Christianity initiated in the Middle Ages a 'deadly tradition' for sodomites (Crompton, 2003: 537), as sodomy was judged as a heresy punishable by torture and death. The first law punishing sodomy in Britain was the 1533 Buggery Act, which 'included acts between men and men, between men and women, men and animals' (Gittins, 1993: 147). Sodomy – which, in many contexts, generally referred to sexual practices between men – had been for many centuries understood as an expression of 'hierarchy and gender,' and as a 'sexual preference without a sexual orientation' (Halperin, 2013: 268–9). While regarded as a perverse act and punishable crime, sodomy did not construct the individual as part of a social category, as homosexuality did.

3. The term 'homophobia' was first theorised by American psychiatrist George Weinberg in *Society and the Healthy Homosexual* (1972). Weinberg described homophobia as 'a fear of homosexuals which seemed to be associated with a fear of contagion, a fear of reducing the things one fought for – home and family. It was a religious fear and it had led to great brutality as fear always does' (quoted in Herek, 2005:7). Significantly, the term homophobia presupposes that homophobes are those who are infected with prejudice, hatred and irrational fear, so, as Gregory Herek explains it, 'the term stood a central assumption of heterosexual society on its head by locating the "problem" of homosexuality not in homosexual people, but in heterosexuals who were intolerant of gay men and lesbians' (8).

4. As Gregory Herek explains, heterosexism entails 'the cultural ideology that perpetuates sexual stigma by denying and denigrating any nonheterosexual form of

behaviour, identity, relationship, or community. Heterosexism is inherent in cultural institutions, such as language and law' (2005: 16).

5. Mother and Baby Homes were operative between 1922 and 1998, and served as 'refuges' for unwed mothers and their babies, often repudiated by their families and the father of the child for 'fear of losing social standing,' in issues involving land inheritance and social respectability (McGarry, 2021). In these institutions, women often received a harsh, punitive treatment. The report estimated that at least 9.000 infants died in Mother and Baby Homes (Leahy, 2021).

6. Run by the Catholic Church in cooperation with the State, Magdalene laundries hosted 'fallen women' and operated in Ireland until the late twentieth century. Young pregnant women who were disowned by their families could end up interned in these convent homes, where, in many cases, they 'became enslaved, often unable to leave, forced to work without pay in the laundries, and subjected to brutal treatment and abuse from the nuns in charge' (Bacik, 2013: 25). In 1993, a mass grave containing 155 unidentified corpses was found in the vicinity of a Magdalene laundry in Dublin, which led to the investigation of these secretive institutions (Ryan, 2011). In 2013, the Irish government issued an apology to the Magdalene women and ordered a compensation scheme for survivors.

7. The Direct Provision scheme was established in 1999 to house asylum seekers and refugees in isolated state-designed accommodation centres. Activist Vukasin Nedeljkovic defines life in these centres as follows: 'Within the Direct Provision scheme, the position allocated to asylum seekers objectifies, infantilises and criminalises them [. . .] They live in ghettoes where families with children are often forced to share small rooms: overcrowding, unhygienic conditions and disease are the results. As if they were children or prisoners, the management controls their food, their movements, the supply of bed linen and cleaning materials, exerting their authority, power and control over them' (2020: 168). In recent years, this reality has come to light not only through activism, but also in the writings of authors like Melatu Okorie and Ifedinma Dimbo.

8. To maintain the romanticised notion of the Catholic family, realities like domestic violence and rape were largely silenced and hidden from public view. This silence was first undermined in the 1970s by Irish feminists who publicly denounced these situations of abuse against women.

9. Despite public awareness that thousands of Irish women have had to travel abroad (often to England) to terminate their pregnancy, abortion has been a taboo topic until very recently. In 2015, Ailbhe Smyth lamented the scarcity of public debates on this issue, denouncing that 'the silence surrounding abortion in this country has been deafening, only punctuated every decade or so by a dreadful human tragedy' (2015: 116). Smyth then mentions the 2012 death of Savita Halappanavar, who was found to be miscarrying, but was refused an abortion on the grounds that the foetal heart was still beating. She died of an infection a week afterwards, a death that could have been prevented had she been given an abortion at hospital. In a way, this tragedy helped mobilise feminist activism on the issue of abortion, which became legal after the 2018 referendum to repeal the Eighth Amendment.

10. In this context of moral conservatism, homosexuality was regarded as an attack against two of the cornerstones of Catholic life: marriage and the family. In this respect, when debates over gay rights and decriminalisation arose in the 1980s and early 1990s, 'the relationship of male homosexuality to religion and to marriage and family, institutions expressly addressed in the Constitution, bec[ame] the main focus of attention and dissent' (Conrad, 2004: 48). Seen as a linchpin of national identity, the Catholic family functioned in this context as a 'keyword for exclusion' (Halperin, 1998: 417), an ideal to be protected from the advent of women's and gay rights movements.

11. In Ireland, this conceptualisation of homosexuality as a negative external influence was already in place in Victorian times. Homosexuality was then formulated as a threat to national identity, and 'both the British colonial powers and the Irish nationalists wrote homosexuality as a kind of foreign "pollution"' (Conrad 2004: 25).

12. In the wake of national independence, both the State and the Catholic Church enforced a cult of domesticity which 'call[ed] for women to eschew public life [. . .] and devote themselves to home and family' (Beaumont, 1999: 94). Legal measures (e.g., marriage bars) were introduced in the early decades of the Irish State, with the outcome that female employment 'stagnated or declined from the 1920s to the 1980s' (Meaney, O'Dowd and Whelan, 2013: 106).

13. Large numbers of young, single women (more than men) migrated from Ireland in the middle decades of the twentieth century. According to Eibhear Walshe, this massive female migration hindered the development of 'any coherent or visible lesbian community in Ireland' (2006b: 40).

14. Given the historical marginalisation and silencing of women, the history of lesbianism in Ireland is highly undocumented, as is also the case elsewhere. Constrained by the institution of the family, women have been for centuries deprived of their personal freedom, which explains why '[female] sexuality appears to have been subordinated to economic survival and the widely propagated concepts of love and romance generally held within marriage' (Diamond, 1984: 10).

15. At the time, homosexuality emerged as a social identity and a 'type of life' (Foucault, [1976] 1998: 43), shaped by cultural and scientific discourses. In his *Nationalism and Sexuality* (1985), George L. Mosse underlines the major contribution of the medical institution to the categorisation of homosexuality as gender inversion. 'The medical stereotype of homosexuality', Mosse explains, 'had fixed the homosexual in place during the nineteenth century: his so-called abnormality was no longer confined to sexual acts, but was part of his psychological makeup, his looks and bodily structure' (37). In this way, the male homosexual arose as the antithesis of normative masculinity and ideal citizenship, was therefore formulated as a threat to national culture.

16. Oscar Wilde became condemned under a clause known as the Labouchère Amendment, which remained in place in independent Ireland, and included the term 'gross indecency' to name any type of 'sexual activity between two men' (Baker, 2004: 96). Under the label of gross indecency, gay sex became liable to prosecution even when practiced privately, with no direct evidence required. Convicted of gross indecency in 1895, Oscar Wilde had been required to define at court 'the love that

dare not speak its name', in reference to a 'coded poem of homosexuality' written by his lover Lord Alfred Douglas (Walshe, 2005: 42). In the century that followed, the shameful nature of gross indecency made 'any intimate contact between men' suspect of homosexual behaviour (Ryan, 2006: 90). A repudiation of male-to-male intimacy, which formed the basis of hegemonic masculinity and homophobia, would become pervasive in twentieth-century Western societies.

17. This situation for lesbians reflects some of the constraints imposed in Victorian times, due to the enforcement of norms of domesticity and femininity which not only defined women as 'incapable of sexual excitement or passion', but also made them 'man's property' under family law (Gittins, 1993: 51, 52). Since there was 'no conceptual framework about passion between women' (Donoghue, 1993: 9), numerous lesbian relationships were perceived as non-sexual romantic friendships, and were usually celebrated as profoundly emotional, in Victorian times and before. One famous, possibly sexual, romantic friendship was that of Lady Eleanor Butler and Sara Ponsoby, two Anglo-Irish women who, in the eighteenth century, eloped together and settled in Llangolen, Wales: 'It was assumed that because the Ladies of Llangolen did not want men, they did not want sex' (Harvey, quoted in Lacey, 2008: 185). What made their relationship possible was their aristocratic status, as both women 'rel[ied] on their class position to gain credit both in financial and social terms' (O'Donnell, 2003: 6). Economic independence has therefore been a vital issue for women to overcome patriarchal restrictions. With the increase in women's employment after World War I, perceptions of female romantic friendships altered significantly, and now 'openly expressed love between women for the most part ceased to be possible' (Faderman, 1981: 20). Lesbians began to be demonised, as it was felt that their sexuality 'turned women away from reproduction and toward masculinism' (Conrad, 2004: 54). Symptomatic of this unrest was the attempt in 1921 to criminalise sex between women, which failed on the grounds that criminalisation would spread awareness of lesbianism. Had this measure been passed at the House of Commons, Brian Lacey opines, 'it would almost certainly form part of [the] legal apparatus in Ireland' (2008: 182), which preserved the anti-gay Victorian law after independence.

18. A member of the British Foreign Office, Roger Casement turned to Irish republicanism after witnessing the Belgian atrocities in the Congo. Involved in the 1916 Rising, Casement was arrested by the British, who circulated his 'Black diaries' (where he described his sexual experiences) as proof of his moral and political 'degeneracy'. In Ireland, Casement's diaries were met with a mixture of shock and disbelief: 'Controversy has raged over the authenticity of these diaries, some Irish republicans feeling unhappy with the notion that one of the leading figures of the 1916 Rising might also have preferred and enjoyed (as the diaries tell us) sex with other men' (Walshe, 1996: 4).

19. Poet Eva Gore-Booth's feminism and her use of 'lesbian themes in her reworking of Celtic myths' (Hanafin, 1998: 416) were soon relegated to silence after independence, in a newly independent Ireland where the developing language of national identity required a 'denial of difference' (Walshe, 1996: 6).

20. These groups organised social events which helped ease the isolation that many homosexuals suffered. For lesbians, who generally enjoyed less freedoms than gay

men, perhaps the most notable social venue of this kind was The Cork Women's
Fun Weekend, facilitated by the Lesbian Cork Collective in the 1980s. These festive
weekends were attended by women from all corners of the country, and 'offered
hope that being a lesbian in Ireland [. . .] did not have to be hidden or seen as
intolerable' (McDonagh, 2017: 73).

21. Kate O'Brien's work enjoyed a 'resurgence' in the 1980s within the Irish feminist
movement, as Tina O'Toole relates (2013: 132). In his study of Kate O'Brien, Eibhear
Walshe (2006b) sees the Irish writer as an inspiring queer figure, and explains how
she, as an expatriate, developed a circle of lesbian friends in London, where she
'clearly evolv[ed] as woman-loving' (41). Though O'Brien never identified publicly
as woman-loving, she became notorious for her defence of sexual freedom. In 1941,
The Land of Spices was banned in Ireland for a single line where the protagonist
unexpectedly finds her father and another man 'in the embrace of love' (O'Brien,
[1941] 2006: 52). This banning sparked an 'outcry', making 'Kate O'Brien something
of an emblematic figure for liberal dissenters' (44). As a well-known personality,
O'Brien returned to Ireland in 1950 and settled in Roundstone, Co. Galway, attract-
ing her London contacts and establishing close friendships with gay men like the
famous actors Michael MacLiammoir and Edward Hilton. Promoted by O'Brien,
this 'lesbian and gay bohemia', though short-lived (she returned to England in
1960), became an early manifestation of a queer subculture in a Catholic Ireland that
was still largely illiberal and censorious (47).

22. In 1974, David Norris and Edmund Lynch founded IGRM to foster collective
action against criminalisation. Despite the widespread belief that anti-gay legislation
was dormant in the 1970s, between 1973 and 1974 43 men were sentenced for gross
indecency, and some of these convictions became a matter of public shaming:
'Careers and family relationships were destroyed' (Ryan, 2014: 108). Many of these
men were humiliated by the judiciary, and one of IGRM's tasks was to defend their
rights. Norris himself, having attended some of these trials, encouraged the accused
men not to remain ashamed and submissive: 'It's not our position to stand with our
heads bowed in the dock and be sentenced and subject to abuse and scorn from the
bench' (quoted in Ryan, 2006: 91).

23. In 1981, LIL maintained that lesbians had only recently started to 'awaken to
their real identity,' invisibility being one of their major problems: 'Many people who
see the word homosexual think only of men' ('Lesbian Women', 1981). As LIL also
claimed, because of the predominant male-defined notions of sexuality and female
acceptability, Irish women were 'discouraged from recognising and asserting an
independent sexuality' ('Lesbian Women').

24. In the context of the 1983 abortion referendum, the National Gay Federation
(NGF) refused to support lesbian feminists. A minority of gay activists, Gays Against
the Amendment (GAA), opposed the more mainstream, conservative approach of
the NGF. This separation between lesbian feminist and mainstream gay activism re-
emerged later in the context of the 1986 referendum, when numerous gay men failed
to understand that the 'legalization of divorce was not just a 'heterosexual' issue but
had major implications for lesbian mothers seeking custody of their children'
(Dunphy, 1997: 253). Generally speaking, one of the main difficulties for Irish
lesbians was gay men's tendency to 'speak on behalf of lesbians without consultation'

(Power, 1995: 146). Partly as a consequence of this, in the early 1990s Irish lesbians began to organise separately, establishing 'the lesbian as a distinct entity rather than being aligned to gay or feminist or any other concern' (O'Donnell, 2008: 1).

25. According to Gerard Rogers (2018: 44–55), this visit led to a resurgence in religious piety and rekindled the Church-State allegiance. Pope John Paul II had preached about Ireland's sacred mission to preserve Catholic morality against the tides of modernity.

26. In the late 1970s, David Norris sued the Irish State on the grounds that criminalisation violated his right to privacy. As a journalist, writer Colm Tóibín attended Norris's trial and witnessed Chief Justice O'Higgins's 1983 verdict, where the judge defended gay criminalisation arguing that: a) gay sex contravenes Christian teaching; b) homosexuality damages the institution of the family; c) a homosexual lifestyle leads to depression and suicide; d) gay sex provokes the spread of venereal infections (Tóibín, 2007). The Irish establishment thus disseminated an idea of homosexuality as prone to misery and disease; a threat to the well-being and integrity of society.

27. The European Court ruled that the Irish Law transgressed the European Convention on Human Rights. Norris' appeal to the European Court had augured well, given Jeff Dudgeon's victory against the United Kingdom, which made the 1967 British gay decriminalisation applicable to a still highly homophobic Northern Ireland in 1982. Norris's (and Irish gay men's) decisive victory occurred when the European Court ruled that the Irish Law transgressed the European Convention on Human Rights.

28. As Tom Inglis relates in his *Moral Monopoly* (1998b), in the 1980s the Irish Catholic Church constantly warned against sexual and moral 'degeneracy', expressing their ideas through 'authoritarian and insensitive promulgations by priests' (204), which castigated homosexuality as intrinsically evil and morally disordered. Drawing on this, Ger Moane contends that, in Ireland, the Catholic Church has counted as 'the primary and most vocal source of condemnatory views of homosexuality, and has provided the main justification for discrimination against, and hatred of, homosexual men and lesbians' (88)

29. In January 1982, Charles Self was killed, presumably, by a gay lover (the murderer was never found, even though the case was reopened in 2008). In the months that followed, the police interviewed hundreds of Dublin gay men about their personal and sexual lives, requiring from them information largely irrelevant to the crime. This situation exposed some of the fractures within the gay movement; whereas the National Gay Federation (NGF) remained cautious and established communication with the police, who assured them that personal information would be destroyed after the resolution of the case, the Dublin Lesbian and Gay Collectives (DLGC) had no doubt that 'the investigation was more concerned with compiling a file on gay men that it was with solving the murder', and thus picketed Pearse Street Garda Station to protest against police intimidation (Boyd et al. 1986: 192). Unlike the NGF, whose major focus was legislative change for gays, the DLGC favoured instead a feminist and socialist approach to their activism. The DLGC edited the book *Out for Ourselves: The Lives of Irish Lesbians and Gay Men* (Boyd et al., 1986), where they openly criticise the NGF, saying that 'the majority see gay rights as a

middle class respectable campaign, [where] there is no working class gay involvement' (85).

30. In September 1982, Declan Flynn was killed in Dublin's Fairview Park by a gang of gay-bashers who had 'the affrontery to boast in court of attacking 150 people' (Healey, 1983). The inquiry into Flynn's murder generated much controversy, not only because the judge decided to give the killers suspended sentences, but also because the police had failed to act on a report they had about 'an organised gang, or gangs, well advanced on a campaign of unusual brutality' (Purcell, 1983). Around the same time, Dolores Lynch (a former prostitute) and her mother had been murdered by a pimp, and, like Flynn's, the killer was leniently treated by the judiciary. Connecting Lynch's and Flynn's cases, the Dublin Lesbian and Gay Collectives (DLGC) publicly insisted that 'Flynn's murder was part of the same pattern as suffered by women who are assaulted or raped, by prostitutes who are beaten or killed' (Casey, 2018: 222).

31. To this scene walked artist Thom McGinty, the 'Diceman', performing an act of public mourning in remembrance of Self and Flynn, a protest which, as Tina O'Toole puts it, 'extended to the lost lives of an entire generation, or more, of Irish queers' (2017: 176).

32. GLEN also sought alliances with other pressure groups, like the Trade Unions. One of their achievements was to have the category of 'sexual orientation' added to the 1990 Prohibition of Incitement to Hatred.

33. Familial homophobia was rampant in Ireland, as attested by a 1990s survey that revealed that 'only 12.5 per cent of Irish people would welcome a gay person into their family' (Mac Gréil, 1997: 372). In the 1980s, the Gay and Lesbian Dublin Collectives also reported stories of horror of young gay men who were beaten up (usually by their fathers) and expelled from home (Boyd et al., 1986: 134).

34. Drawing on this language of the family promoted by GLEN, politician Maire Geoghegan Quinn explained that: 'When, in 1993, as minister for justice, I decided to decriminalize homosexuality, I did so because I met people. Women with the tears unwiped. Mothers of gay sons' (2015).

35. At the time, the realities of abuse taking place in institutions like the Magdalene laundries came to public attention. These scandals also involved reported cases of sexual abuse of minors by priests in Catholic schools. For a detailed account, see Donnelly and Inglis, 2010.

36. As Carol Coulter explains (1997), the anti-divorce campaigners fuelled the fears of the sixty per cent of married women who did not work outside the home. Their message was that divorce largely devalues the family-centred role of the stay-at-home wife and mother, causing her economic insecurity and increasing her chances of being abandoned. It was further argued that divorce could only benefit family destroyers, namely the unfaithful husband who neglects his familial responsibilities and the 'predator female' – stereotyped as a working woman who prioritises her personal desires and her career over marriage and motherhood (Coulter, 286). In a country where a majority of married women depended on a male breadwinner, the anti-divorce argument struck a chord with the electorate. Divorce was passed by a very slim majority (50.5%) and its legalisation saw 'wild claims as to the demise of the family' (Conroy, 1997: 76).

37. For Irish lesbians at the time, meaningful instances of political assertion included Emma Donoghue's appearance at The Late Late Show, the popularity of a lesbian music group called Zazry, and the demonstrations in Cork in support of Donna McAnnellan, who had been dismissed for kissing another woman at work.

38. Too many Irish lesbians in 1990s Ireland, Ger Moane relates, still 'lived in total secrecy and isolation, deprived of access to their children, or prevented from being with their lover during illness' (1995: 87).

39. To increase lesbian visibility, LOT sponsored the 1996–9 project LEA (Lesbian Education Awareness), under the EU's programme NOW (New Opportunities for Women). In its final year, following GLEN's strategy for gay decriminalisation, LEA members mounted a billboard campaign, asking Irish parents to recognise, love and accept their lesbian daughters. According to O'Donnell, this campaign – which was 'largely concerned with issues of coming out'– aptly illustrates how Irish society was not ready for profound debates about legal inequalities, social injustices and the effects of lesbophobia, as these matters were not to the 'forefront' (O'Donnell, 2008: 8).

40. The Celtic Tiger period was characterised by sustained high levels of economic growth due to the introduction of neoliberal and free-market policies. Thanks to this change in the economy, Irish society gradually became more confident and outward looking. Unfortunately, this patina of national success concealed unpalatable social realities, since the liberal policies of this period created a growing inequality in access to housing, education and healthcare.

41. Harassment and discrimination against homosexuals continued to be common in 1990s Ireland, as 'the level of homophobia in Irish population [was] still very high and quite disturbing' (Mác Gréil, 1997: 451). In his *Occasions of Sin*, Diarmaid Ferriter further indicates that 'research conducted in 24 countries between 1999 and 2002 suggested Ireland was one of the most homophobic countries in the western world' (2009: 509).

42. In more recent years, blatant discrimination began to be progressively replaced by what has been termed as 'homonegativity', whereby 'the objections are not that gay men and lesbian women are immoral, sinful, or evil but, rather, that these groups have all the rights they need, and should stop asking for more' (Morrison et al. 2005: 221). Homonegativity became salient, for example, in the arena of family rights.

43. Single lesbians and gays could adopt, but same-sex couples could not do so jointly. As already noted, queer family units already existed, so the non-recognition of same-sex parenthood meant that children had '[no] legal claim on both their carers' (Kavanagh, 2009: 179).

44. The main pro-marriage associations were GLEN (Gay and Lesbian Equality Network), Marriage Equality and ICCL (Irish Council for Civil Liberties).

45. Yvonne Murphy (2016: 326) notes that same-sex marriage passed by a margin of 467,307 votes (1,201,607 for, 734,300 against). All constituencies but one voted in favour of the amendment.

46. This is a global trend that Kay Siebler discusses at length in *Learning Queer Identity in the Digital Age* (2017). In today's increasingly dominant digital culture, which transmits the values of homonormativity, there is a 'very specific narrative of how sex, gender, and sexuality intersect: lesbians need to be sexy porn fantasies or butchy andro boys on their way to a trans identity; gay men are girly femme,

domestic divas, or performing the six-pack ab homoerotic sexy ideal; trans people are on their way to surgery/hormones that 'correct' the body they were born with to align with their gender' (4).

47. *Quare Fellas* was launched by Basement Press, an imprint of the feminist Attic Press, which began a series of gay and lesbian titles in the wake of gay decriminalisation. Eibhear Walshe contrasts this publishing project with another collection, *Alternative Loves: Gay Irish Stories* (edited by David Marcus in 1994, launched by the mainstream Mercier Press), an anthology containing stories from well-established authors (e.g., William Trevor, Edna O'Brien and Sean O'Faolain). 'In comparison to the *Quare Fellas* collection', Walshe relates, '*Alternative Loves* plays it safe, using mainstream, 'straight' writers (in both senses!) to articulate same-sex desire, and, as a result, often falling back into the conventions of destruction and disturbance' (1996: 166). Two of the short stories included in this volume – Eamon Somers's 'Nataí Bocht' and Keith Ridgway's 'Graffiti' – belong to the *Quare Fellas* collection.

CHAPTER ONE

1. Single mothers were, for example, harshly punished and vilified because of their transgression to the so-called Catholic family, and became 'socially isolated or exiled by public opinion' (Conroy, 1997: 76).

2. In one of these articles, we read: 'Don't tell your husband [about your lesbianism] until you're separated. He might use it as a weapon to drag you through the courts and make a show of you' (Harri and Laing, 1985: 32).

3. A common belief was that homosexuals were highly educated and middle-class. In *Equality Now for Lesbians and Gay Men* (1990), the Irish Council for Civil Liberties emphasise that 'despite false myths, lesbians and gay men are in every social class and every part of the country' (8).

4. An explanation of the difficulties of coming out for Irish women is provided by Joni Crone, who sees this process as particularly complex, more than in the case of men: 'We have been socialized into a mothering role as helpers, assistants and carers. 'Coming out' as an Irish lesbian involves undoing much of our conditioning' (1995: 61).

5. This sexual sin was reinforced by the Victorian assumption that women were asexual by nature: 'Sexual excitement was defined by many doctors as an exclusively male preserve and power, and, because it was inherently male, it was therefore inappropriate for women' (Gittins, 1993: 51). This gendering of sexuality as a 'male preserve' stereotyped women as passive, censoring the female body and sexual desires – an obvious example in Catholic Ireland is the asexual and abnegated Virgin Mary, an icon of ideal femininity.

6. A situation similar to the one described by Richards has persisted until recently in Ireland, since, even in the more liberal years of the Celtic Tiger, 'public space was still treacherous for both gays and lesbians' (Conrad, 2004: 53).

7. Prior to Vatican II, nuns were expected to live in total abnegation. Friendships were discouraged, and 'the expression of individuality, through dress, opinions or actions was frowned upon' (Beale, 175).

8. Writing in 1990s Ireland, LGBTI+ activists Suzy Byrne and Junior Larkin explained that Irish bisexuals remained more invisible than homosexuals: 'When they are in opposite sex relationships, bisexuals are presumed to be heterosexual and when they are in a same-sex relationship they are presumed to be gay. Society tends to reject the idea of bisexuality as a legitimate sexual orientation even more than it rejects homosexuality' (1994: 91).

9. Helen and Joanna had relationships with men, but it is their first kiss together that is described as sensuous and deeply meaningful: 'Kissed lips, cheeks, lips again. So softly they could have been butterfly kisses' (74).

10. Ann Norton, for example, concludes that '*The High Road* presents a potential remedy for women's mistaken erotic obsessions, suggesting the specific embrace of lesbian love as a healthy replacement for men's cruelty and domination' (2006: 100).

11. In his study, Ó Conchubhair further explains that, in the early twentieth century, the novel in Irish emphasised 'native Irish speakers' 'Irishness', their physical superiority, their deliverance from degeneration, and their higher moral values' (2005: 14). From the 1950s onwards, the critic argues, novelists refused to 'speak for either Irish-language writing or Irish culture' (216), focusing instead on individual lives and identities: 'The problems of today, the lovers and hates, the human rights and responsibilities, desires and doubts of modern men and women are fearlessly dealt with' (Ó Conchubhair, 231). In a 1992 article, Pádraig Standún himself claimed that this 'fearlessness' of the Irish-language novel still had no parallel in the Irish novel written in English: 'We encourage the artistic, the imaginative, the wild in our people [. . .] Strangely enough, there has been more freedom and encouragement in this area in the Irish than in the English language' (224).

12. As Alan Titley observes in his study of twentieth-century Irish-language prose, Standún uses an alternative language of Christian ethics in his fiction: 'Standún has admitted that his novels are simply a means of disseminating Christianity. His Christianity, however, is not always the stuff of conforming beliefs but is concerned with setting the oak of orthodoxy against the reed of bending life' (2007: 18). In *A Woman's Love*, for example, the religious Bridie reconciles her Catholicism with her growing desire and affection for Therese, whom she had previously judged as having 'neither religion nor morality' (59). Bridie is also the daughter of a strong-minded woman who condemns the old ways of her generation: 'I knew a woman that broke the handle of the brush on her daughter's back because the priest read her form the altar for being pregnant and single. Was that Christianity? The religion of being respectable was a lot stronger than the religion of Jesus Christ' (108).

13. Bridie becomes jealous, for example, when Therese talks about her experiences with another woman in London, whom she plans to visit on a business travel: 'I don't like you going over there, without me knowing if you'll be staying with her or not' (215). And, when Bridie's ex-husband returns to Ireland, Bridie assures an insecure Therese that she would never abandon her for him: 'You're not in competition with John. Or if you are you have the competition won' (215).

14. Standún spares no details of the gender violence intrinsic in John's patriarchal thinking. Emasculated and infuriated, John fantasises about raping Therese, punishing her with his phallus to 'teach' her a lesson: '"I'd love to fuck the living

daylights out of [Therese],' he told himself, not for the pleasure it would give her but for the pain. He'd ram her until she'd split in two' (234).

15. At work, for example, Therese confronts the heightened hostility of her colleagues, who expel her from one of the projects because 'the image of the Board has to be considered' (221).

CHAPTER TWO

1.   Her outspokenness at the time frightened some other gay and lesbian activists. 'A lot of lesbians and gay people', Dorcey intimates in an interview, 'were frightened because they were closeted at the time, and I was the only one who wasn't' (Coppola, 2015: 230).

2.   This negative stereotype of lesbianism has also been challenged years later in some studies that emphasise Irish lesbians' high levels of self-realisation with regard to their sexual orientation. While an overwhelming majority of younger lesbians report being 'very comfortable' with their sexuality (Mallon, 2013: 28), mid-life lesbians indicate that, in spite of having experienced discrimination, they greatly value 'the sense of being bold or different, of refusing to conform, of being subversive and outside the norm' (Moane, 2008: 138).

3.   The concept of 'male gaze' was first used by Laura Mulvey in 'Visual Pleasure and Narrative Cinema' (1975), who argued that patriarchal cultures tend to construct 'the image of woman as (passive) raw material for the (active) gaze of man' (17). This concept thus serves as a critique of how women have traditionally been displayed as 'objects [. . .] rather than as independent entities whose value is distinct from how they are viewed by men' (Griffin, 2017).

4.   For example, he believes that Martina cannot really be a lesbian, because she is 'too fundamentally healthy, and too fond of the admiration of men' (70). Instead of describing Martina, the husband voices here his own masculine needs: 'The thing he really prized [was] her vulnerability, her need to confide' (75).

5.   A majority of Irish people voted against divorce legislation in 1986. Divorce was finally introduced in the 1995 referendum by a very slim majority.

6.   Section 37.1 was a present, real threat for many teachers, especially after the infamous 1982 Eileen Flynn case, the teacher who was dismissed because she was an unmarried mother living with her partner, a separated man.

7.   In her analysis of Dorcey's use of second-person narratives, Heather Ingman further explains that this stylistic choice 'breaks the boundaries between the self and the other' and suggests that 'the semiotic world inhabited by lesbian lovers has the potential to disrupt and change the symbolic' (2007: 62). The 'symbolic' order here refers to the hetero-patriarchal discourses still affecting women's lives.

8.   This is not so different from Edna O'Brien's approach in *The High Road*, though Dorcey's scenes are more explicitly sexual.

9.   Incredulous like the husband in the eponymous story, Malachy asks his wife: 'What can she possibly give you that I can't? What could any woman give to you? What more do you want?' (270).

10. See McIntosh, 1992; Kitzinger and Wilkinson, 1995; Golden, 1999; Swann and Anastas, 2003.

11. In a number of scenes, Katherine also imagines Malachy's anger about being abandoned for a woman, fearing that he will take revenge by claiming custody of their children. *Biography of Desire* hence reminds us that, at this time 'there [were] particular problems for lesbians who attempt to talk with their husbands about their sexuality' (Boyd et al., 1986: 64), since lesbianism was perceived by many men as an attack against their masculinity and patriarchal dividend.

12. As Abigail Palko argues, rather than being a realistic recreation of a custody case, this imagined legal battle serves as '[Katherine's] opportunity to defend herself and explore her past' (2016: 209). In these personal explorations, Katherine also pictures herself answering questions about her own mother. The imaginary judge asks Katherine: 'Would you tell the court about your relationship with your mother, Mrs Newman? Were you close to her?' (91). Katherine believes she would react to these questions with 'disdain' (91), but her imagination betrays her own insecurities and emotional conflicts. When she confessed her love of Nina to her mother, Katherine became devastated: 'I saw tears welling in her eyes and saw that her cheeks were flushed and dark [. . .] We didn't talk about you again after that' (138). The mother's painful reaction hints at a cultural discourse in which mothers were made to feel ashamed and inadequate on account of their children's homosexuality. Such situation, as Dorcey's novel illustrates, increased familial homophobia and led to much suffering and incomprehension within families.

13. Dorcey dramatises Nina's role as a devoted mother in numerous scenes, showing how she overcompensates in her motherly role. When Lizzie is hospitalised, Nina offers to stay by her while Elinor continues working, which provokes Katherine's jealousy: 'Why can't Elinor take care of her?' (217). At the ailing child's bed, Nina cannot avoid reconsidering whether she should go or stay: 'She had sat, holding the warm, damp hand in her own and planned her betrayal. At times when Lizzie writhed suddenly, as though in pain, or called out in her sleep, Nina imagined that her thoughts must be transmitting themselves to the fitful consciousness and she felt smitten with guilt. And it was impossible to leave' (231).

CHAPTER THREE

1. This chapter focuses on this sexual subculture from the viewpoint of same-sex attracted men, but this does not imply that women do not engage in cruising or similar sexual behaviours. Writing in an American context, Denise Bullock expands conventional definitions of cruising to include similar behaviours among non-heterosexual women (2004).

2. Writer Tom Lennon draws on this gay stigma when, in *When Love Comes to Town* (1993), a depressed teenager broods over his homosexual feelings, afraid to become somebody who 'spend[s] [his] Sunday afternoons in a stinking toilet' (15). This book is analysed in Chapter Four.

3. In the 1970s, many gay communities in the US and the UK had embraced cruising as 'a political opposition to heterosexual monogamous ideology' (Edwards, 1994: 114). The more recent 'sacrifice' of cruising within gay subcultures is seen by some theorists as a consequence of a homonormative culture which adopts the sexual morality of ideal heterosexuality.

4. For example, a 2000s British study reported that numerous men went cruising simply because 'they enjoyed the activity sexually, the excitement or thrill, and the anonymity' (Ashford, 2007: 509). In his acclaimed *The Swimming-Pool Library* (1988), English novelist Alan Hollinghurst also describes the allure of cruising thus: 'It was strangers who by their very strangeness quickened my pulse and made me feel I was alive – that and the irrational sense of absolute security that came from the conspiracy of sex with men I had never seen before' (188).

5. Precisely in this way, historian George Chauncey indicates that cruising has a long history, which pre-dates the evolution of gay liberation: 'The most striking difference between the dominant sexual culture of the early twentieth century and that of our era is the degree to which the earlier culture permitted men to engage in sexual relations with other men, often on a regular basis, without requiring them to regard themselves – or to be regarded by others – as gay' (1994: 65).

6. 'At the Station' is translated from Irish by Katherine Duffy.

7. About his 1999 gay Bildungsroman *Sna Fir*, the writer remarks: 'People told me that it opened their eyes, and that I had forced them to think in ways they hadn't done before' (Ó Siadhail and Ó Conghaile, 2005: 58).

8. In his analysis of *Sna Fir*, Pádraig Ó Siadhail describes the character's evolution thus: 'By the end [of the book] John Paul has questioned why he is queer and recognized that he has come a long way experientially and emotionally during that year, whatever the future has in store for him' (2010: 149).

9. This excerpt from *Sna Fir* is taken from an unpublished translation by Nuala Ní Chonchuir and Gabriel Rosenstock, which critic Ed Madden used in a research article (2013).

10. Somers's narrator fails to engage in conversation with the boy, but he nonetheless develops a sincere concern for his welfare: 'For most of his two hours I stood on the pan in the next cubicle watching over him, wondering when his agony would end' (21).

11. In 1980s Ireland, gay organisations received calls of distressed young people who 'cr[ied] for help' and shared stories 'of angry parents and a suitcase in the hall' (Boyd et al., 1986: 134). Familial homophobia will also be explored in Chapter Four.

12. Somers foregrounds the personal transformation of the teenager, now that he no longer feels isolated. Glad to perceive Nataí Bocht's newly discovered happiness, the narrator remarks: 'There was no doubt he had changed. He looked, well, just more proud, more at ease with himself. His shoulders were held back and his head was up, looking at the world, insisting he had a place' (24).

13. As Peadar and the narrator are being beaten up, Nataí Bocht emerges from inside the cubicle, stabs one of the attackers and escapes, never to be seen again. Because the teenager saved them, Peadar and the narrator share fond memories of Nataí Bocht: 'He keeps us together' (27).

14. *Hawthorn and Child* is a postmodernist, highly experimental, detective story set in London.

15. Rather than simply accepting his enjoyment of gay sex, 2nd Person in 'Graffitti' imagines himself as part of a 'ritual': 'It was the ritual that drew him here, the sense that he was a figure in an age-old dance, unconscious of the steps, sure-footed. He took part and moved on. He hadn't started it' (36). In Chapter Five, we shall discuss in more detail how Ridgway's 'Andy Warhol' also recreates a repressed gay character who experiences this split between his sexual acts and his own sense of self.

16. The narrator, an experienced cruiser, tells us some men 'may get frightened and rush off or get violent and beat you up' (16).

17. These complaints, as related in the Introduction, gained momentum in the context of the 1982 murder of Declan Flynn by a gang of gay-bashers.

18. Unfortunately, after the 1998 Good Friday Agreement, which put an end to sectarian violence, homophobia continued to be 'commonplace', and still 'produced deadly violence' (Curtis, 2013: 146). Commenting on Iris Robinson's 2008 remark that homosexuality is an 'abomination', Jennifer Curtis argues that this Unionist politician's blatant homophobia reflects the hostility of heteronormative Northern Ireland against the 'increased visibility of LGBT people and increased legal protections for gay people' (2013: 146). Hence, even though homosexuals became more visible in post-Troubles Northern Ireland, this new situation at times provoked the reactionary attitudes of nationalist and religious factions.

19. In one of the scenes, Danny, while recognising its influence, amusingly observes one mural which 'showed a throng of rifle-walking proletarians, all stripped to the waist, all swathed in a giant Irish tricolour, necks as thick as their heads, biceps like tree trunks, nipples you could have hung your hat on, fists like hams' (160).

20. It is Danny that first discovers the identity of Henry. Danny, who, as an IRA man, had committed atrocities for the sake of a united Ireland, cannot shoot the enemy, Henry, and thus feels emasculated, 'betrayed by his own cowardice' (173).

21. This coming together of an IRA member and a British soldier gives O'Connor the chance to reflect on the roots and causes of terrorism, accounting for 'the traumatic social and psychological impact' on people, and the 'moral choices forced upon [them]' (Storey, 2004: 150). O'Connor explicitly describes the terror caused by the IRA; Danny's first 'job' was to shoot a policeman until 'the rifle burnt [his] hands,' the man's 'intestines spilling out onto the ground' (168). A context to Danny's hatred is also given in the story. Talking to Henry, Danny recalls how his father had been killed by the UVF (Ulster Volunteer Force), and how his cousin was tortured: 'Every inch of his flesh was covered with tiny jagged stab wounds' (179). Henry, on his part, features as a young, idealist soldier who hardly knew about the Northern Irish conflict: 'Private Henry Woods shook his head. He said he wouldn't have believed these things could happen in Britain' (179).

22. Deep at night in Victoria Park, Henry, acting on Danny's information, digs a hole where a secret stash of IRA money is kept, but he is ambushed by fellow British soldiers, who start shooting at him without exchanging a word: 'Bullets [. . .] ripped open his handsome face' (186). Danny is also killed while waiting for Henry; his car explodes just as he starts the ignition.

CHAPTER FOUR

1. One of the novels in this chapter, by the Northern Irish Damian McNicholl, is an American publication.

2. In the field of education, the Church's institutional power remains strong. Ivana Bacik calls attention to the fact that 'over 90 percent of the 3,200 state-funded primary schools ('national schools') are owned and controlled by the Catholic Church' (2013: 19).

3. At the age of 28, McKee was shot dead in 2019 while covering a riot between the police and members of the New IRA in Derry. Since she was also an activist for LGBTI+ rights, McKee's death sparked public debates in Northern Ireland about the legalisation of same-sex marriage.

4. An international figure in the 1970s and 1980s, Hogan vanished from public life in the 1990s, and, in 1994, 'seem[ed] to have been on the verge of a breakdown' (McCrum, 2004). In the late 2000s, in a controversial legal case, he pleaded guilty of sexually assaulting a 15-year-old boy, but the judge gave him a suspended sentence due to Hogan's deteriorated mental health. It was argued that 'Hogan had suffered a lot during his formative years and that he now suffered greatly from alienation and isolation and from serious problems of consistent depression' (Roche, 2009).

5. In recent years, this history of gay exile came to the fore in some of the personal testimonies given by gay men in the context of the 2015 same-sex marriage referendum. See for example David Hoctor's article 'I needed to leave Ireland to come out as a gay man' (2015) and Niall O Sullivan's 'Ireland was not the place to be a young gay man' (2013).

6. For a detailed analysis about the ways in which Susan was changed by her time in London, see Murray (2006).

7. The novel appeared in 2004 in the United States (where the author lives), and McNicholl recently explained that he decided to revise *A Son Called Gabriel* for its 2017 edition: 'With the advent of legal same-sex marriage in the U.S., I knew I had to rewrite a fundamental part of the novel. I needed to depict scenes of hope and happiness' (Weber, 2017). This analysis centres on the 2004 text, as it is closer to the author's original inspirations when writing about gay sexuality in a 1970s Northern Irish rural context. His second novel, *The Moment of Truth* (2017), is another coming-of-age narrative which develops in a challenging context. This time the story focuses on a woman, Kathleen Boyd, who wants to become a bullfighter in 1950s Mexico.

8. If homosexuality/masturbation was linked with sexual vice, heterosexuality was popularly associated with romance and sexual respectability. A 17-year-old Gabriel starts to date Fiona, as he hopes that she will be his 'salvation' (294). Though marginally, McNicholl depicts here how women became victims of a hetero-patriarchal system that pushed same-sex attracted men into strategies of deceit and concealment. As sociologist Paul Ryan remarks in his study on 1970s Catholic Ireland, because there was for women 'an emphasis on chastity and courtship,' many gay men entered heterosexual relationships with relative ease while leading 'a dual sexual life' (2003: 79).

9. Gabriel's mother is clearly affected by the culture of sexual prudery of the time. Within Gabriel's home, the mother's reticence on sexual matters is sometimes rendered humorously. When she gives a vague explanation of what sex is, Gabriel, as an innocent child, concludes that two men may also perform the 'sacred act' together: 'I just thought sexual intercourse was such a wonderful gift from God that it was for all kinds of people to enjoy together' (128). With regard to this culture of sexual prudery in Catholic Ireland, Tom Inglis notes how 'the denial of sexuality in previous generations has had the effect of inculcating in older people an incompetence in talking not just about the sexual aspects of their lives, but their pleasures, desires, emotions' (1998: 166).

10. As discussed in Chapter Two, Section 37.1 remained operative in Irish law until 2015, which meant that Church-run schools – around 90% – could legally dismiss the workers who were perceived to transgress the religious ethos of the institution.

11. It is only those who oppose the moral rules of the Church that offer Neil acceptance and support on account of his sexuality. One of them is his friend Becky (herself similarly oppressed by Catholic sexual morality), who shares her secret and reveals her affair with a married man.

12. Family Solidarity published in 1990 *The Homosexual Challenge* in their attempt to deter the forces of social change. One of their arguments is that, in order to 'protect the young' and prevent the 'advent of AIDS' (7, 14), male homosexuality should remain illegal.

13. In the story, Neil also has preconceived notions about older gays, popularly characterised as immoral sexual predators. In his first adventure in the gay scene, Neil meets Jack, 'Uncle Sugar', a middle-aged gay man he befriends, even if he silently despises him as a 'disgusting pervert' (97). His negative perception of him changes when 'Uncle Sugar' heroically recues Neil from a gang of queer bashers.

14. As one reviewer puts it, Oísin and the other young characters of the story 'find themselves caught between the shackles of staunch Catholicism and the shadows of lingering terrorism in post-ceasefire Crossmaglen' (Bradley, 2001: 18).

15. In early 2000s Northern Ireland, the context of Gregory's *Snapshots*, large numbers of young homosexuals felt they needed to migrate in order to be able to lead fulfilling lives as adults. The results of a study conducted between 2005 and 2008 reveal that 'a majority of same-sex-attracted 16-year-olds (64% of men and 60% of women) intend to leave Northern Ireland' (Schubotz and O'Hara, 2011: 501).

16. At some point in the story, Jude has trouble identifying himself as a homosexual, because 'it makes [him] think of someone wired up wrong. Like you're in a clinic and there's no cure' (77).

17. Gregory creates in his book a confident gay protagonist who enjoys the liberal culture of his time, but the story also depicts a still visible 2000s culture of sexual shame concerning homosexuality. Anto had several relationships with 'closet cases' (161), the last one being Kieran, who 'started spray-painting his bedroom with verses from the Bible' (61).

CHAPTER FIVE

1. As Ann Nolan and Fiona Larkan argue, 1980s Ireland was not a unique case in terms of its adherence to strict moral codes, but the key difference was that, contrary to other nations, important liberal measures in relation to sexual, reproductive health were delayed until the early 1990s (264). In 1990, Ireland's first sex education programme was introduced, and the selling of condoms was deregulated in 1993.

2. GHA had produced in 1985 their own AIDS information leaflet, but it 'met with considerable opposition' due to its sexual explicitness (Nolan, 2018: 116).

3. A national survey about AIDS awareness found that 'considerable overspill to Ireland exists from the British TV,' since 'British TV channels are received by 75% of households in Ireland' (Harkin and Hurley, 1988: 25).

4. Because of the contagion paranoia, in 1989 a third of Irish people believed that 'AIDS c[ould] be contracted from toilet seats and eating utensils and through kissing or hugging' (Power, 1989).

5. Like 'At the Station', 'Lost in Connemara' is included in Ó Conghaile's collection of translated stories, *The Colours of Man* (2012). 'Lost in Connemara' is translated from Irish by Katherine Duffy.

6. Interestingly, there is a similar scene in Maura Richards's *Interlude* (1982), where an outraged Irish-speaking man suddenly shifts into English to curse one of the women, who had identified herself as a lesbian (the scene is set in the West of Ireland). This man, Emma Donoghue points out in her analysis of *Interlude*, 'will not let their terms into his native language; the unnatural women are exiled into English' (1995: 166).

7. The priest's use of the word 'plague' merits special attention, since, as Maurice J. Casey observes, it 'was imported to Ireland through the availability of the British tabloids propagating the expression' (2018: 229).

8. *The Green Road*, for example, won the Irish novel of the year in 2015. *The Gathering* received the 2007 Man Booker Prize.

9. In the US and elsewhere, this cruelty against AIDS victims not only derived from exaggerated fears about HIV infection, but also from the ways in which the general public placed all the blame on those infected with the virus. An activist in America at the time, Douglas Crimp, describes the situation thus: 'Most people dying of AIDS are very young, and those of us coping with these deaths, ourselves also young, have confronted great loss entirely unprepared [. . .] Apart from the deaths, we contend with the gruesome illness itself, acting as caretakers [. . .] Through the turmoil imposed by illness and death, the rest of society offers little support or even acknowledgment. On the contrary, we are blamed, belittled, excluded, derided' (1989: 15).

10. Setting, according to Eibhear Walshe, is 'the most radical element' of *The Blackwater Lightship*, as this AIDS narrative develops 'within the heartland of the Irish novel, the Irish country homestead, the home of an elderly Irish grandmother' (2013: 87).

11. Declan is 'adopted' by his friends, but one of his frustrations remains not having a place of his own, as he tells his sister: 'I'd love to have a real house to go back to – you know, a house of my own' (197). Though briefly, Tóibín addresses in his text a key problem affecting many AIDS victims at the time, since, as stated by the 1992

National AIDS Strategy Committee, patients were usually 'discharged from institutional care without adequate planning for suitable accommodation' (National AIDS Strategy, 'Report'). Likewise, in a leaflet of the 2002 Dublin Pride – collected in a folder of the Irish Queer Archive –, it was reported that 'many individuals diagnosed with the disease suffer additional discrimination through losing their jobs or being evicted from, or refused, accommodation' ('Leaflet').

12. In various and meaningful ways, gay friendship acquires in the novel a meaning that has been conventionally attached to the romanticised nuclear, heterosexual family. This 'friends as family' model, Tóibín's novel suggests, is not necessarily incompatible with one's biological family. Even though 'a topic that recurs frequently in AIDS narratives [is] the tensions and jealousies that erupt between the AIDS patient's biological relatives and the members of his queer family' (Palmer, 2012: 42), Declan's biological and alternative families eventually come together as one functional unit. Though they are initially regarded as an uncomfortable presence (especially by the mother, Lily), the friends become accepted, as their stay in the house proves essential for the well-being of Declan. Moreover, as Matthew Ryan notes, by depicting an alternative family for Declan, Tóibín effects '[a] liberal reconstruction of social relations', in which traditional categories of Irish identity, like the Catholic family, 'are not dissolved but reworked to accommodate the assertion of late twentieth-century fluidity of self-formation' (2008: 23). Rather than being supportive of a liberalism that rejects tradition, Tóibín attempts to position Ireland as a mature, pluralist society which embraces diversity of its population.

13. References abound in the text as to the religiosity of Dora, the grandmother, and her daughter, Lily. Another religious character is Paul, Declan's gay friend, who felt a 'very special grace' in his non-official Catholic wedding in Brussels (173).

14. This is partly so, the text suggests, because of the role of the mass media (which Tóibín had criticised in a 1991 newspaper article, 'Time to be Positive about AIDS'). As one critic puts it, 'Tóibín presents an almost utopian vision of television as a potent medium for informing and educating the predominantly rural, Catholic population of Ireland' (Matthews, 2019: 292). If as a teenager Helen enjoyed watching The Late Late Show, when 'hardly a Saturday night passed without a group of women wanting rights, or a priest in dispute with the hierarchy' (64), Dora, the grandmother, 'watched documentaries and [. . .] knew about AIDS and the search for a cure and the long illness' (47).

15. A 2019 survey, though, did indicate that '93% of people think there needs to be more information on HIV in Ireland' (Dunne, 2019).

CHAPTER SIX

1. *I Know my Own Heart* retells the story of Anne Lister (1791–1840), a British landowner and one of the first 'modern' lesbians, who wrote of her romantic relationships in her diaries.

2. As a literary historian, Donoghue has investigated British and Irish lesbian history, as exemplified by her monograph *Passions Between Women: British Lesbian Culture between 1668 and 1801* (1993) and her chapter in *Lesbian and Gay Visions of*

Ireland (O'Carroll and Collins, 1995), where she discusses the cultural contributions of key figures such as Eva Gore Booth, Kate O'Brien and Elizabeth Bowen.

3. Along the same lines, Ger Moane explained in 1995 that 'explicitly feminist ideals do not necessarily inform lesbian organizing in the 1990s to the same extent as they did in the 1970s and 1980s' (94).

4. This sense of the homonormative in liberal Ireland manifests itself in various ways, as seen, for instance, in the analyses of Jarlath Gregory's *G.A.A.Y.* (Chapter Four) and Colm Tóibín's *The Blackwater Lightship* (Chapter Five).

5. Maria's most significant act of unspoken lesbian desire occurs almost at the end of the story, when she enters Ruth's wardrobe and feels her velvet clothes while masturbating: 'Maria reached under [Ruth's] nightshirt and touched herself for the first time since she could remember' (184). In her reading of this passage, Emma Young points out that, while velvet is 'a vernacular term for the vagina' (2013: 8), Donoghue invokes 'the closet as part of [Maria's] coming out,' thus engaging 'with socially recognized metaphors that surround homosexuality and play[ing] on them to raise awareness of homosexual invisibility and silence' (2013: 9). In this way, Donoghue's *Stir-fry* traces Maria's emergence from a culture of shame and silence regarding same-sex desire.

6. This type of process is also present in some of Dorcey's texts, like 'The Husband' and 'Introducing Nessa' in *A Noise from the Woodshed*.

7. Because of the descriptions that Donoghue provides, it becomes clear that this GaySoc is established at University College Dublin (UCD). The UCD GaySoc remained unauthorised until 1990. When it was officially recognised, it had to face the hostility of academics and students alike. Writing for the *Irish Independent* in March 1990, John Walshe observes: 'A college paper has revealed that 10 UCD academics have tried to prevent the college's Gay and Lesbian Society being officially recognised. The academics had warned that students could become 'emotionally kidnapped' through encounters with an organised homosexual movement before their psychosexual identity was crystalised.' In 2004, the same UCD GaySoc had to remove their posters announcing their 'Rainbow Week', which displayed the image of two men who are about to kiss, with the message 'Love is Good'. Mrs Marven, the organiser, 'conveyed her disappointment about the amount of negative feedback the campaign received throughout 'Rainbow Week' from students and staff alike. She also stated that she had received insulting emails and phone calls from various academic staff' (Horan and Hewenham, 2004).

8. Now familiarised with the egalitarian ethos of feminism, Maria warns Ruth about Jael's exploitative behaviour: 'I still don't see why we can't make Jael shift her lazy arse and do a bit of housework. I mean, you wear that No Means No T-shirt to college all the time, but you're not much good at saying no once you come home' (168).

9. One of the passages, which has been often quoted in previous analyses of the novel, may even read as a 'didactic' description on clitoral stimulation: 'The hood of the clitoris was not a hood to take off, only to push back. In fact, the whole thing was a series of folds and layers, a magical Pass the Parcel in which the gift was not inside the wrappings but was the wrappings. If you touched the glans directly it would be too sharp, like a blow. It was touching it indirectly, through and with the hood, that felt so astonishing' (257). The clitoris – customarily censored by a dominant

patriarchal culture – is pictured here while Pen masturbates thinking about Cara. By foregrounding Pen's sexual desires during her grieving process, Donoghue helps create a language of lesbian eroticism at a time when, as also discussed in the analysis of *Stir-fry*, women's same-sex passions were largely unknown to the wider society.

10. Writing in an American context that resembles the one Donoghue describes, Vicky Whipple underlines the scarcity of resources available for lesbian widows, and how this social silence extends to their experiences of marginalisation: 'Some of us were treated as if we did not exist, faced having our relationship ignored or minimized' (2006: 67). Hence, as Whipple suggests, lesbian widows must confront a life-changing loss, but they are often denied a position as primary mourners. In Ireland and elsewhere, lesbians and gay men have frequently suffered disenfranchised grief. See also Shernoff (1997); Piatczanyn, Bennett and Soulsby (2016).

11. For instance, Mr Wall expects Pen's family at the funeral, and later tells her that she has been 'like a daughter' to him (277) and that, when she moved in with them, she 'made Cara much happier' (206).

12. It has often been the case, for example, that the surviving partner attends the funeral only as a friend, not as the life companion of the deceased: 'These experiences compound feelings of anger, sorrow and isolation and serve to disenfranchise the individual from mourning rituals that may assist facilitation of grief' (Green and Grant, 2008: 284).

13. In her 1993 *Contemporary Lesbian Writing: Dreams, Desire, Difference*, Paulina Palmer explains the emergence of this libertarian model of as follows: '[The libertarian model of lesbianism] s[ought] to challenge and supplant many of the ideas promulgated by the Lesbian Feminist Movement. Accusing lesbian feminists of attempting to desexualise lesbianism and 'sanitize' female sexuality by encouraging women to conform to a politically correct standard, they foreground the importance of sexual practice and a lesbian erotics. Instead of defining lesbian sexual attraction in terms of 'identification', they see 'difference' as the motivating impulse of desire' (14).

14. Pen, for instance, talks of her monogamy, a bastion of female virtue in the past, in the following terms: 'How very foolish I had been, in this age of pic-'n'-mix consumerism, to have slept with only one woman in the thirteen years since I discovered the whole business. Now I was left high and dry and loverless' (122).

15. Cara's final betrayal, as the protagonist sees it, was that she told her lovers that she and Pen had an open relationship, conveniently obscuring the fact that her partner was being faithful to her. Upon discovering Cara's distortion of their relationship, Pen cannot suppress her fury: 'My face met me in the mirror. So near, it looked chalky and monstrous' (50).

16. As Silvia Brandi (2007) explains in her analysis of the 2004 Referendum, historically, Ireland had been a country of mass emigration, and this pattern changed radically during the years of economic prosperity of the Celtic Tiger, when large numbers of workers from Eastern Europe, China and Africa were drawn to the country's prosperous economy. Xenophobic attitudes flourished in Ireland, and the so-called non-nationals began to be perceived as a threat to the country's well-being and prosperity.

17. In her internalised role as the feminine partner of the couple, Síle appears to assume that she should be the one to change her life and move to Canada for the sake of her relationship.

CHAPTER SEVEN

1. This term signals the disappearance of the kind of Catholicism that was 'a defining characteristic of Irish nationalism, that had a 'monopoly' on the Irish religious market [. . .], that had a strong relationship with state power, that elevated the status of cleric to extraordinarily high levels, and that emphasised the evils of sexual sin' (Ganiel, 2016: 3–4). The 2018 referendum on abortion exemplifies this transition towards a post-Catholic Ireland.

2. The boss, whom Paul feared, intimates that he has a gay son. The boss, however, expresses his acceptance of Paul's homosexuality in the language of individualism and the liberal economy, but not so much in terms of inclusion and understanding: 'All I care about is your performance here' (230).

3. Chapters One and Two analyse lesbian novels where the topic of same-sex parenthood is also present.

4. As a result, Fiachra Ó Súilleabháin indicates, gay parents in Ireland feel forced to employ socially visible tactics of 'family validation' to gain the community's acceptance (2017: 509). Conducted elsewhere, other studies on same-sex parenting found that gay fathers 'presented conflicts for the society' and that 'lesbian couples were accepted somewhat more easily' (Miller, 2001: 228).

5. Several scenes, like the following one, have Paul giving love and affection to her child: 'She is your hope and joy. You place your face to hers and experience a warm glow inside' (20). While he regrets marrying Anne, he truly loves his daughter and is afraid of losing her.

6. Catherine's teenage angst resurfaces at various points of the narrative. In one of the scenes, Catherine, seeing that James ignores her, contemplates harming herself: 'The skin on her arms, those mornings: so alive with the desire to be cut' (351).

7. It is worth noting that, as the story progresses, McKeon also challenges the conventional binaries between city/modernity and town/conservatism. On a visit to her town, Longford, Catherine has a hilarious conversation with her aunt Fidelma, whose sexual ethics represents a reversal of traditional Catholic morality: 'Ride all around you, Catherine [. . .] and don't bother your arse marrying any one of them. That's my advice to you' (273).

8. Later in the story, McKeon further explores this 'alliance' between straight women and gays by having the other female friends –Zoe, Amy and Lorraine– insisting on going to a gay club with James and Liam (the boyfriend). Whilst Emmet and Conor (the straight male friends) quickly leave because they are uncomfortable around gays smiling at them, the girls display a sense of self-congratulation as they see Liam and James dancing together: 'The girls were smiling at each other, as though together they had achieved something, together they had brought something into being' (341).

9. Although James tends to remain silent about his own suffering, this silence is also enforced by Catherine herself, as is made evident in the following quotation: 'Maybe if she had not been so tired herself, [. . .] Catherine would just have let him sit there, moaning like that; she would have known that it was only the booze talking, and the tiredness, and whatever else was eating at him – things she had not, after all, really tried to talk to him about yet, things that any real friend would probably by now have encouraged him to talk about' (160).

10. Some excerpts of this analysis have been previously published in Carregal-Romero (2015).

11. Similar observations were made in Chapter Four, in the analysis of Gregory's *Snapshots*.

12. This is the case of a 14-year-old girl – known as 'X' to protect her identity – who, after becoming pregnant as a result of rape, was stopped from travelling to England with her parents to undergo an abortion. This was a very public case that 'drove thousands of people to demonstrations across the country – for both pro-life and pro-choice campaigns' (O'Carroll, 2012).

13. Immersed in the case of the X girl, Grace muses on the possibility to find her in prison: 'It occurred to her, gently, pleasantly, that she may end up meeting the girl in prison. Murderers, the two of them. Grace would look after her, become her friend. Together they would move on from the places where they had been fixed' (274).

14. Lovett was a 15-year-old girl in Granard (Co. Longford) who, in 1984, gave birth on her own and died with her baby beside a grotto.

15. Rodger's *Being Gay in Ireland: Resisting Stigma in the Evolving Present* (2018) is a study that warns about the high prevalence of psychological damage in a significant proportion of today's gay population in Ireland.

16. Again, as also observed in Chapters Three and Five, Ridgway's characters frequently bear the burden of internalised homophobia.

17. His fiction is highly critical of the neoliberal ethos of Celtic Tiger Ireland. In her analysis of *The Parts*, Katherine O'Donnell notes that, even though the poor in 'are occluded in the noise of the economic boom [and] repressed from the dominant social imaginary,' they nonetheless 'haunt the text' (2013: 91).

18. Excerpts of this analysis have previously been published in Carregal-Romero (2019).

19. A study conducted between 2009 and 2012 found that 'in Ireland, academic policy and advocacy research have tended to focus almost exclusively on female sex work' (Maginn and Ellison, 2014: 370).

20. In his 2010s study of male prostitution, sociologist Paul Ryan confirms a lower preponderance of street-based sex work, pointing out that 'the widespread use of mobile applications by the gay community has occurred within a context of socio-economic and political change that has transformed the nature of male sex work in Ireland' (2016: 1714). A substantial number of young men now entering prostitution – Ryan studies the cases of Brazilian immigrants in Dublin – 'capitalize on wider trends within society like the proliferation of social media, the continued sexualization of the male body and the increasing popularity of gym selfies' (1721). We should note, however, that Ryan's recent study concerns itself with Brazilian immigrants, and not with teenage, underage rent boys, who are the type of prostitute Ridgway depicts in his texts.

21. One (in)famous case in 1994 brought male prostitution to public attention, when a Minister was found in Dublin's Phoenix Park with a rent boy. However, instead of promoting social debates on the conditions of street prostitution, the media high-lighted the politician's tarnished reputation and his claim that he did not know that the boy was a prostitute. A 1997 article in *The Irish Times* did give a glimpse into the

ugliest side of this underworld, after a middle-aged man had slept with a rent boy and found him dead in bed beside him the following morning. The boy's death was caused by 'a combination of alcohol and drug abuse,' and the story reported that he came from 'a dysfunctional family.' The boy hailed from an unfortunate background, and social services had failed to protect the minor's welfare.

22. I draw here on Joe Kort's definitions of sexual orientation and sexual preference. He uses such distinction when explaining the differences between homosexual men and SMSM (Straight Men who have Sex with Men): 'A gay man's sexual orientation is characterized by lasting aesthetic attraction to, romantic love of, and sexual attraction almost exclusively towards those of the same gender [. . .] In contrast, SMSM might fantasise about men, but their primary sexual and romantic attractions are toward women. They are heterosexual men who for a variety of reasons engage in sexual behaviour with other men [. . .] In understanding SMSM, a significant distinction is that between sexual preference and sexual identity. Sexual preferences are about various desires, positions, and fantasies one might have, whereas sexual identity is about how one self-identifies in terms of straight, gay, or bisexual' (2008).

23. For example, the rent boys in McGrath's documentary relate that teenagers as young as 12 entered prostitution, but 'when you reach the age of 20, you're too old' (1993). Another rent boy, interviewed by Kearins, tells us that 'the punters they do like 'em a bit young and all so I do often pretend I'm only sixteen' (2000: 45).

24. As Derek Hand observes in his review, 'this acknowledgement of form indicates the difficulty that exists in the telling', a difficulty that mirrors 'the characters' struggle to project themselves in the stories they create' (2003).

25. Ridgway's rent boy character is pimped by his older brother, and the money he makes helps sustain his mother financially.

26. This is a sexual conduct that has gained immense popularity in the neo-liberal culture of today: 'Whereas in gay liberation the answer to roles was to "shed" them, in later decades they were picked up, polished and redeployed for the purposes of sexual excitement' (Jeffreys, 2003: 13).

27. The same topic is explored in Chapter Four, in the analysis of Gregory's *G.A.A.Y.* Gregory's novel, though, does not problematise this liberal sexual culture.

28. Kevin is used as a guinea pig for a potent drug a corrupt doctor is testing – a situation which clearly exemplifies rent boys' extremely marginal status. Kevin eventually saves himself and decides to escape from Dublin.

29. Founded 2003, BeLonG To is Ireland's national service for lesbian, gay, bisexual, and transgender young people.

CHAPTER EIGHT

1. Investigating the lesbian past proves to be an arduous task. Whereas historical evidence for male homosexuality in Europe 'arises from major scandals and from court records', this type of documentation is 'just not available for women' (Lacey, 2008: 181). Even though lesbianism has never been criminal in England or Ireland,

this 'legal silence', Emma Donoghue notes in *Passions Between Women* (1993), meant that 'law-makers preferred to keep [lesbianism] unthinkable, while going ahead and punishing women who loved women on vaguer chargers of lewdness and fraud' (18).

2. Campaigners Gráinne Healy, Brian Sheehan and Noel Whelan explain that 'the referendum campaign required hundreds of gay and lesbian people, their parents, and their adult children to become champions for family diversity. Hundreds wrote letters to newspapers, posted on social media or started conversations about why marriage equality mattered' (2016: 111).

3. The enactment of the same-sex marriage bill, Yvonne Murphy points out, 'ensured that any potential reform of matters such as adoption, guardianship, and assisted reproduction were dealt with separately and irrespective of the outcome of the Marriage Referendum' (2016: 320).

4. For example, Australian supporters of marriage equality have looked at Ireland when designing their own campaign: 'Just like the Irish referendum, Australian Yes campaigners want to make the vote a conversation about "real people's lives" rather than a political debate' (Pollak, 2017).

5. Donoghue addresses reactionary attitudes and political controversies of the time concerning Catholic emancipation in Ireland, the need to protect England from outside influences, the anti-French sentiment derived from the Revolution, or the vilification of the working classes as a result of their revolts. For a detailed analysis on how these issues parallel political developments in the early 2000s, see Bensyl (2009).

6. The real Damer had destroyed her papers.

7. These lines, which Donoghue found quoted in Hester Thrale Piozzi's *Thraliana* (unpublished until 1942), became the writer's initial inspiration for *Life Mask*, as she explains in her 'Author's Note' (605–8). 'DAMN HER' is clearly intended as a pun on Anne Damer's surname.

8. In *Passions Between Women*, Donoghue relates that: "'Tommy' seems to have been a home-grown slang word for a woman who had sex with women. The first such use I have found is in a satire of 1773 [. . .] 'Tommy' may derive from 'tom boy', 'tom lad' or 'tom rig', all names for boyish, uncontrollable girls' (1993: 5).

9. Donoghue's novel also queers the figure of Horace Walpole by having Damer talk about his homosexuality: 'He knew what it was to love one's own sex and to be vilified for it, maybe, but not ashamed' (603). However, as a conservative politician, Donoghue's Walpole emerges as somebody who, in his public life, voices the discourse of hatred towards sodomites. In his conversation with the French ambassador, he states: 'I'm proud to report that my own [nation] is pre-eminent in the punishment of sodomites. We won't have such monsters on British soil' (306).

10. The Great Famine, as Emily Mark-Fitzgerald reminds us, 'devastated Irish culture, language and social demographics, form[ing] the basis for the massive Irish diaspora' (2013: 1).

11. Barry's *Days Without End* thus documents the 'irony' of the Irish involvement in the Indian wars (Campbell, 2018: 231). As a soldier, Thomas finds other Irish comrades who share tales of horror about their Famine days and voyages to America. The dehumanisation they suffered, Barry suggests, somehow mirrors these boys' capacity for cruelty: 'We were thought worthless. Nothing people [. . .] Irish boys all stuffed with anger. Bursting into flame' (148).

12. In recent years, drag was also used as a political strategy in Panti Bliss's 2014 'Noble Call' at the Abbey Theatre, where she gave everyday examples of Irish homophobia. Panti Bliss's successful 'Noble Call' provoked no public outrage, but the opposite happened when her alter ego, Rory O'Neill, was denounced after his condemnation of Iona Institute's homophobia on a RTÉ programme (under the threat of legal action, RTÉ paid €85.000 to the offended party and eliminated Rory O'Neill's video from their website). According to Fintan Walsh, this situation 'effectively meant that homophobia could not now be called out in public' (2015: 104).

13. The only line describing their love-making reads as follows: 'And then we quietly fucked and then we slept' (33).

14. Nonetheless, as one reviewer points out, the ease with which Winona welcomes her new life and accepts her adoptive parents 'belies the trauma of Indian dislocation' (Simpson Smith, 2017).

15. The title itself, for example, is a reference to Flann O'Brien's *At Swim, Two Birds* (1939). For an analysis of intertextuality in O'Neill's novel, see Cardin (2006).

16. Ironically, though, as Eibhear Walshe reminds us, the middle-class, patriarchal and Catholic nationalism that prevailed after revolution 'led to a suppression of a number of counter-discourses (i.e. feminism, radical socialism, lesbianism, the homoerotic)' (1997: 3).

17. In *The Myth of Manliness in Irish National Culture, 1880–1922* (2011), Joseph Valente provides an insightful overview of the feminisation and bestialisation of the Irish under the masculinised power of the British: 'Whereas feminization implied that the political rights of the Irish were vested in their British masters, such as a wife's suffrage was understood to be vested in her "lord and master", the burden of simianisation was to throw into question that the Irish properly owned any political rights in the first place. The former represented colonial rule as companiable protection, the latter as exigent control' (13).

18. For example, O'Neill learned that, whereas the nation had often been represented as an old woman, between 1910 and 1920 Ireland was masculinised and transformed into 'a youth with a bare chest' (Conner, 2007: 76). When reading about the fighters in war, O'Neill also perceived that the young men 'talk[ed] about the love they had for their comrades, nothing would be equal to that' (Conner, 77). Their love for their comrades thus compared with their commitment to fight for an independent Ireland.

19. The homoerotic element of official nationalism is, for example, represented by Pádraig Pearse, both in Irish culture and in O'Neill's novel. His presence in O'Neill's text, though, is only marginal, when MacMurrough remarks that Pearse's love of Ireland is 'in the boys' (326). In 1914, Pearse's unambiguously gay poem, 'Little Lad of the Tricks', engendered 'great consternation' on its publication, and his homosexual sensibility became 'edited out' in post-revolutionary times (Walshe, 1997: 4–5).

20. According to Foucault, 'the disappearance of [male romantic] friendship as a social relationship and the transformation of homosexuality into a social, political and medical problem are part of the same process' (cited in Simpson, 1994: 279).

21. MacMurrough replicates the famous words from Lord Alfred Douglas's poem 'Two Loves', which were used as evidence of their relationship during Oscar Wilde's trials for 'gross indecency'. Throughout the text, MacMurrough consciously models himself on Wilde.

22. As Sarah Cole points out, Hellenism is a cultural manifestation of late Victorianism, and was perceived as a 'viable idea to help combat a sense of cultural deterioration and to compete with dominant values surrounding Christianity, capitalism and the middle-class family' (2003: 24).

23. Apparently, this harsh treatment against homosexuals coexisted with a social pressure to keep their sexual transgressions hidden. Between 1962 and 1972, there were 455 convictions for homosexual offences, but these 'indecent' cases were not reported 'down to concerns about offending public sensibilities' (Gallagher, 2016).

24. The same doctor advises Cyril not to watch too much television. At this time, when the country was opening up culturally, a widespread assumption was that homosexuality was a 'immoral import, a foreign vice borrowed by a previously pure Ireland from America and Britain' (Lacey, 2008: 6).

25. With aversion therapy, psychiatrists attempted to re-orient homosexual people to heterosexual preferences: 'Specific treatments in various countries included aversion therapies delivering painful electric shocks to homosexual men at the wrists, calves, feet or genitals as they fantasised or viewed images of undressed males; administering emetic medication (such as apomorphine) to produce vomiting while similar materials were viewed; administration of testosterone followed by showing films of nude or semi-nude women; playing tape recordings every 2 hours outlining the alleged adverse effects of homosexual behaviour (in association with emetic medication); and, later, repeatedly playing tape recordings outlining the alleged positive consequences of no longer being homosexual' (Kelly, 2017: 209).

26. B. D. Kelly underlines how 'neither homosexuality nor aversion therapy were explicitly mentioned by Ireland's 1966 Commission of Inquiry on Mental Illness". Cases of homosexual conduct, Kelly observes, were placed in 'a section devoted to "sexual deviates"' (2017: 210).

27. Significantly, whereas many AIDS narratives focus on the gay victim, Boyne contemplates the human tragedy of the disease from the perspective of a hetero-sexual. The equation gay sexuality=AIDS=punishment=death makes Julian, as a heterosexual, suffer even more and receive his diagnosis with utter bewilderment and disbelief: 'I can't possibly have that disease. Do I look like a queer? I'm normal, for Christ's sake!' (377).

BIBLIOGRAPHY

PRIMARY SOURCES

Barry, Sebastian, *Days Without End* (London: Faber & Faber, 2016).

Boyne, John, *The Heart's Invisible Furies* (London: Penguin, 2017).

Cullen, Linda, *The Kiss* (Dublin: Attic Press, 1990).

Donoghue, Emma, *Stir-fry* (London: Penguin, 1994).

—— *Hood* (London: Penguin, 1995).

—— *Life Mask* (London: Virago, 2004).

—— *Landing* (Orlando, Austin, New York, San Diego and London: Harcourt, 2007).

Dorcey, Mary, 'A Country Dance', in *A Noise from the Woodshed* (London: Onlywomen Press, 1989), pp 44–63.

—— 'The Husband', in *A Noise from the Woodshed* (London: Onlywomen Press, 1989), pp 64–80.

—— 'Introducing Nessa', in *A Noise from the Woodshed* (London: Onlywomen Press, 1989), pp 130–59.

—— *Biography of Desire* (Dublin: Poolbeg Press, 1996).

Enright, Anne, *The Green Road* (London: Penguin, 2015).

Gregory, Jarlath, *Snapshots* (Dublin: Sitric Books, 2001).

—— *G.A.A.Y.: One Hundred Ways of Loving a Beautiful Loser* (Dublin: Sitric Books, 2005).

Hogan, Desmond, *The Ikon Maker* (Dublin: The Lilliput Press, [1976] 2013).

—— *Farewell to Prague* (Champaign, London and Dublin: Dalkey Archive Press, [1995] 2013).

Lennon, Tom, *When Love Comes to Town* (Dublin: O'Brien Press, 1993).

—— *Crazy Love* (Dublin: O'Brien Press, 1999).

McGuinness, Frank, 'Chocolate and Oranges', in *Paprika* (Dublin: O'Brien Press, 2018), pp 39–46.

McKeon, Belinda, *Tender* (London: Picador, 2015).

McNicholl, Damian, *A Son Called Gabriel* (New York: CDS Books, 2004).

O'Brien, Edna, *The High Road* (London: Penguin, 1988).

Ó Conghaile, Micheál, 'Father', in *Fourfront: Contemporary Stories Translated from the Irish* by Micheál Ó Conghaile, Pádraic Breathnal, Dara O'Conaola and Alan Titley (Conamara: Cló Iar-Chonnachta 1998), pp 20–7.

—— 'At the Station', in *The Colours of Man* (Conamara: Cló lar-Chonnacht, 2012), pp 133–9.

—— 'Lost in Connemara', in *The Colours of Man* (Conamara: Cló lar-Chonnacht, 2012), pp 207–20.

O'Connor, Joseph, 'The Hills Are Alive', in *True Believers* (London: Flamingo, 1992), pp 159–89.

O'Neill, Jamie, *At Swim, Two Boys* (London: Scribner, [2001] 2017).

Richards, Maura, *Interlude* (Dublin: Ward River Press Ltd, 1982).

Ridgway, Keith, 'Graffiti', in Brian Finnegan, ed., *Quare Fellas: New Irish Gay Writing* (Dublin: Basement Press, 1994), pp 31–42.

—— *The Long Falling* (London: Faber & Faber, 1998).

—— 'Angelo', in *Standard Time* (London: Faber & Faber, 2001), pp 195–248.

—— *The Parts* (London: Faber & Faber, 2003).

—— 'Andy Warhol', in Sarah Gilmartin and Declan Meade, eds., *Stinging Fly Stories: Celebrating our First 20 Years 1998–2018* (Dublin: The Stinging Fly Press, 2018), pp 333–45.

Somers, Eamon, 'Nataí Bocht', in Brian Finnegan, ed., *Quare Fellas: New Irish Gay Writing* (Dublin: Basement Press, 1994), pp 13–28.

Standún, Pádraig, *A Woman's Love* (Dublin: Poolbeg, 1994).

Tóibín, Colm, *The Blackwater Lightship* (London: Picador, 1999).

—— 'The Pearl Fishers', in *The Empty Family* (London: Viking, 2010), pp 46–89.

SECONDARY SOURCES

Adachi, Ken, 'Edna O'Brien Takes the High Road', in Alice Hughes Kersnowski, ed., *Conversations with Edna O'Brien* (Jackson: UP of Mississippi, 2014), pp 49–52.

Ahmed, Sarah, 'Interview with Judith Butler', in *Sexualities*, 19.4, 2016, pp 482–92.

Asher, Rachel, 'Ireland, the Same-Sex Partnership Debate, and the Normal Sexual Citizen', in *Journal of Bisexuality*, 9.3&4, 2009, 477–89.

Ashford, Chris, 'Sexuality, Public Space and the Criminal Law: The Cottaging Phenomenon', in *The Journal of Criminal Law*, 71.6, 2007, pp 506– 19.

Bacik, Ivana, 'The Politics of Sexual Difference: The Enduring Influence of the Catholic Church', in Noreen Giffney and Margrit Shildrick, eds., *Theory on the Edge: Irish Studies and the Politics of Sexual Difference* (London and New York: Palgrave MacMillan, 2013), pp 17–28.

Backus, Margot Gayle, '"More Useful Washed and Dead": James Connolly, W.B. Yeats, and the Sexual Politics of 'Easter 1916', in *Interventions*, 10.1, 2008, pp 67–85.

Baker, Paul, '"Unnatural Acts": Discourses of Homosexuality within the House of Lords debates on gay male law reform', in *Journal of Sociolinguistics*, 8.1, 2004, pp 88–106.

Balls, Richard, 'Man Awoke to Find Teenage Rent Boy Dead in Bed Beside Him', in *The Irish Times*, 12 April 1997, https://www.irishtimes.com/news/man-awoke-to-find-teenage-rent-boy-dead-in-bed-beside-him-1.61344, accessed 20 Oct. 2018.

Barron, Michael and Simon Bradford, 'Violence, Bodies, and Young Gay Men's Identities', in *Youth & Society*, 39.2, 2007, pp 232–61.

Barros-del Río, María Amor, 'Fragmentation and Vulnerability in Anne Enright's *The Green Road* (2015): Collateral Casualties of the Celtic Tiger in Ireland', in *International Journal of English Studies*, 18.1, 2018, pp 35–51.

Beale, Jenny, *Women in Ireland: Voices of Change* (Basingstoke and London: Macmillan, 1986).

Beaumont, Caitríona, 'Gender, Citizenship and the State in Ireland, 1922–1990', in Scott Brewster, Virginia Crossman, Fiona Beckett and David Alderson, eds., *Ireland in Proximity: History, Gender, Space* (London: Routledge, 1999), pp 94–108.

Bell, James G. and Barbara Perry, 'Outside Looking In: The Community Impacts of Anti-Lesbian, Gay, and Bisexual Hate Crime', in *Journal of Homosexuality*, 62.1, 2015, pp 98–120.

Bensyl, Stacia, 'Swings and Roundabouts: An Interview with Emma Donoghue', in *Irish Studies Review*, 8.1, 2000, pp 73–81.

—— 'Emma Donoghue's *Life Mask*: Post 9/11 rhetoric and Lesbian Identity', in Sonja Tiernan and Mary McAuliffe, eds., *Sapphists and Sexologies. Histories of Sexualities: Volume 2* (Newcastle: Cambridge Scholars, 2009), pp 41–55.

Bowyer, Susanah, 'Queer Patriots: Sexuality and the Character of National Identity in Ireland', in *Cultural Studies*, 24.6, 2010, pp 801–20.

Boyd, Clodagh, Declan Doyle, Bill Foley, Brenda Harvey, Annette Hoctor, Maura Molloy and Mick Quinlan, *Out for Ourselves: The Lives of Irish Lesbians and Gay Men* (Dublin: Dublin Lesbian and Gay Men's Collectives and Women's Community Press, 1986).

Boyne, John, 'The Catholic Priesthood Blighted My Youth and the Youth of People Like Me', in *The Guardian*, 3 Oct. 2014, https://www.theguardian.com/lifeandstyle/2014/oct/03/john-boyne-novelist-catholic-church-abuse-priesthood-boy-in-striped-pyjamas, accessed 10 Nov. 2020.

—— 'Introduction', in *At Swim, Two Boys* by Jamie O'Neill (London: Scribner, 2017), pp v–viii.

Bradley, Lara, 'Gay Goings-on in Crossmaglen', *The Belfast News Letter*, 12 July 2001, p. 18.

Brandi, Silvia, 'Unveiling the Ideological Construction of the 2004 Irish Citizenship Referendum: A Critical Analytical Approach', in *Translocations*, 2.1, 2007, pp 26–47.

Bridges, Tristan and C.J. Pascoe, 'Masculinities and Post-Homophobias?', in G.J. Pascoe and Tristan Bridges, eds., *Exploring Masculinities: Identity, Inequality, Continuity and change* (Oxford: Oxford UP, 2016), pp 412–23.

Bullock, Denise, 'Lesbian Cruising: An Examination of the Concept and Methods', in *Journal of Homosexuality*, 47.1, 2004, pp 1–31.

Butler, Jonathan, '"The Terror of Being Watched": Panopticism and Social Discipline in Keith Ridgway's *The Long Falling*', in Marti D. Lee and Ed Madden, eds., *Irish Studies: Geographies and Genders* (Newcastle: Cambridge Scholars, 2008), pp 60–8.

Butler, Judith, *Excitable Speech: A Politics of the Performative* (London: Routledge, 1997).

—— 'Critically Queer', in Anna Trip, ed., *Gender* (London and New York: Palgrave, 2000), pp 154–67.

—— 'Performativity, Precarity and Sexual Politics', in *AIBR: Revista de Antropología Iberoamericana*, 4.3, 2009, pp i–xiii.

—— 'Rethinking Vulnerability and Resistance', in Judith Butler, Zeynep Gambetti and Leticia Sabsay, eds., *Vulnerability in Resistance* (Durham and London: Duke UP, 2016), pp 12–27.

Byrne, Suzy and Junior Larkin, *Coming Out* (Dublin: Martello Books, 1994).

Cahill, Susan, *Irish Literature in the Celtic Tiger Years 1990-2008: Gender, Bodies, Memory* (London: Bloomsbury, 2011).

Campbell, Neil, '"The Seam of Something Else Unnamed": Sebastian Barry's *Days Without End*', in *Western American Literature*, 53.2, 2018, pp 231–52.

Cardin, Bertrand, 'Intertextual Re-creation in Jamie O'Neill's *At* Swim, *Two Boys*', in *Estudios Irlandeses*, 1, 2006, pp 23–31.

Carregal-Romero, José, 'Sexuality and the Culture of Silence in Colm Tóibín's "The Pearl Fishers"', in *Atlantis: Journal of the Spanish Asssociation of Anglo-American Studies*, 37.1, 2015, pp 69–83.

—— 'The Cultural Narratives of AIDS, Gay Sexuality, and the Family in Colm Tóibín's *The Blackwater Lightship*', in *PLL: Papers on Language and Literature*, 52.4, 2016, pp 350–73.

—— 'Gay Fiction, Homophobia and Post-Troubles Northern Ireland: An Interview with Jarlath Gregory', in *Estudios Irlandeses*, 14, 2019, pp 198–206.

—— 'The Social Silencing of Male Prostitution in Keith Ridgway's 'Angelo' and *The Parts*', in *New Hibernia Review*, 23.1, 2019, pp 122–37.

Casey, Maurice J., 'Radical politics and gay activism in the Republic of Ireland, 1974–1990', in *Irish Studies Review*, 26.2, 2018, pp 217–36.

Casey, Moira. '"If Love's a Country": Transnationalism and the Celtic Tiger in Emma Donoghue's *Landing*', in *New Hibernia Review*, 15.2, 2011, pp 64–79.

Cavalier, Elizabeth S., 'Men at Sport: Gay Men's Experiences in the Sport Workplace', in *Journal of Homosexuality*, 58.5, 2011, pp 626–46.

Charczun, Anna, '"Can I Write About It Yet?": The Influence of Politics on Literary Representations of Lesbians in Irish Women's Writing', in *Studi Irlandesi*, 10, 2020, pp 43–62.

Chauncey, George, *Gay New York: Gender, Urban Culture, and the Making of the Gay Male World, 1890-1940* (New York: Basic Books, 1994).

CHE: Campaign for Homosexual Equality, *Attacks on Gay People: A Report of the Commission on Discrimination* (London: CHE, 1990), Irish Queer Archive, National Library of Ireland, Ms 45,978/1.

Clair, Robin Patric, *Organizing Silence: A World of Possibilities* (New York: State University of New York Press, 1998).

Clarke, Jim, 'Male Prostitution and Health', in *Irish Health.com*, 2002, http://www.irishhealth.com/article.html?id=3387, accessed 31 Jan. 2018.

Clewell, Tammy, *Mourning, Modernism and Postmodernism* (London and New York: Palgrave MacMillan, 2009).

Cole, Sarah, *Modernism, Male Friendship, and the First World War* (Cambridge: Cambridge UP, 2003).

Conan, Catherine, 'Narration as Conversation: Patterns of Community-making in Colm Tóibín's *The Empty Family*', in *Journal of the Short Story in English*, 63, 2014, http://jsse.revues.org/1485, accessed 4 Dec. 2018.

Conaty, Donal, 'The Alarming Spread of AIDS Among the London Irish', in *The Irish Times*, 8. Aug. 1989, Irish Queer Archive, National Library of Ireland, Ms 45, 999/1.

Connell, Raewyn, *Gender and Power* (Oxford: Blackwell, 1995).

Conner, Marc C., '"To Bring All Loves Home": An Interview with Jamie O'Neill', in *New Hibernia Review*, 11.2, 2007, pp 66–78.

Conrad, Kathryn, 'Queer Treasons: Homosexuality and Irish National Identity', in *Cultural Studies*, 15.1, 2001, pp 124–37.

—— *Locked within the Family Cell: Gender, Sexuality and Political Agency in Irish National Discourse* (Madison: U of Wisconsin P, 2004).

Conroy, Pauline, 'Lone Mothers: The Case of Ireland', in J. Lewis, ed., *Lone Mothers in European Welfare Regimes: Shifting Policy Logics* (London and Bristol: Jessica Kingsley Publishers, 1997), pp 76–95.

Coppola, Maria Micaela, 'Mary Dorcey: The Poet's Gaze and Scalpel', in *Studi irlandesi*, 5, 2015, pp 225–52.

Costello-Sullivan, Kathleen, *Mother/Country: Politics of the Personal in the Fiction of Colm Tóibín* (Bern: Peter Lang, 2012).

Coulter, Carol, '"Hello Divorce, Goodbye Daddy": Women, Gender and the Divorce Debate', in Anthony Bradley and Maryann Gialanella Valiulis, eds., *Gender and Sexuality in Modern Ireland* (Amherst: U of Massachusetts P, 1997), pp 275–98.

Cregan, David, 'Irish Theatrical Celebrity and the Critical Subjugation of Difference in the Work of Frank McGuinness', in *Modern Drama*, 47.4, 2004, pp 671–85.

Crimp, Douglas, 'Mourning and Militancy', in *October*, 51, 1989, pp 3–18.

Crompton, Louis, *Homosexuality and Civilization* (Cambridge, Massachusetts, and London: Harvard UP, 2003).

Crone, Joni, 'Lesbians: The Lavender Women of Ireland', in Íde O'Carroll and Eoin Collins, eds., *Lesbian and Gay Visions of Ireland: Towards the Twenty-First Century* (London and New York: Cassell, 1995), pp 60–70.

Cronin, Michael G., '"He's My Country": Liberalism, Nationalism, and Sexuality in Contemporary Irish Gay Fiction', in *Eire-Ireland*, 39.3&4, 2004, pp 250–67.

—— Cronin, Michael G., 'Review of *Nights Beneath the Nation* by Denis Kehoe', in *Stinging Fly*, 11.2, 2008–09, https://stingingfly.org/review/nights-beneath-nation/, accessed 24 Nov. 2020.

—— *Impure Thoughts: Sexuality, Catholicism and Literature in Twentieth-Century Ireland* (Manchester: Manchester UP, 2012).

—— Cronin, Michael G., '"Our Nameless Desires": The Erotics of Time and Space in Contemporary Irish Lesbian and Gay Fiction', in Liam Harte, ed., *The Oxford Handbook of Modern Irish Fiction* (Oxford: Oxford UP, 2020), pp 567–83.

Curtis, Jennifer, 'Pride and prejudice: gay rights and religious moderation in Belfast', in *The Sociological Review*, 61.2, 2013, pp 141–59.

de Brún, Sorcha, 'History Repeating Itself: Men, Masculinities, and "His Story" in the Fiction of Micheál Ó Conghaile', in *Éire-Ireland*, 52.1&2, 2017, pp 17–48.

Delaney, Paul, 'Introduction', in Paul Delaney, ed., *Reading Colm Tóibín* (Dublin: The Liffey Press, 2008), pp 1–20.

Diamond, Sara, 'Discovering Lesbian History: From Invert-to-dyke to Feminist', in *Rites*, June 1984, Irish Queer Archive, National Library of Ireland, Ms 46,005/2.

Doka, Kenneth J., 'Disenfranchised Grief', in *Bereavement Care*, 18.3, 1999, pp 37–9.

Donoghue, Emma, *Passions Between Women* (London: Harper Collins, 1993).

—— 'Noises from Woodsheds: Tales of Irish lesbians 1886–1989', in Íde O'Carroll and Eoin Collins, eds., *Lesbian and Gay Visions of Ireland: Towards the Twenty-First Century* (London and New York: Cassell, 1995), pp 158–70.

—— *What Sappho Would Have Said: Four Centuries of Love Poems Between Women* (London: Hamish Hamilton, 1997).

Donnelly, Susie and Tom Inglis, 'The Media and the Catholic Church in Ireland: Reporting Clerical Child Sex Abuse', in *Journal of Contemporary Religion*, 25.1, 2010, pp 1–19.

Donoghue, Emma and Abigail L. Palko, 'Emma Donoghue, in Conversation with Abby Palko', in *Breac: A Digital Journal of Irish Studies*, 17 July 2017, https://breac.nd.edu/articles/emma-donoghue-in-conversation-with-abby-palko/, accessed 10 June 2018.

Donohoe, Katie, '2018 HIV Figures Hit Record High In Ireland', in *Gay Community News*, 4 Jan. 2019, https://gcn.ie/2018-hiv-figures-hit-record-high-ireland/, accessed 5 May 2019.

—— 'HIV and Sexual Health Front and Centre at this Year's Dublin Pride as ACT UP to Lead Parade with U=U message', in *Gay Community News*, 29 June 2019b, https://gcn.ie/hiv-sexual-health-front-centre-years-dublin-pride-act-up-lead-parade-uu-message/, accessed 10 Sep. 2019.

Dorcey, Mary, 'Interview', in Íde O'Carroll and Eoin Collins, eds., *Lesbian and Gay Visions of Ireland: Towards the Twenty-First Century* (London and New York: Cassell, 1995), pp 25–44.

Douglas, Carol Anne, 'Lesbian Nuns: Breaking the Silence', in *Off Our Backs*, 14.10, 1984, p. 19.

Doyle, Rob, '*A Farewell to Prague/ The Ikon Maker* by Desmond Hogan', in *The Stinging Fly* 26.2, 2013, https://stingingfly.org/review/farewell-prague-ikon-maker/, accessed 18 Jan. 2019.

Duggan, Lisa, 'The New Homonormativity: The Sexual Politics of Neoliberalism', in Russ Castronovo and Dana D. Nelson, eds., *Materializing Democracy: Toward a Revitalized Cultural Politics* (Durham and London: Duke UP, 2002), pp 175–95.

Duggan, Marian, *Queering Conflict: Examining Lesbian and Gay Experiences of Homophobia in Northern Ireland* (London: Routledge, 2012).

Dunne, Peter, 'New HIV Diagnosis Numbers in Ireland Higher In 2018 Than During AIDS Crisis in '80s And '90s', in *Gay Community News*, 26 Feb. 2019, https://gcn.ie/new-hiv-diagnosis-numbers-ireland/, accessed 10 May 2019.

—— 'New HIV Diagnosis Rates in Ireland Almost Double the European Average', in *Gay Community News*, 3 Dec. 2019, https://gcn.ie/hiv-diagnosis-ireland-double-european-average, accessed 30 Jan. 2020.

Dunphy, Richard, 'Sexual Identities, National Identities: The Politics of Gay Law Reform in the Republic of Ireland', in *Contemporary Politics*, 3.3, 1997, pp 247–65.

Edwards, Tim, *Erotics & Politics: Gay Male Sexuality, Masculinity and Feminism* (London: Routledge, 1994).

Ehrhardt, Michael, 'About the Inner Sanctum of the Self', in *The Gay and Lesbian Review Worldwide*, 29 Aug. 2013, https://glreview.org/article/about-the-inner-sanctum-of-the-self/, accessed 10 June 2019.

Equality Authority, *Implementing Equality for Lesbians, Gays and Bisexuals* (Dublin: Equality Authority, 2003).

Esposito, Veronica Scott, 'Damian McNicholl Interview', in Conversational Reading. Veronica Scott Esposito's Blog, 13 June 2005, http://conversationalreading.com/damian-mcnicholl-interview/, accessed 5 March 2018.

Faderman, Lillie, *Surpassing the Love of Men* (London: The Women's Press, 1981).

Fahie, Declan, '"Spectacularly Exposed and Vulnerable" – How Irish Equality Legislation Subverted the Personal and Professional Security of Lesbian, Gay And Bisexual Teachers', in *Sexualities*, 19.4, 2016, pp 393–411.

Family Solidarity, *The Homosexual Challenge Analysis and Response* (Dublin: Dublin Family Solidarity, 1990).

Fantaccini, Fiorenzo and Samuele Grassi, 'Emma in Borderlands: Q&A with Emma Donoghue', in *Studi Irlandesi*, 1, 2011, pp 397–406.

Ferriter, Diarmaid, *Occasions of Sin: Sex and Society in Modern Ireland* (London: Profile Books, 2009).

Finnegan, Brian, 'Introduction', in Brian Finnegad, ed., *Quare Fellas: New Irish Gay Writing* (London: Basement Press, 1994), pp 5–12.

—— 'Exploitation of Children Will Shore Up Deeply Held Beliefs in the Anti-Gay Marriage Campaign', in *Gay Community News*, 5 Jan. 2015, https://gcn.ie/children-and-gay-marriage/, accessed 1 March 2019.

FitzPatrick Dean, Joan, 'Self-Dramatization in the Plays of Frank McGuinness', in *New Hibernia Review*, 3.1, 1999, pp 97–110.

Fogarty, Anne, 'The Ear of the Other: Dissident Voices in Kate O'Brien's *As Music and Splendour* and Mary Dorcey's *A Noise from the Woodshed*', in Eibhear Walshe, ed., *Sex, Nation and Dissent in Irish Writing* (Cork: Cork UP, 1997), pp 170–201.

Foucault, Michel, *The History of Sexuality: Vol. 1*, translated by Robert Hurley (London: Penguin Books, [1976] 1998).

France, Nadine Ferris, Steve H. Macdonald, Ronan R. Conroy, Elaine Byrne, Chris Mallouris, Ian Hodgson, Fiona Larkan, '"An unspoken world of unspoken things": A Study Identifying and Exploring Core Beliefs Underlying Self-Stigma Among People Living with HIV and AIDS in Ireland', in *Swiss Medical Weekly*, 145.w1420, 2015.

Gaffney, Christine, 'Coming Out of Heterosexuality, Coming Into Lesbianism', in Maire Leane and Elizabeth Kiely, eds., *Sexualities and Irish Society: A Reader* (Dublin: Orpen Press, 2014), pp 219–40.

Gallagher, Conor, 'Gay Community Recalls Dark Days Before Decriminalisation', in *The Irish Times*, 30 Nov. 2016, https://www.irishtimes.com/news/social-affairs/gay-community-recalls-dark-days-before-decriminalisation-1.2886652, accessed 2 Aug. 2018.

Ganiel, Gladys, *Transforming Post-Catholic Ireland: Religious Practice in Late Modernity* (Oxford: Oxford UP, 2016).

Gay Health Action, 'Press Release', 1 April 1987, Irish Queer Archive, National Library of Ireland, Ms 45, 999/14.

Geoghegan Quinn, Maire, 'Decriminalisation of homosexuality was just the beginning', in *The Irish Times,* 14 May 2015, https://www.irishtimes.com/opinion/decriminalisation-of-homosexuality-was-just-the-beginning-1.2211452, accessed 3 Feb. 2018.

Ghaziani, Amin, 'Post-Gay Collective Identity Construction', in *Social Problems*, 58.1, 2011, 99–125.

Gibney, Rosemary, Patricia Carey, Izzy Kamikaze and Kate Frances, 'Unity Without Uniformity: Lesbians in Ireland in the 1990s', in Gabriele Griffin, ed., *Feminist Activism in the 1990s* (London: Taylor & Francis, 1995), pp 158–68.

Ging, Debbie, 'All-Consuming Images: New Gender Formations in post-Celtic Tiger Ireland', in Debbie Ging, Michael Cronin and Peadar Kirby, eds., *Transforming Ireland: Challenges, Critiques and Resources* (Manchester: Manchester UP, 2009), pp 52–70.

Gittins, Diana, *The Family in Question: Changing Households and Familiar Ideologies* (London: MacMillan, 1993).

Gleeson, Sinéad, '"I write because I don't quite know how to live": Interview with Keith Ridgway', in *The Irish Times*, 14 July 2012, https://www.irishtimes.com/culture/books/i-write-because-i-don-t-quite-know-how-to-live-1.536333, 22 March 2018.

Goggin, Mark, 'Gay and Lesbian Adolescence', in Susan Moore and Doreen Rosenthal, eds., *Sexuality in Adolescence* (London: Routledge, 1993), pp 102–23.

Golden, Carla, 'Diversity and Variability in Women's Sexual Identities', in John Corvino, ed., *Same Sex: Debating the Ethics, Science, and Culture of Homosexuality* (Maryland: Rowman & Littlefield Publishers, 1999), pp 149–66.

Grant, Linda, 'Public Lives: The Bishop and the Lesbian. Emma Donoghue is Ireland's most Famous Lesbian', in *The Guardian*, 22 March 1995, p. 8.

Green, Lorraine and Victoria Grant, '"Gagged Grief and Beleaguered Bereavements?": An Analysis of Multidisciplinary Theory and Research Relating to Same Sex Partnership Bereavement', in *Sexualities*, 11.3, 2008, pp 275–300.

Griffin, Gabriele, 'Male Gaze', in *A Dictionary of Gender Studies* (Oxford: Oxford UP, 2017) Online version.

Gutenberg, Andrea, 'Coming-Out Story', in David Herman, Mandred Jahn and Marie-Laure Ryan, eds., *Routledge Encyclopedia of Narrative Theory* (London: Routledge, 2010), p. 73.

Haines, Kari M., C. Reyn Boyer, Casey Giovanazzi and M. Paz Galupo, '"Not a Real Family": Microaggressions Directed toward LGBTQ Families', in *Journal of Homosexuality*, 65.9, 2018, pp 1138–51.

Halperin, David M., 'Pal O' Me Heart', in *London Review of Books*, 22 May 2003, https://www.lrb.co.uk/v25/n10/david-halperin/pal-o-me-heart, accessed 2 May 2018.

—— 'How to Do the History of Male Homosexuality', in Donald E. Hall, Annamarie Jagose, Andrea Bebell and Susan Potter, eds., *The Routledge Queer Studies Reader* (London: Routledge, 2013), pp 262–86.

Hanafin, Patrick, 'Rewriting Desire: The Construction of Sexual Identity in Literary and Legal Discourse in Postcolonial Ireland', in *Social and Legal Studies*, 7.3, 1998, pp 409–29.

Hand, Derek, 'Young Writers with Promise: *Snapshots* by Jarlath Gregory', in *The Irish Times*, 7 July 2001, p. 68.

—— 'Dislocated in Dublin', in *The Irish Times*, 18 Jan. 2003, http://www.ricorso.net/rx/library/criticism/revue/Hand_D/Hand_D1.htm, accessed 30 Nov. 2018.

Hannon, Patrick, 'AIDS: Moral Issues', in *Studies: An Irish Quarterly Review*, 79.314, 1990, pp 102–15.

Hansen, Arlen J., 'Short Story', in *Britannica*, 12 Nov. 2020, https://www.britannica.com/art/short-story, accessed 29 Dec. 2020.

Harkin, Anna May and Mary Hurley, 'National survey on public knowledge of AIDS in Ireland', in *Health Education Research*, 3.1, 1988, pp 25–9.

Harri, Kate and Carol Laing, 'Lesbian Mothers', in *Out Magazine*, 1.4, June/ July 1985, pp 30–2, Irish Queer Archive, National Library of Ireland, Ms 45,996 /2.

Harris, Katharine, "'Part of the project of that book was not to be authentic": Neo-Historical Authenticity and its Anachronisms in Contemporary Historical Fiction', in *Rethinking History*, 21.2, 2017, pp 193–212.

Haughey, Nuala, 'Romanian Community Spirit Slow to Take Off', in *The Irish Times*, 2 Aug. 2002, https://www.irishtimes.com/news/romanian-community-spirit-slow-to-take-off-1.1090563, accessed 10 Sep. 2018.

Healey, Joseph, 'After Declan Flynn...', in *Hot Press*, March 1983, Irish Queer Archive, National Library of Ireland, Ms 46,005 /4.

Health Education Bureau, 'AIDS –Information Booklet', 1987, Irish Queer Archive, National Library of Ireland, Ms 45, 999/14.

Healy, Gráinne, Brian Sheehan and Noel Whelan, *Ireland Says Yes: The Inside Story of How the Vote for Marriage Equality Was Won* (Sallins: Merrion Press, 2016).

Herek, Gregory M., 'Beyond 'Homophobia: Thinking About Sexual Prejudice and Stigma in the Twenty-First Century', in *Journal of NSRC*, 1.2, 2005, pp 6–24.

Higgins, Agnes, Louise Doyle, Carmel Downes, Rebecca Murphy, Danika Sharek, Jan DeVries, Thelma Begley, Edward McCann, Fintan Sheerin, Siobháin Smyth, *The LGBT Ireland Report: national study of the mental health and wellbeing of lesbian, gay, bisexual, transgender and intersex people in Ireland* (Dublin: GLEN and BeLonG To, 2016).

Hoctor, David, 'I needed to leave Ireland to come out as a gay man', in *The Irish Times*, 5 May 2015, https://www.irishtimes.com/life-and-style/abroad/generation-emigration/i-needed-to-leave-ireland-to-come-out-as-a-gay-man-1.2200482, accessed 6 Oct. 2017.

Hogan, Desmond, 'Jimmy', in *Larks' Eggs: New and Selected Stories* (Dublin: Lilliput Press, [1987] 2005), pp 71–82.

Hollinghurst, Alan, *The Swimming-Pool Library* (London: Penguin, [1988] 2015).

Holmquist, Kathryn, "'Married guys, all they want is to touch and feel another guy": Kathryn Holmquist Meets the Author of a New Study of this Invisible Subculture', in *The Irish Times*, 15 March 2000, p. 13.

Horan, Niamh and Pamela Hewenham, 'Staff and Students Voice Objections over LGB Posters', in *The University Observer*, 10, 18 Feb. 2004, p. 1, Irish Queer Archive, National Library of Ireland, Ms 45,949 /6.

Hug, Chrystel, *The Politics of Sexual Morality in Ireland* (London: MacMillan, 1999).

Hughes, Christine Marie, *Multivalent Masculinities in the Northern Irish Post-Conflict Novel*, unpublished PhD dissertation (Belfast: Ulster University, 2019).

Inglis, Tom, *Lessons in Irish Sexuality* (Dublin: UCD Press, 1998).

—— *Moral Monopoly: The Rise and Fall of the Catholic Church in Ireland*, 2nd edition (Dublin: UCD Press, 1998b).

—— 'Origins and Legacies of Irish Prudery: Sexuality and Social Control in Modern Ireland', in *Eire-Ireland*, 40.3&4, 2005, pp 9–36.

Ingman, Heather, *Twentieth-Century Fiction by Women: Nation and Gender* (Aldershot: Ashgate, 2007).

Irish Council for Civil Liberties, *Equality Now for Lesbians and Gay Men* (Dublin, 1990).

'*The Irish Times* view on the Mother and Baby Homes report: a culture of silence and shame', in *The Irish Times*, 12 Jan. 2021, https://www.irishtimes.com/opinion/editorial/the-irish-times-view-on-the-mother-and-baby-homes-report-a-culture-of-silence-and-shame-1.4456594, accessed 14 Jan. 2021.

Jeffers, Jennifer M., *The Irish Novel at the End of the Twentieth Century* (London and New York: Palgrave, 2002).

—— 'Trends in the Contemporary Irish Novel: Sex, Lies, and Gender', in *Literature Compass*, 1, 2003, pp 1–31.

Jeffreys, Sheila, *Unpacking Queer Politics* (Cambridge: Polity Press, 2003).

Johnson, Paul, 'Ordinary Folk and Cottaging: Law, Morality, and Public Sex', in *Journal of Law and Society*, 34.4, 2007, pp 520–43.

Jonas, Norman W., *Gay and Lesbian Historical Fiction: Sexual Mystery and Post-Secular Narrative* (London and New York: Palgrave, 2007).

Jordan, Justine, 'Interview. Sebastian Barry: "You get imprisoned in a kind of style, I could feel it leaning on me"', in *The Guardian*, 21 Oct. 2016, https://www.theguardian.com/books/2016/oct/21/sebastian-barry-interview-days-without-end, accessed 3 April 2018.

Kavanagh, Eimear, 'Same-Sex Marriage or Partnership and Adoption: Debate for Ireland', in *Critical Social Thinking: Policy and Practice*, 1, 2009, pp 165–83.

Kearins, Evanna, *Rent: The Secret World of Male Prostitution in Dublin* (Dublin: Marino Books, 2000).

Kelly, B. D., 'Homosexuality and Irish psychiatry: Medicine, law and the changing face of Ireland', in *Irish Journal of Psychological Medicine*, 34.3, 2017, pp 209–15.

Kennedy, Finola, *Cottage to Crèche: Family Change in Ireland* (Dublin: Institute of Public Administration, 2001).

Kiberd, Declan, 'Dig in Dangerous Waters', in *The Irish Times*, 8 Sep. 2001, http://www.jamieoneill.com/atswim/reviews/irish.html, accessed 2 June 2019.

Kiersey, Nicholas J., '"Retail Therapy in the Dragon's Den": Neoliberalism and Affective Labour in the Popular Culture of Ireland's Financial Crisis', in *Global Society*, 28.3, 2014, pp 356–74.

Kimmel, Michael, 'Masculinity as Homophobia', in Harry Brod and Michael Kaufman, eds., *Theorizing Masculinities* (Thousand Oaks: Sage, 1994), pp 119–41.

Kirby, Peadar, *Celtic Tiger in Collapse: Explaining the Weaknesses of the Irish Model* (London and New York: Palgrave MacMillan, 2010).

Kitchin, Rob, 'Sexing the City: The Sexual Production of Nonheterosexual Space in Belfast, Manchester and San Francisco', in *City: Analysis of Urban Trends, Culture, Theory, Policy, Action*, 6.2, 2002, pp 205–18.

Kitzinger, Celia and Sue Wilkinson, 'Transitions from Heterosexuality to Lesbianism: The Discursive Production of Lesbian Identities', in *Developmental Psychology*, 31.1, 1995, pp 95–104.

Kristeva, Julia, *Strangers to Ourselves* (New York: Columbia UP, 1991).

Kort, Joe, 'Straight Men Who Have Sex With Men (SMSM)', in *GLBTQ Encyclopedia*, 2008, http://www.glbtqarchive.com/ssh/straight_men_who_S.pdf, accessed 1 Nov. 2017.

Lacey, Brian, *Terrible Queer Creatures: Homosexuality in Irish History* (Dublin: Wordwell Ldt, 2008).

Laing, Carol, 'The Invisible Lesbian', in *Out Magazine*, 1.3, April/ May 1985, p. 17, Irish Queer Archive, National Library of Ireland, Ms 45,995/14.

Lawson, Anthea, 'In Dublin's Unfair City', in *The Guardian*, 9 March 2003, https://www.theguardian.com/books/2003/mar/09/fiction.features, accessed 10 March 2018.

LEA (Lesbian Education Awareness), 'Annual report 1998', Irish Queer Archive, National Library of Ireland, Ms 45,988/8.

'Leaflet of Dublin Pride 2002', National Library of Ireland, Irish Queer Archive, Ms 46,013/10.

Leahy, Pat. 'Mother and Baby Homes Report finds "rampant" infant mortality, "appalling" conditions for thousands', in *The Irish Times*, 12 Jan. 2021, https://www.irishtimes.com/news/social-affairs/mother-and-baby-homes-report-finds-rampant-infant-mortality-appalling-conditions-for-thousands-1.4456447, accessed 3 Feb. 2021.

Leonard, Sue, 'One-Sitting Reads', in *Books Ireland*, 275, 2005, pp 94–5.

—— 'Book review: *The Heart's Invisible Furies*', in *Irish Examiner*, 4 March 2017, https://www.irishexaminer.com/viewpoints/books/book-review-the-hearts-invisible-furies-444309.htm, accessed 20 March 2017.

'Lesbian Women', Leaflet of the National Gay Federation, Irish Queer Archive, National Library of Ireland, Ms 45,938 /3.

Ley, David J., 'Overcoming Religious Sexual Shame', in *Psychology Today*, 23 Aug. 2017, https://www.psychologytoday.com/us/blog/women-who-stray/201708/overcoming-religious-sexual-shame, accessed 10 June 2018.

LOT (Lesbians Organising Together), 'Annual Report, 1993', Irish Queer Archive, National Library of Ireland, Ms 45,988/6.

LOT (Lesbians Organising Together), 'Annual Report, 1995', Irish Queer Archive, National Library of Ireland, Ms 45,988 /6.

McCabe, Ian, Michael Acree, Finbar O'Mahony, Jenny McCabe, Jean Kenny, Jennifer Twyford, Karen Quigley and Edel McGlanaghy, 'Male Street Prostitution in Dublin: A Psychological Analysis', in *Journal of Homosexuality*, 58.8, 2011, pp 998–1021.

McClenaghan, Brendí, 'Invisible Comrades: Gays and Lesbians in the Struggle', in Angela Bourke et al., eds., *The Field Day Anthology of Irish Writing: Volume IV* (Cork: Cork UP in association with Field Day, 2002), pp 1062–4.

McCourt, John, '"All Stories Overlap": Reading Keith Ridgway's Short Fiction', in *Journal of the Short Story in English*, 63, 2014, pp 229–40.

McCrum, Robert, 'The Vanishing Man', in *The Guardian*, 14 Nov. 2004, https://www.theguardian.com/books/2004/nov/14/fiction.features2, accessed 10 April 2019.

McDonagh, Patrick James, '"Homosexuals Are Revolting": Gay & Lesbian Activism in the Republic of Ireland 1970s–1990s', in *Studi irlandesi*, 7, 2017, pp 65–91.

McDonald, Ronan, 'Strategies of Silence: Colonial Strains in Short Stories of the Troubles', in *The Yearbook of English Studies*, 35, 2005, pp 249–63.

McGarry, Patsy, 'Many Men Refused to Marry Pregnant Women "over fear of losing social standing"', in *The Irish Times*, 12 Jan. 2021, https://www.irishtimes.com/news/social-affairs/many-men-refused-to-marry-pregnant-women-over-fear-of-losing-social-standing-1.4456304, accessed 20 Jan. 2021.

McGrath, Liam, *Boys for Rent* (short documentary), in *Vimeo*, 1993, https://vimeo.com/116162119, accessed 20 Feb. 2018.

Mac Gréil, Mícheál, *Prejudice in Ireland Revisited* (Maynooth: Survey and Research Unit, 1997).

McGurren, Catherine, '"Damning Men's Souls": The Evolution of Irish Prostitution Memoirs', in *Études Irlandaises*, 39.1, 2014, pp 73–86.

McKee, Lyra, 'A Letter to My 14-year-Old Self', in *The Guardian*, 19 April 2019 [2014], https://www.theguardian.com/commentisfree/2019/apr/19/lyra-mckee-letter-gay-journalism-northern-ireland, accessed 20 June 2019.

McKenna, Neil, 'The Joys of Cottaging', in *New Statesman*, 11.528, 30 Oct. 1998, p. 8.

McIntosh, Mary, 'The Homosexual Role', in Edward Stein, ed., *Forms of Desire: Sexual Orientation and the Social Constructionist Controversy* (London: Routledge, 1992), pp 152–64.

Mac Risteaird, Seán, 'Coming Out, Queer Sex, and Heteronormativity in Two Irish-language Novels', in *Studi Irlandesi*, 10, 2020, pp 63–75.

Madden, Ed. '"Here, of all places": Geographies of Sexual and Gender Identity in Keith Ridgway's *The Long Falling*', in *South Carolina Review*, 43.1, 2010, pp 20–32.

—— 'Queering the Irish Diaspora: David Rees and Padraig Rooney', in *Eire-Ireland*, 47.1&2, 2012, pp 172–200.

—— 'Queering Ireland, in the Archives', in *Irish University Review*, 43.1, 2013, pp 184–220.

—— 'Get Your Kit On: Gender, Sexuality, and Gay Rugby in Ireland', in *Eire-Ireland*, 48.1&2, 2013b, pp 246–81.

Maginn, Paul and Graham Ellison, 'Male Sex Work in the Irish Republic and Northern Ireland', in V. Minichiello and J. Scott, eds., *Male Sex Work and Society* (New York: Harrington Park Press, 2014), pp 367–401.

Mahoney, Christina Hunt, *Contemporary Irish Literature: Transforming Tradition* (London and New York: Palgrave, 1998).

Mallon, Aoife, 'Colourful Voices: The Experience of Young Lesbians Combating Homophobia and Heteronormativity', in *Women & Gender Studies Series*, 13.1, 2013, pp 24–47.

Mannix-McNamara, Patricia; Emmanuel O'Grady; Eva Devaney and Didier Jourdan, 'Tackling social and health inequalities: vulnerability among the young lesbian, gay and bisexual population in Ireland', in *Psychology & Sexuality*, 4.3, 2013, pp 268–82.

Mark-Fitzgerald, Emily, *Commemorating the Irish Famine: Memory and the Monument* (Liverpool: Liverpool UP, 2013).

Matthews, Graham John, 'Family Caregivers, AIDS Narratives, and the Semiotics of the Bedside in Colm Tóibín's *The Blackwater Lightship*', in *Critique: Studies in Contemporary Fiction*, 60.3, 2019, pp 289–99.

Meaney, Gerardine, Mary O'Dowd and Bernardette Whelan, *Reading the Irish Woman: Studies in Cultural Encounter and Exchange, 1714–1960* (Liverpool: Liverpool UP, 2013).

Medd, Jodie, '"Patterns of the Possible": National Imaginings and Queer Historical (Meta)Fictions in Jamie O'Neill's *At Swim, Two Boys*', in *GLQ: A Journal of Lesbian and Gay Studies*, 13.1, 2007, pp 1–31.

Mikalson, Kaarina, '"The Best Tradition of Womanhood": Negotiating and Reading Identities in Emma Donoghue's *Landing*', in *Canada and Beyond: A Journal of Canadian Literary and Cultural Studies*, 7, 2018, pp 51–60.

Miller, John C., '"My Daddy Loves Your Daddy": A Gay Father Encounters a Social Movement', in Mary Bernstein and Renate Reimann, eds., *Queer Families, Queer Politics: Challenging Culture and the State* (New York: Columbia UP, 2001), pp 221–30.

Minton, Stephen James, Torunn Dahl, Astrid Mona O' Moore and Donnely Tuck, 'An exploratory survey of the experiences of homophobic bullying among lesbian, gay, bisexual and transgendered young people in Ireland', in *Irish Educational Studies*, 27.2, 2008, pp 177–91.

Moane, Ger, 'Living Visions', in Íde O'Carroll and Eoin Collins, eds., *Lesbian and Gay Visions of Ireland: Towards the Twenty-First Century* (London and New York: Cassell, 1995), pp 86–95.

—— 'Building Strength Through Challenging Homophobia: Liberation Workshops with Younger and Midlife Irish Lesbians', in *Journal of Gay & Lesbian Social Services*, 20.1&2, 2008, pp 129–45.

Morgensen, Scott Lauria, 'Settler Homonationalism: Theorizing Settler Colonialism within Queer Modernities', in *GLQ*, 16.1&2, 2010, pp 105–31.

Morrison, Todd G.; Paula Kenny and Aoife Harrington, 'Modern Prejudice Toward Gay Men and Lesbian Women: Assessing the Viability of a Measure of Modern Homonegative Attitudes Within an Irish Context', in *Genetic, Social, and General Psychology Monographs*, 131.3, 2005, pp 219–50.

Morrison, Todd G.; Ronan Harrington and Daragh T. McDermott, 'Bi Now, Gay Later: Implicit and Explicit Binegativity Among Irish University Students', in *Journal of Bisexuality*, 10.3, 2010, pp 211–32.

Moss, Stephen, 'Interview. Costa winner Sebastian Barry: "My son instructed me in the Magic of Being Gay"', in *The Guardian*, 1 Feb. 2017, https://www.theguardian.com/books/2017/feb/01/sebastian-barry-costa-book-award-2017-days-without-end-interview-gay-son, accessed 5 March, 2018.

Mosse, George L., *Nationalism and Sexuality: Respectability and Abnormal Sexuality in Modern Europe* (New York: Howard Fertig, 1985).

—— *The Image of Man: The Creation of Modern Masculinity* (New York: Oxford UP, 1996).

Mowlabocus, Sharif, 'Revisiting Old Haunts Through New Technologies: Public (homo)sexual Cultures in Cyberspace', in *International Journal of Cultural Studies* 11.4, 2008, pp 419–39.

Mulhall, Anne, 'Queer in Ireland: "Deviant" Filiation and the (Un)holy Family', in Lisa Downing and Robert Gillett, eds., *Queer in Europe* (London: Ashgate, 2011), pp 99–112.

—— 'The Republic of Love', in *Critical Legal Thinking*, 23 June 2015, http://criticallegalthinking.com/2015/06/23/the-republic-of-love/, accessed 16 July 2019.

Mullally, Una, 'Preventative HIV Drug Must be Made Available', in *The Irish Times*, 23 Oct. 2017, https://www.irishtimes.com/opinion/una-mullally-preventative-hiv-drug-must-be-made-available-1.3264837, accessed 5 May 2019.

Mullen, Patrick, 'Queer Possession and the Celtic Tiger: Affect and Economics in Belinda McKeon's *Tender*', in *Lit: Literature Interpretation Theory*, 28.1, 2017, pp 75–95.

Mulvey, Laura, 'Visual Pleasure and Narrative Cinema', in *Screen*, 16.3, 1975, pp 6–18.

Murphy, Patrick J; David Hevey; Siobhán O'Dea; Neans Ní Rathaille and Fiona Mulcahy, 'Serostatus Disclosure, Stigma, Resistance, and Identity Management Among HIV-Positive Gay Men in Ireland', in *Qualitative Health Research*, 26.11, 2016, pp 1459–72.

Murphy, Robinson, 'The Politics of Rebirth in Colm Tóibín's "Three Friends" and "A Long Winter"', in *Irish Studies Review*, 17.4, 2009, pp 485–98.

Murphy, Yvonne, 'The Marriage Equality Referendum 2015', in *Irish Political Studies*, 31.2, 2016, pp 315–30.

Murray, Tony, 'Curious Streets: Diaspora, Displacement and Transgression in Desmond Hogan's London Irish Narratives', in *Irish Studies Review*, 14.2, 2006, pp 239–53.

Nagel, Joane, 'Masculinity and Nationalism: Gender and Sexuality in the Making of Nations', in *Ethnic and Racial Studies*, 21.2, 1998, pp 242–69.

National AIDS Strategy Committee, 'Report of the Sub-Committee on the Care and Management of Persons with HIV/AIDS to the National AIDS Strategy Committee', 13 April 1992, Irish Queer Archive, National Library of Ireland, Ms 46,005 /12.

Nealon, Christopher. *Foundlings: Lesbian and Gay Historical Emotion Before Stonewall* (Durham and London: Duke UP, 2001).

Nedeljkovic, Vukasin, 'Direct Provision and Asylum Archive: Power and Surveillance', in Constanza del Río and José Carregal, eds., *Revolutionary Ireland 1916–2016: Historical Facts & Social Transformations Re-Assessed* (Brighton: Edward Everett Root, 2020), pp 167–81.

Nolan, Ann, 'The Gay Community Response to the Emergence of AIDS in Ireland: Activism, Covert Policy, and the Significance of an "Invisible Minority"', in *Journal of Policy History*, 30.1, 2018, pp 105–27.

Nolan, Ann and Fiona Larkan, 'Vectors and Transnationality in the Adoption of a Liberal Public Health Response to HIV and AIDS in Ireland', in *Global Social Policy*, 16.3, 2016, pp 253–67.

Norton, Ann, 'From Eros to Agape: Edna O'Brien's Epiphanies', in Kathryn Laing, Sinéad Mooney and Maureen O'Connor, eds., *Edna O'Brien: New Critical Perspectives* (Dublin: Carysfort Press, 2006), pp 83–102.

O'Brien, Carl, 'Rates of LGBT Self Harm, Suicide are Horrific, says McAleese', in *The Irish Times*, 22 March 2016, https://www.irishtimes.com/news/social-affairs/rates-of-lgbt-self-harm-suicide-are-horrific-says-mcaleese-1.2583054, accessed 7 June 2019.

O'Brien, Cormac, 'Performing POZ: Irish Theatre, HIV Stigma, and "Post-AIDS" Identities', in *Irish University Review*, 43.1, 2013, pp 74–85.

—— 'HIV and AIDS in Irish Theatre: Queer Masculinities, Punishment, and "Post-AIDS" Culture', in *Journal of Medical Humanities*, 41, 2020, pp 123–36.

O'Brien, Kate, *The Land of Spices* (London: Virago, [1941] 2006).

O'Callaghan, Claire, 'Re-claiming Anne Damer/re-covering Sapphic History: Emma Donoghue's *Life Mask*', in Katherine Cooper and Emma Short, eds., *The Female Figure in Contemporary Historical Fiction* (London and New York: Palgrave, 2012), pp 134–52.

O'Carroll, Sinead, 'Twenty Years on: A Timeline of the X Case', in *The Journal*, 23 Feb. 2012, https://www.thejournal.ie/twenty–years-on-a-timeline-of-the-x-case-347359-Feb2012/, accessed 15 May 2018.

Ó Conchubhair, Brian, 'The Novel in Irish Since 1950: From National Narrative to Counter-Narrative', in *The Yearbook of English Studies*, 35, 2005, pp 212–31.

—— 'Introduction', in *The Colours of Man* by Micheál O' Conghaile (Conamara: Cló Iar-Chonnacht, 2012), pp 9–15.

O'Connor, Pat, 'Defining Irish Women: Dominant Discourses and Sites of Resistance', in *Éire-Ireland*, 30.3, 1995, pp 177–87.

O'Connor, William, 'Prelude to a Vision: The Impact of AIDS on the Political Legitimacy and Political Mobilization of Gay Men in Ireland', in Íde O'Carroll and Eoin Collins, eds., *Lesbian and Gay Visions of Ireland: Towards the Twenty-First Century* (London and New York: Cassell, 1995), pp 183–97.

O'Cuilleanáin, Cormac, 'Irish Publishers: A Nation Too Often', in *The Crane Bag*, 8.2, 1984, pp 115–23.

O'Donnell, Katherine, 'Lesbianism', in Brian Lalor, ed., *The Encyclopaedia of Ireland* (London: Gill and Macmillan, 2003), http://hdl.handle.net/10197/2894, accessed 1 Feb. 2019.

—— 'Lesbian Lives and Studies in Ireland at the Fin de Siécle', in Mary McAuliffe and Sonja Tiernan, eds., *Tribades, Tommies and Transgressors. Histories of Sexualities: Volume 1* (Newcastle: Cambridge Scholars, 2008), pp 1–26.

—— '*The Parts:* Whiskey, Tea, and Sympathy', in Pilar Villar-Argáiz, ed., *Literary Visions of Multicultural Ireland: The Immigrant in Contemporary Irish Literature* (Manchester: Manchester University Press, 2013), pp 188–200.

—— 'Keith Ridgway', in Michael R. Molino, ed., *Dictionary of Literary Biography Vol. 386: Twenty-First-Century Irish Fiction Writers* (Farmington Hills: Gale, 2020), pp 263–71.

O'Faolain, Nuala, 'Decriminalising Homosexuality Will Have Far-reaching Effects', in *The Irish Times*, 6 Dec. 1993, Irish Queer Archive, National Library of Ireland, Ms 45,999 /1.

O'Higgins-Norman, James, 'Still Catching Up: Schools, Sexual Orientation and Homophobia in Ireland', in *Sexuality & Culture*, 13.1, 2009, pp 1–16.

O'Higgins-Norman, Michael Goldrick and Kathy Harrison, *Addressing Homophobic Bullying in Second-Level Schools* (Dublin: The Equality Authority, 2010).

Oliva, Juan Ignacio, 'Overtones and Disturbances in Jamie O'Neill's Dissidence Novels', in *Revista Canaria de Estudios Ingleses*, 68, 2014, pp 185–93.

Olszewska, Kinga, *Wanderers Across Language: Exile in Irish and Polish Literature in the Twentieth Century* (London: Legenda, 2007).

O'Neill, Jamie, 'Jamie O'Neill reading *At Swim, Two Boys*', in *Youtube*, 2015, https://www.youtube.com/watch?v=E2TCbbHeRzg, accessed 10 Aug. 2019.

O'Reilly, Elizabeth, 'Anne Enright', in *British Council Literature*, 2008, https://literature.britishcouncil.org/writer/anne-enright, 28 Sep. 2019.

O'Rourke, Michael, Aideen Quilty, Michael Barron, Eibhear Walshe, Kathryn Conrad and Moynagh Sullivan, 'Roundtable: Are We Queer Yet?', in *Irish University Review*, 43.1, 2013, pp 12–54.

Ó Siadhail, Pádraig, 'Odd Man Out: Micheál Ó Conghaile and Contemporary Irish language Queer Prose', in *The Canadian Journal of Irish Studies*, 36.1, 2010, pp 143–61.

Ó Siadhail, Pádraig and Micheál Ó Conghaile, 'An Fear Aniar: An Interview with Micheál Ó Conghaile', in *The Canadian Journal of Irish Studies*, 31.2, 2005, pp 54–9.

Ó Súilleabháin, Fiachra, 'Vigilant Dads: Exploring Gay Men's Parenting Experiences in Contemporary Ireland', in Máire Leane and Elizabeth Kiely, eds., *Sexualities and Irish Society: A Reader* (Dublin: Orpen Press, 2014), pp 173–90.

—— 'Expanding "Irish Family" Repertoires: Exploring Gay Men's Experiences as Parents in the Republic of Ireland', in *Journal of GLBT Family Studies*, 13.5, 2017, pp 498–515.

O'Sullivan, Niall, 'Ireland Was Not the Place to be a Young Gay Man', in *The Irish Post*, 15 April 2013, https://www.irishpost.com/news/ireland-was-not-the-place-to-be-a-young-gay-man-5126, accessed 11 June 2019.

O'Toole, Emer, 'Guerrilla Glamour: The Queer Tactics of Dr. Panti Bliss', in *Éire-Ireland*, 52.3&4, 2017, pp 104–21.

O'Toole, Tina, 'Ce' Leis Tu ? Queering Irish Migrant Literature', in *Irish University Review*, 43.1, 2013, pp 131–45.

—— 'Making a Scene: The Diceman's Queer Performance Activism and Irish Public Culture', in *Études Irlandaises*, 42.1, 2017, pp 169–85.

Palko, Abigail L., *Imagining Motherhood in Contemporary Irish and Caribbean Literature* (London and New York: Palgrave, 2016).

Palmer, Paulina, *Contemporary Lesbian Writing: Dreams, Desires, Difference* (Ballmoor: Open UP, 1993).

—— *Lesbian Gothic: Transgressive Fictions* (London and New York: Cassell, 1999).

—— *The Queer Uncanny: New Perspectives on the Gothic* (Cardiff: U of Wales, 2012).

Peach, Linden, *The Contemporary Irish Novel: Critical Readings* (London and New York: Palgrave Macmillan, 2004).

Pelan, Rebecca, 'Undoing That Other Conquest: Women's Writing from the Republic of Ireland', in *The Canadian Journal of Irish Studies*, 25.1&2, 1999, pp 126–46.

Persson, Åke, '"Do Your Folks Know that You're Gay?": Memory and Oral History as Education and Resistance in Colm Tóibín's *The Blackwater Lightship*', in Hedda Friberg, Irene Gilsenan Nordin and Lene Yding Pedersen, eds., *Recovering Memory: Irish Representations of Past and Present* (Newcastle: Cambridge Scholars, 2007), pp 149–69.

Piatczanyn, Steven A; Kate M. Bennett and Laura K. Soulsby, '"We Were in a Partnership That Wasn't Recognized by Anyone Else": Examining the Effects of Male Gay Partner Bereavement, Masculinity, and Identity', in *Men and Masculinities*, 19.2, 2016, pp 167–91.

Pine, Emilie, 'Commemorating Abuse: Gender Politics and Making Space', in *UCD Scholarcast*, 2013, https://www.ucd.ie/scholarcast/transcripts/Gender_politics_and_making_space.pdf, accessed 15 Aug. 2018.

Pollak, Sorcha, 'Australian Campaign for Marriage Equality Follows Irish Model', in *The Irish Times*, 24 Sep. 2017, https://www.irishtimes.com/news/ireland/irish-news/australian-campaign-for-marriage-equality-follows-irish-model-1.3232036, accessed 10 June 2018.

Power, Joseph, 'False Fears on AIDS Spread Persist, Survey Finds', in *Irish Independent*, 1 Dec. 1989, Irish Queer Archive, National Library of Ireland, Ms 45,999/23.

Power, Maria, 'Lesbians Organizing Together (LOT) in Dublin', in Gabriele Griffin, ed., *Feminist Activism in the 1990s* (London: Taylor & Francis, 1995), pp 139–57.

Prendiville, Patricia, 'Ireland', in Kate Griffin and Lisa A. Mulholland, eds., *Lesbian Motherhood in Europe* (London and New York: Cassell, 1997), pp 133–40.

—— *LOT: Lesbian Information and Resource Pack: A Learning and Development Tool Towards Inclusion* (Dublin: LOT [Lesbians Organizing Together], 1998).

Purcell, Sean, 'The Killing That Should Have Been Prevented', in *The Irish Press*, 9 March 1983, Irish Queer Archive, National Library of Ireland, Ms 46,005 /4.

Quinn, Antoinette, 'Speaking the Unspoken: The Poetry of Mary Dorcey', in *Colby Quarterly*, 28.4, 1992, pp 227–38.

—— 'New Voices from the Woodshed: The Novels of Emma Donoghue', in Liam Harte and Michael Parker, eds., *Contemporary Irish Fiction: Themes, Tropes, Theories* (London and New York: Palgrave, 2000), pp 145–67.

Quinn, John R, 'The Lost Language of the Irish Gay Male: Textualization in Ireland's Law and Literature (or the Most Hidden Ireland)', in *Columbia Human Rights Law Review*, 26, 1995, pp 552–677.

Ramello, Stefano, 'Behind the Mask: A Typology of Men Cruising for Same-Sex Acts', in *Identity: An International Journal of Theory and Research*, 13, 2013, pp 73–94.

Reeser, Todd W, *Masculinities in Theory: An Introduction* (Chichester: Wiley-Blackwell, 2010).

Reimers, Eva, 'Primary Mourners and Next-of-kin – How Grief Practices Reiterate and Subvert Heterosexual Norms', in *Journal of Gender Studies*, 20.3, 2011, pp 251–62.

Reygan, Finn C. G., 'The School-Based Lives of LGBT Youth in the Republic of Ireland', in *Journal of LGBT Youth*, 6.1, 2009, pp 80–9.

Reygan, Finn and Geraldine Moane, 'Religious Homophobia: The Experiences of a Sample of Lesbian, Gay, Bisexual and Transgender (LGBT) People in Ireland', in *Culture and Religion*, 15.3, 2014, pp 298–312.

Rich, Adrienne, 'Compulsory Heterosexuality and Lesbian Existence', in *Signs: Journal of Women in Culture and Society*, 5, 1980, pp 531–60.

Ridgway, Keith. *Hawthorn & Child* (London: Granta Books, 2012).

Roche, Barry, 'Writer Sentenced for Sexual Abuse of Teen', in *The Irish Times,* 5 Oct. 2009, https://www.irishtimes.com/news/writer-sentenced-for-sexual-abuse-of-teen-1.847249, accessed 20 Nov. 2020.

Rodgers, Gerard, *Being Gay in Ireland: Resisting Stigma in the Evolving Present* (Lanham: Lexington Books, 2018).

RTÉ Written Archives, 'Reaction to Lesbian Nuns 1985', https://www.rte.ie/archives/exhibitions/1379-a-glimpse-into-rte-written-archives/381435-lesbian-nuns-on-the-late-late-show/, accessed 10 Nov. 2018.

Rustin, Susanna, 'A Life in Books: Colm Tóibín', in *The Guardian*, 25 Oct. 2010, https://www.theguardian.com/books/2010/oct/25/colm-toibin-brooklyn-family-interview, accessed 2 Feb. 2016.

Ryan, Alice, 'The Coming-of-Age-Novel After Joyce: *A Portrait of the Artist as a Young Man,* 1916–2016: Readings and Talks by Belinda McKeon, Paul Murray and Éilís Ní Dhuibhne', in *Dublin James Joyce Journal*, 9, 2016, pp 135–7.

Ryan, Carol, 'Irish Church's Forgotten Victims Take Case to U.N.', in *The New York Times,* 25 May 2011, https://www.nytimes.com/2011/05/25/world/europe/25iht-abuse25.html, accessed 26 Feb. 2019.

Ryan, Matthew, 'Abstract Homes: Deterritorialisation and Reterritorialisation in the Work of Colm Tóibín', in *Irish Studies Review*, 16.1, 2008, pp 19–32.

Ryan, Paul, 'Coming Out, Fitting In: The Personal Narratives of Some Irish Gay Men', in *Irish Journal of Sociology*, 12.2, 2003, pp 68–85.

—— 'Coming Out of the Dark: A Decade of Gay Mobilisation in Ireland, 1970–80', in Linda Connolly and Niamh Hourigan, eds., *Social Movements and Ireland* (Manchester: Manchester UP, 2006), pp 86–105.

—— 'The Pursuit of Gay and Lesbian Citizenship Rights', in Máire Leane and Elizabeth Kiely, eds., *Sexualities and Irish Society: A Reader* (Dublin: Orpen Press, 2014), pp 101–26.

—— '#Follow: Exploring the Role of Social Media in the Online Construction of Male Sex Worker Lives in Dublin, Ireland', in *Gender, Place & Culture*, 23.12, 2016, pp 1713–24.

Said, Edward W., *Reflections on Exile and Other Literary and Cultural Essays* (London: Granta Books, 2001).

Sanches, Zusanna, 'Long-distance *Landing*: Emma Donoghue and her Experience of Otherness in Canada', in *Anglo Saxonica*, 3.2, 2011, pp 297–307.

Schneider, Ana-Karina, 'Postnationalism, Postfeminism, and Other "Posts" in Anne Enright's Fiction', in *Studies in the Novel*, 50.3, 2018, pp 400–18.

Schubotz, Dirk and Helen McNamee, '"I Knew I Wasn't Like Anybody Else": Young Men's Accounts of Coming Out and Being Gay in Northern Ireland', in *Child Care in Practice*, 15.3, 2009, pp 193–208.

Schubotz, Dirk and Malachai O'Hara, 'A Shared Future? Exclusion, Stigmatization, and Mental Health of Same-Sex–Attracted Young People in Northern Ireland', in *Youth & Society*, 43.2, 2011, pp 488–508.

Schulman, Sarah, *Ties that Bind: Familial Homophobia and its Consequences* (New York: The New Press, 2009).

Sedgwick, Eve Kosofsky, *Epistemology of the Closet* (Berkeley: U of California P, 2008).

Share, Perry, Mary P. Corcoran and Brian Conway, *Sociology of Ireland*, 4th edn (Dublin: Gill & Macmillan, 2012).

Shernoff, Michael, 'Mental Health Considerations of Gay Widowers', in *Journal of Gay & Lesbian Social Services*, 7.2, 1997, pp 137–55.

Siebler, Kay, *Learning Queer Identity in the Digital Age* (London and New York: Palgrave, 2017).

Sinfield, Alan, *Gay and After* (London: Serpent's Tail, 1998).

Simpson, Mark, *Male Impersonators: Men Performing Masculinity* (London and New York: Cassell, 1994).

Simpson Smith, Katy, 'A Dreamlike Western with a Different Kind of Hero', in *The New York Times*, 3 Feb. 2017, https://www.nytimes.com/2017/02/03/books/review/days-without-end-sebastian-barry.html, accessed 10 Nov. 2017.

Smith, James M., 'The Politics of Sexual Knowledge: The Origins of Ireland's Containment Culture and the Carrigan Report (1931)', in *Journal of the History of Sexuality*, 13.2, 2004, pp 208–33.

Smyth, Ailbhe, 'Foreword', in David Marcus, ed., *Alternative Loves: Irish Gay and Lesbian Stories* (Dublin: Martello, 1994), pp v–viii.

—— 'Telling the Truth About Women's Lives', in *Estudios Irlandeses*, 10, 2015, pp 115–8.

Smyth, Gerry, *The Novel and the Nation: Studies in the New Irish Fiction* (London: Pluto Press, 1997).

Smyth, Fiona, 'Cultural Constraints on the Delivery of HIV/AIDS Prevention in Ireland', in *Social Science and Medicine*, 46.6, 1998, pp 661–72.

Standún, Pádraig, 'Making Flesh of the Word', in *The Furrow*, 43.4, 1992, pp 222–5.

—— 'Getting Our Ass Out of the Ditch', in *The Furrow*, 55.9, 2004, pp 506–8.

Stepien, Magdalena, 'From Peripheries to the Centre: The Quest for One's Self in Keith Ridgway's *The Long Falling*', in Pawel Schreiber, Joanna Malicka and Jakub Lipski, eds., *The Central and the Peripheral: Studies in Literature and Culture* (Newscastle: Cambridge Scholars, 2013), pp 117–27.

Storey, Michael L., *Representing the Troubles in Irish Short Fiction* (Washington: The Catholic University of America Press, 2004).

Stulberg, Lisa M., *LGBTQ Social Movements* (Cambridge: Polity Press, 2018).

Swann, Stephanie K. and Jeane W. Anastas, 'Dimensions of Lesbian Identity During Adolescence and Young Adulthood', in *Journal of Gay & Lesbian Social Services*, 15.1–2, 2003, pp 109–125.

Sweetman, Rosita, 'A Collapse in Belief', in *Books Ireland*, 70, 1983, pp 13–4.

Tasker, Yvonne and Diane Negra, 'Introduction: Feminist Politics and Postfeminist Culture', in Diane Negra and Yvonne Taskers, eds., *Interrogating Postfeminism: Gender and the Politics of Popular Culture* (Durham and London: Duke UP, 2007), pp 1–26.

Thompson, Helen, 'Uncanny and Undomesticated: Lesbian Desire in Edna O'Brien's *Sister Imelda* and *The High Road*', in *Women's Studies*, 32.1, 2003, pp 21–44.

—— 'Edna O'Brien', in Caitriona Moloney and Helen Thompson, eds., *Irish Women Writers Speak Out: Voices from the Field* (Syracuse: Syracuse UP, 2003b), pp 197–205.

—— 'Emma Donoghue', in Caitriona Moloney and Helen Thompson, eds., *Irish Women Writers Speak Out: Voices from the Field* (Syracuse: Syracuse UP, 2003c), pp 169–80.

Tierney, Eoin, 'Interview – Belinda McKeon', in *Totally Dublin*, 1 July 2015, http://www.totallydublin.ie/more/features-more/interview-belinda-mckeon/, accessed 22 Feb. 2018.

Titley, Alan, 'Twentieth-Century Irish Prose', in Séamus Mathúna and Ailbhe Ó Corráin, eds., *Celtic Literatures in the Twentieth Century* (Moscow: Languages of Slavonic Culture, 2007), pp 7–30.

Tóibín, Colm, 'Time to be Positive About AIDS', in *Sunday Independent*, 22 Dec. 1991, Colm Tóibín Papers, National Library of Ireland, Ms 44,490 /6.

—— *Love in Dark Time: Gay Lives from Wilde to Almodóvar* (London: Picador, 2001).

—— 'Foreword', in Glen O'Brien, ed., *Coming Out: Irish Gay Experiences* (Dublin: Currach Press, 2003), pp 9–11.

—— 'A Brush with the Law', in *The Dublin Review*, 28, 2007, http://thedublinreview.com/a-brush-with-the-law, accessed 10 Sep. 2017.

—— 'Among the Flutterers', in *London Review of Books*, 32.16, 19 Aug. 2010, https://www.lrb.co.uk/v32/n16/colm-toibin/among-the-flutterers, accessed 8 Sep. 2017.

Ue, Tom, 'An extraordinary act of motherhood: a conversation with Emma Donoghue', in *Journal of Gender Studies*, 21.1, 2012, pp 101–6.

Valente, Joseph, 'Race/Sex/Shame: The Queer Nationalism of *At Swim Two Boys*', in *Éire-Ireland*, 40.3&4, 2005, pp 58–84.

—— *The Myth of Manliness in Irish National Culture, 1880-1922* (Urbana, Chicago and Springfield: University of Illinois Press, 2011).

Vicinus, Martha, 'Introduction', in Martha Vicinus, ed., *Lesbian Subjects: A Feminist Studies Reader* (Bloomington and Indianapolis: Indiana UP, 1996), pp 1–14.

Walsh, Fintan, 'Introduction', in Fintan Walsh, ed., *Queer Notions: New Plays and Performances from Ireland* (Cork: Cork UP, 2010), pp 1–16.

——— "Cyberactivism and the Emergence of #TeamPanti", in *Theatre Research International*, 40.1, 2015, pp 104–7.

——— *Queer Performance and Contemporary Ireland: Dissent and Disorientation* (London and New York: Palgrave, 2016).

Walshe, Eibhear, 'Sexing the Shamrock', in *Critical Survey*, 8.2, 1996, pp 159–67.

——— 'Introduction', in Eibhear Walshe, ed., *Sex, Nation and Dissent in Irish Writing* (Cork: Cork UP, 1997), pp 1–15.

——— 'The First Gay Irishman? Ireland and the Wilde Trials', in *Éire- Ireland*, 40.3&4, 2005, pp 38–57.

——— 'The Vanishing Homoerotic: Colm Tóibín's Gay Fictions', in *New Hibernia Review*, 10.4, 2006, pp 122–36.

——— 'Invisible Irelands: Kate O'Brien's Lesbian and Gay Social Formations in London and Ireland in the Twentieth Century', in *SQS Journal*, 1.1, 2006b, pp 39–48.

——— '"A Different Story to Tell": The Historical Novel in Contemporary Irish Lesbian and Gay Writing', in Borbála Faragó and Moynagh Sullivan, eds., *Facing the Other: Interdisciplinary Studies on Race, Gender and Social Justice in Ireland* (Newcastle: Cambridge Scholars, 2008), pp 137–49.

——— *A Different Story to Tell: The Writings of Colm Tóibín* (Sallins: Irish Academic Press, 2013).

Walshe, John, 'UCD academics warn on gays', in *Irish Independent,* 17 March 1990, Irish Queer Archive, National Library of Ireland, Ms 46,005 /7.

Weber, Katharine, 'Three Novels Set in Ireland Past and Present', in *The New York Times,* 6 Oct. 2017, https://www.nytimes.com/2017/10/06/books/review/a-son-called-gabriel-damian-mcnicholl-ireland.html, 19 Dec. 2020.

Weekes, Anne Owens, 'A Trackless Road: Irish Nationalisms and Lesbian Writing', in Kathryn Kirkpatrick, ed., *Border Crossings: Irish Women and National Identities* (Tuscaloosa: The University of Alabama Press, 2000), pp 123–56.

Weeks, Jeffrey, *Invented Moralities: Sexual Values in an Age of Uncertainty* (Cambridge: Polity P, 1995).

Whelan, Christopher T. and Bertrand Maître, 'Levels and Patterns of Material Deprivation in Ireland: After the "Celtic Tiger"', in *European Sociological Review*, 23:2, 2007, pp 139–54.

Whipple, Vicky, *Lesbian Widows: Invisible Grief* (London: Harrington Park Press, 2006).

——— 'Addressing the Needs of Lesbian Widows', in *Journal of LGBT Issues in Counseling*, 1.1, 2006b, pp 61–74.

Whyte, Pádraic, 'Young Adult Fiction and Youth Culture', in Valerie Coghlan and Keith O'Sullivan, eds., *Irish Children's Literature and Culture: New Perspectives on Contemporary Writing* (London: Routledge, 2011), pp 71–84.

Wiesenfarth, Joseph, 'An Interview with Colm Tóibín', in *Contemporary Literature*, 50.1, 2009, pp 1–27.

'Women's Report', in National Gay Conference, 1982, Irish Queer Archive, National Library of Ireland, Ms 45,940 /10.

Wondrich, Roberta Gefter, 'Exilic Returns: Self and History outside Ireland in Recent Irish Fiction', in *Irish University Review*, 30.1, 2000, pp 1–16.

Woods, Gregory, *A History of Gay Literature: The Male Tradition* (New Haven and London: Yale University Press, 1998).

Woods, Jeannine, 'Trans-formations of Gendered Identities in Ireland', in Conn Holohan and Tony Tracy, eds., *Masculinity and Irish Popular Culture* (London and New York: Palgrave, 2014), pp 27–41.

—— 'Dragging up the Past: Subversive Performance of Gender and Sexual Identities in Traditional and Contemporary Irish Culture', in Pilar Villar-Argáiz, ed., *Irishness on the Margins: Minority and Dissident Identities* (London and New York: Palgrave, 2018), pp 17–36.

Wright, Abbe, 'An Interview with John Boyne', in *Read it Forward*, Oct. 2017, https://www.readitforward.com/author-interview/john-boyne/, accessed 2 Aug. 2018.

Yeates, Padraig, 'State AIDS Campaign not Reaching those Most at Risk', in *The Irish Times*, 19. Nov. 1993, Irish Queer Archive, National Library of Ireland, Ms 45,999/23.

Yebra, José M., 'The Interstitial Status of Irish Gayness in Colm Tóibín's *The Blackwater Lightship* and *The Master*', in *Estudios Irlandeses*, 9, 2014, pp 96–106.

Young, Emma, 'No Place like Home: Re-writing "Home" and Re-locating Lesbianism in Emma Donoghue's *Stir-fry* and *Hood*', in *Journal of International Women's Studies*, 14.4, 2013, pp 5–18.

Index